The Battle over School Prayer

LANDMARK LAW CASES

AMERICAN SOCIETY

Peter Charles Hoffer

N. E. H. Hull

Series Editors

RECENT TITLES IN THE SERIES

Murder in Mississippi, Howard Ball
The Vietnam War on Trial, Michal R. Belknap
Sexual Harassment and the Law, Augustus B. Cochran III
The DeShaney Case, Lynne Curry
Brown v. Board of Education, Robert M. Cottrol, Raymond T. Diamond,
and Leland B. Ware
The Battle over School Prayer, Bruce J. Dierenfield
Nazi Saboteurs on Trial, Louis Fisher
The Great New York Conspiracy of 1741, Peter Charles Hoffer
Griswold v. Connecticut, John W. Johnson
M'Culloch v. Maryland: *Securing a Nation*, Mark R. Killenbeck
The Slaughterhouse Cases, Abridged Edition, Ronald M. Labbé
and Jonathan Lurie
Mapp v. Ohio, Carolyn N. Long
Dred Scott *and the Politica of Slavery*, Earl M. Maltz
The Snail Darter Case, Kenneth M. Murchison
Animal Sacrifice and Religious Freedom, David M. O'Brien
The Yoder *Case*, Shawn Francis Peters
The Insular Cases *and the Emergence of American Empire*,
Bartholomew H. Sparrow
San Antonio v. Rodriguez *and the Pursuit of Equal Education*, Paul Sracic
Slave Law in the American South, Mark V. Tushnet
The Confederacy on Trial, Mark A. Weitz
The Times and Trials of Anne Hutchinson, Michael P. Winship
Race and Redistricting, Tinsley E. Yarbrough
The Battle for the Black Ballot, Charles L. Zelden

For a complete list of titles in the series go to www.kansaspress.ku.edu

BRUCE J. DIERENFIELD

The Battle over School Prayer

How *Engel v. Vitale* Changed America

UNIVERSITY PRESS OF KANSAS

© 2007 by the University Press of Kansas

All rights reserved

Published by the University Press of Kansas (Lawrence, Kansas 66045), which was organized by the Kansas Board of Regents and is operated and funded by Emporia State University, Fort Hays State University, Kansas State University, Pittsburg State University, the University of Kansas, and Wichita State University

Library of Congress Cataloging-in-Publication Data

Dierenfield, Bruce J., 1951–

The battle over school prayer : how Engel v. Vitale changed America /
Bruce J. Dierenfield.

p.   cm. — (Landmark law cases and American Society)

Includes bibliographical references and index.

ISBN 978-0-7006-1525-4 (cloth : alk. paper) — ISBN 978-0-7006-1526-1
(pbk. : alk. paper)   1. Engel, Steven I. — Trials, litigation, etc.   2.
Vitale, William J. — Trials, litigation, etc.   3. Prayer in the public
schools — Law and legislation — United States.   4. Prayer in the public
schools — Law and legislation — New York (State)   5. Church and
state — United States.   I. Title.

KF228.E54D54   2007

344.73'0796—dc22

2007003909

British Library Cataloguing-in-Publication Data is available.

Printed in the United States of America

10 9 8 7 6 5 4 3 2 1

The paper used in this publication meets the minimum requirements of the
American National Standard for Permanence of Paper for Printed Library Materials
z39.48-1992.

CONTENTS

Editors' Preface *vii*

Preface *ix*

Acknowledgments *xi*

Introduction *1*

1. "Forced Worship Stinks in God's Nostrils" *5*

2. "Christ Loves All But the Hypocrites" *26*

3. "Good Fences Make Good Neighbors" *46*

4. "The One-Size-Fits-All Prayer" *67*

5. "The Day I Stopped Believing in God" *86*

6. "Why Are These People So Afraid of God?" *111*

7. "Almighty God Has Been Given His Walking Papers" *137*

8. "The Most Hated Woman in America" *163*

9. "My God, What's Wrong with That Man?" *187*

Afterword *213*

Chronology *219*

Relevant Cases *223*

Major U.S. Supreme Court Religion Cases *225*

Bibliographic Essay *227*

Index *239*

What landmark U.S. Supreme Court decision was more openly disregarded than *Worcester v. Georgia*, greeted with more shock and criticism than *Dred Scott v. Sandford*, affected more school districts than *Brown v. Board of Education*, and brought together conservative Roman Catholics and fundamentalist Protestants in common cause a decade before *Roe v. Wade*? The answer is *Engel v. Vitale* (1962), the celebrated and infamous "school prayer decision."

In *Engel*, five Nassau County, New York, families challenged the constitutionality of the New York State Regents' nondenominational prayer. The prayer was read at the beginning of all public school classes. The High Court had already held that classrooms could not be used for religious instruction, but schools could cooperate with "released time programs." With reported juvenile delinquency on the rise, fears of "godless communism" dominating politics, and the precedent of released time in New York schools already vindicated, local school boards like those in New Hyde Park decided that a simple prayer, recited without comment, during which a student might leave the room or remain silent, would save the nation from a dire fate. Some objected that the prayer was a meaningless exercise, and others found it offensive, but most students joined the exercise.

There was nothing new in that — from the inception of compulsory public education in America, school prayer and Bible reading were common. From Thomas Jefferson to Jesse Helms, U.S. politicians have clashed over the proper tie between the church and the state in our democratic republic. The issues are controversial ones. Many immigrant parents found the first school book selections insulting, for they featured anti-Catholic propaganda. But Catholics were caught in a difficult situation. They believed that religious instruction belonged in the schools. The issue of school-mandated devotions split Christians into factions, and the factions struggled for control of school boards. Thus when Protestants and Catholics agreed that the New York Regents' prayer was an acceptable compromise, an observer might have concluded that the issue was resolved.

But *Engel* forced the courts to take a closer look at what Jefferson called the "wall of separation" between church and state. The First

Amendment applied that concept to the U.S. Constitution, and the Fourteenth Amendment, as read by the justices in the twentieth century, imposed the First Amendment upon the states. The First Amendment guaranteed freedom of worship, barred the establishment of a state religion, and prevented the federal government from giving preferential treatment to any faith, sect, or church. Did the New York prayer violate the First Amendment rights of the petitioners? It did, according to a six to one ruling of the Court (one justice was ill and another newly confirmed).

Bruce Dierenfield's account of the case, its protagonists, and its aftermath is set in the larger context of religious education in the schools. It makes compelling reading. He has tracked down and interviewed all the parties and rendered the complex legal and religious arguments into clear and concise explanations. With fairness to all and malice toward none, to borrow from another landmark text, Dierenfield takes the reader behind the scenes at the school board meetings and the deliberations of the Supreme Court to find real people wrestling with deeply personal issues. His pen portraits of these men and women bring them to life. In two concluding chapters, he traces the response and the impact of *Engel*. Now that religion and politics are once more made uneasy bedfellows, Dierenfield's work is must reading.

PREFACE

I grew up with the landmark decision of *Engel v. Vitale* (1962), which barred organized prayers in U.S. public schools. My father, Richard B. Dierenfield, professor emeritus of education at Macalester College in St. Paul, Minnesota, was one of the country's leading authorities on religious practices in public education just as the U.S. Supreme Court decided *Engel*. He became something of an academic celebrity, writing a widely quoted book, being interviewed by major newspapers, appearing on national television programs, and testifying before Congress. Shortly after *Engel* was decided, my father was on sabbatical leave in Guildford, England, and, although we are Presbyterian, I attended the seventh grade in St. Bede's Church of England Secondary School. For the first time in my formal education, I was required to say the Lord's Prayer, listen to verses of the King James Bible being read, and bow my head when a student leader said grace at lunch. I also had to pass a class in Anglican theology that was taught by the local vicar.

Religious activities were an occasional part of my public schooling in St. Paul, Minnesota, as well. At Horace Mann Elementary School, I felt special when a Christian missionary group gave me a free New Testament Bible, even if the print was small. Christmas was the most conspicuous religious observance at Horace Mann, and we exchanged gifts in homeroom around a decorated evergreen tree. At Henry Sibley High School in West St. Paul, I was a member of an acclaimed choir that sang at Sunday morning worship services at Lutheran churches. Every December, our Christmas program in the school gymnasium featured sacred music and a disembodied voice of "God" reading prophetic verses from the book of Isaiah. Gar Lockrem, the longtime and much-admired director, patterned the program after one at Concordia College, his Lutheran alma mater. As Christmas rehearsals became more intense, Art Birnbaum, a fellow choir member and a Jew, objected to their sectarian focus. He was looked upon as a troublemaker and ignored. These experiences, as well as my father's career-long interest in the *Engel* decision, prompted me to study this fascinating case, particularly to discover how the case had arisen.

This book provides an introduction to the history of religious practices in U.S. public education, especially organized school prayer, the judiciary's most significant decisions concerning them, and the social and political fallout from such decisions. Space constraints, it should be noted, prevent a consideration of all, or even most, of the innumerable incidents and many state and federal district court cases involving religion in the public school classroom. Chapter 1 describes the extent of devotions in colonial America and the subsequent conflicts that developed in their wake. Chapter 2 looks at pressures on the local level to oust religion in public schools and the backlash to retain — even expand — such devotions, as well as the changing judicial philosophy on behalf of religious minorities. Chapter 3 considers the first significant establishment case — *Everson v. Board of Education* (1947) — and then examines the major two released time decisions — *McCollum v. Board of Education* (1948) and *Zorach v. Clauson* (1952).

The heart of the book, and its major contribution, comes in Chapters 4–7, when it examines closely the human side and constitutional implications of *Engel v. Vitale* (1962), the first of five school prayer cases decided by the U.S. Supreme Court. It focuses especially on the Herricks School District in the town of North Hempstead in Nassau County on Long Island, where the case arose, and on the plaintiffs and their ten children (listed alphabetically by family [last] name — parents first, then children, starting with the oldest): Steven, Thelma, and Michael Engel; Monroe, Julia, and Cynthia Lerner; Daniel, Ruth, Judith, David, and Naomi Lichtenstein; Lenore, Wendy, David, and Jeanne Lyons; and Lawrence, Frances, Daniel, and Joseph Roth.

The remaining chapters discuss the U.S. Supreme Court's school prayer decisions that followed *Engel*. Chapter 8 looks at two companion cases that confirmed and expanded that epic case — *Abington v. Schempp* (1963) and *Murray v. Curlett* (1963). The last chapter looks at several major cases that have occurred since the early 1960s, including *Wallace v. Jaffree* (1985), *Lee v. Weisman* (1992), and *Santa Fe Independent School District v. Doe* (2000). Because each of these cases presented a different circumstance involving organized school prayer, the Court felt obliged to strengthen its proscription of it still further.

ACKNOWLEDGMENTS

Canisius College, the Jesuit institution in Buffalo, New York, where I have worked for twenty years, provided generous support for this project in a variety of ways, including several sabbaticals and summer research grants. My research assistants, who have provided vital legwork, include Chantal Bartels, Jennifer Dodd, Stephen Evers, Ion Ghetie, Nicole Graci, Dean Kotlowski, Gail McDonald, Kelly McQuillan, Keith Muse, Megan Puchalski, Catherine Scanlon, Kathleen Smith, and Katie Starr. I was similarly assisted by the departmental work-study students: Sarah Cosgrove, Kristen Downey, Alexandria Fox, Gretchen Hollmer, Mark Hollmer, Kathleen Kemp, Jennifer Meisenburg, Mark Muoio, Maria Pascucci, Anton Strgagic, and Jacquelyn Wagner. The Canisius library reference staff—Jessica Blum, Karen Bordonaro, Betsey Higgins, Anne Huberman, Pat McGlynn, Lisa Sullivan, and Janelle Toner — has been invaluable. Interlibrary loan technician Sally DiCarlo secured countless books and periodicals. Barbara Boehnke, the acquisitions librarian, purchased many books I requested. Several secretaries, including Sylvia Bigler, Dena Bowman, and Sharon Wiese, transcribed interviews, typed parts of this manuscript, made telephone calls and photocopies, and ordered books from other libraries. Students in my honors seminars on "Church and State in American History" and "Social Movements in the Twentieth Century" asked challenging questions as we studied the meaning of the First Amendment and the activism of the religious right. In this regard, I owe much to my mentor, Erling Jorstad, a professor of modern U.S. history at St. Olaf College in Northfield, Minnesota.

A number of other institutions made this work possible. I received grants from the National Endowment for the Humanities, the Gerald R. Ford Presidential Library, the New York State Archives, and Indiana University's Lilly Library. The Institute for Advanced Study at Indiana University made writing a pleasure during one summer. As I visited many libraries, including the Carnegie Library of Pittsburgh, Pennsylvania; Senator John Heinz Pittsburgh Regional History Center in Pittsburgh; Long Island Studies Institute at Hofstra University; Shelter Rock Public Library in Albertson, New York; Library of Congress; presidential libraries of John F. Kennedy, Gerald Ford, Jimmy

Carter, and Ronald Reagan; Dirksen Congressional Center, Pekin, Illinois; Princeton University's Seeley G. Mudd Library; and Syracuse University's George Arendts Research Library, the staffs were uniformly helpful. Barbara Bernstein, executive director of the Nassau, New York, chapter of the American Civil Liberties Union (ACLU), provided historical information about the organization and telephone numbers for former members to continue the search. Repeated telephone queries to the Historical Genealogy Department of the Allen County Public Library of Fort Wayne, Indiana, and the Rauh Jewish Archives of the Historical Society of Western Pennsylvania, were answered promptly. My long-lost cousin, Ellen Dierenfeld [*sic*], then chief nutritionist for the Bronx Zoo, kindly welcomed me into her home, which I used as a base to visit Nassau County on Long Island, where the school prayer case arose.

Groups on the front lines in the struggle to safeguard religious freedom were particular useful sources for this project. I have long studied and written about the Minnesota chapter of the ACLU, which was for years the organization's most aggressive chapter on church-state issues. In addition, I cofounded and served as president of the Western New York chapter of Americans United for Separation of Church and State. The difficulties in organizing group activities gave me a healthy respect for activist groups on both sides of this persistently nettlesome issue. This book, however, is not intended as a polemic, but as a narrative history of religious practices, especially school prayer, in U.S. public schools.

I especially want to thank several of the plaintiffs in *Engel v. Vitale* and their children (Steven Engel, Michael Engel, Madeleine Engel Koenig; Monroe Lerner, Julia Lerner, Cynthia Lerner Franken; Ruth Lichtenstein and Naomi Lichtenstein; Rita Lichtenstein; Wendy Lyons, Jeanne Lyons, and Douglas Lyons; and Daniel Roth) for their recollections of the case. This is the first book to include interviews from all five families who participated in the suit. Others refused to be interviewed, most notably Joe Roth, the lead petitioner's younger son and a highly successful Hollywood movie producer. In a 1990 interview with *Premiere* magazine, Joe's older brother, Daniel Roth, explained, "There's not a lot of reminiscing. . . . Much more talk about today and tomorrow and very little about yesterday." Their father, Lawrence Roth, never sought publicity, and when he died at age ninety-one in 2005, there was no obituary. His fitting memorial would be public schools where learning is preeminent and prayers are never recited.

Steven Engel insists that there was "nothing special" about any of the plaintiffs, and he requested that this book focus on the critical constitutional issues raised by the case. As will be plain in the pages that follow, I declined to follow this advice to reveal the personal side of the story, though it greatly prolonged the undertaking. What follows is the first in-depth social, political, and constitutional history of one of the most controversial Supreme Court cases in U.S. history.

I also am grateful for interviews with other key figures in the *Engel* case, including attorneys (Herbert Balin, William Butler, Bertram Daiker, Thomas Ford, and Stanley Geller), the trial judge (Bernard Meyer), school board members (George Farber and Frank Picciano), school officials (Magill Shipman), teachers (Walter Bemak, Michael Carbone, Scott Finegan, Joe Hagan, Michael Klopfer, Rita Leidner, Harold Lovins, Paul Mott, Frederick Pedersen, Sidney Schaffer, Magill Shipman, John Snyder, and David Stollwerk), librarians (Elizabeth Bartle), and students (Peter Arest, Alice Milner Cutler, Barbara Kantowitz Kalvert, Nancy Lehr Lee, Ellen Kahn Masters, Stuart Masters, George Peck, Sandy Poliakin Rosen, Thomas Roth, Susan Chiusano Russo, Susan Spizz Stollwerk, and Jill Poliakin Wood), for their invaluable recollections of the *Engel* case. I corresponded with other Herricks alumni, including Frank Biondo, Charles Caputo, David Fisher, David Marshak, Marion Polon, and David Rubin. To understand a related court case and political activism for and against religion in public education, I interviewed John Buchanan, James Terry McCollum, Louise Ruhlin, and Chalmers Wylie. My research assistant, Kathleen Smith, interviewed Vashti Cromwell McCollum and Dannel McCollum.

I received research assistance from several other people associated with the Herricks School District. Linda Steel, administrative assistant to the superintendent of the Herricks public schools, located a treasure trove of archival material on the case that has not previously been examined. Michael Klopfer hunted down materials in the basement of the Herricks administrative building and read back issues of the *Herricks Highlander.* Elizabeth Bartle, a retired librarian at Searingtown School, retrieved valuable information about that school, which set off the school prayer fight. Barbara Kantowitz Kalvert, a member of Herricks' graduating class of 1963, kindly gave me a copy of her senior thesis at Barnard College, which includes valuable local information on the case.

Some of my research has appeared previously in scholarly articles and essays: "The Amen Amendment: Doomed to Failure?" *Religion and Education* 22 (Fall 1995): 40–48; "'A Nation under God': Ronald Reagan and the Crusade for School Prayer," in *Ronald Reagan's America*, ed. Eric Schmertz, et al. (Westport, CT: Greenwood Press, 1997), pp. 215–247; "Rooting out Religion: Devotions in Minnesota Public Schools since 1950," *Minnesota History* 58, no. 3 (Winter 1993): 294–311; "Secular Schools? Religious Practices in New York and Virginia Public Schools since World War II," *Journal of Policy History* 4, no. 4 (1992): 361–388; "'Somebody Is Tampering with America's Soul': Congress and the School Prayer Debate," *Congress and the Presidency* 24, no. 2 (Autumn 1997): 167–204; "Steven Engel and Lawrence Roth: 'The Supreme Court Has Held That God Is Unconstitutional,'" in *100 Americans Making Constitutional History*, ed. Melvin Urofsky (Washington, D.C.: Congressional Quarterly Press, 2004), pp. 48–51; "*Engel v. Vitale*," in *The Public Debate over Controversial Supreme Court Decisions*, ed. Melvin Urofsky (Washington, D.C.: Congressional Quarterly Press, 2006), pp. 215–225. Part of this study was presented to an annual meeting of the American Historical Association. I thank the respondents — Paul Murphy, Mark Tushnet, and William Barnard — for their incisive comments.

Particular thanks go to the manuscript readers, including Sr. Patricia Brady, Rev. John Bucki, S.J., Derek Davis, Richard Dierenfield, Donald Drakeman, Fr. Robert Drinan, S.J., Charles Haynes, Peter Charles Hoffer, John Johnson, Jonathan Lurie, Al Menendez, and Melvin Urofsky. They have been helpful and encouraging, even when they could not accept every part of the manuscript. Brian Kantz, Sue Banchich, Jeff Paterson, and David Stollwerk carefully edited the manuscript.

I want particularly to thank Michael Briggs, editor-in-chief at the University Press of Kansas, for his extended patience while I tracked down the principals in the case and fleshed out what has, until now, been a story with more of an ending than a beginning.

It is my family who means the most and to whom I owe the greatest debt. They truly know how long it has taken to write this story, and their love has been steadfast from beginning to end. My parents, Richard and Yvonne Dierenfield, have been everything a son could ask for. Their example, their deep wisdom, and their faith in my abilities have always carried me through whatever task I undertook. My brother, David, and his family, my uncle Charles and cousin Lili and my mother-in-law, June Murphy, and her family (Pat Murphy and Millie Khemakhem; Loretta, Jim, and Mike Nuessle; and Maureen and John Martin) have been interested in and supportive of my work in a general sense. My historian wife Kate continues to serve as an invaluable sounding board for my work and to handle matters large and small that would have otherwise delayed this manuscript even more. This book is dedicated to our talented daughter Elizabeth, the light of our lives.

The Supreme Court Decision

The beginning of America's downfall, many conservatives maintain, can be pinpointed rather specifically. According to David Barton, an influential fundamentalist Christian and vice chair of the Texas Republican Party, that day was June 25, 1962. It was then, he declared, that the "U.S. Supreme Court kicked God out of public schools" in the *Engel v. Vitale* decision. From that moment on, Barton asserts, 39 million students and 2 million teachers "were barred from doing what had been done since our nation's founding — pray in school." As a direct result, he maintains, the United States entered into a downward spiral that threatens to destroy the world's greatest nation. Life is, supposedly, worse in every way than it was before 1962. Educational achievement, as measured by SAT scores, has plummeted, and the incidence of illegitimate births, the divorce rate, drug use, racial unrest, public protests, and violence have skyrocketed. For Barton, who graduated from Oral Roberts University and founded an educational organization called WallBuilders, the cause is unmistakable.

For others, religion in the public schools meant something different — isolation and harassment. Walter Dellinger, a former law clerk for U.S. Supreme Court Justice Hugo Black and the solicitor general in Bill Clinton's administration, remembers how much he disliked going to public school in Charlotte, North Carolina, in the early 1950s. On Thursdays, eleven-year-old Walter, who was raised in a blue-collar, Irish Catholic home, awoke with "a dull aching pain in the pit of [his] stomach," because a Bible teacher was coming to teach a one-hour "nondenominational" class. In reality, the fifth-grade Bible class was Protestant. Although students could be excused upon a parent's written request, Walter's mother agonized over whether to send such a note to the school. She finally did so, persuaded by her parish priest's warning that such instruction would subject Walter to "an occasion of sin." As the hands on the clock moved inexorably toward 10 a.m., Walter's classmates, except for a Jewish boy named Victor Burg, eagerly awaited the Bible class, which would give them a welcome break from arithmetic and English grammar. As the Bible teacher arrived with an armful of comics, films, and snacks, the regular teacher announced, "Walter and Victor should now leave the room." As an embarrassed Walter exited the classroom, he felt the stinging stares of his classmates, who wondered why he could not stay for cookies and Kool-Aid, coloring pictures of Jesus, and singing hymns. Walter and Victor headed to the library, where they shelved books.

Young Walter's story was far from unique, as the statistics in Table I.1 reveal.

In Alabama, religious activities dominated some public schools as late as the 1990s, because school officials and most parents regarded religion (i.e., Protestant Christianity) as the indispensable means to enter heaven, to promote discipline in class, and to fight society's secular and materialistic tendencies. As the thinking went, the more religion the better. The De Kalb and Pike County public schools provided many examples. The evangelical Ponderosa Bible Camp offered religious instruction during class time. Teachers said grace before lunch in the cafeteria and solicited students to pray or read

Table I.1 Religious Practices in U.S. Public Schools, 1960

Practice	Percentage
Christmas celebration	87.9
Baccalaureate services	86.8
Thanksgiving celebration	76.8
Easter celebration	57.8
Gideon Bible distribution	42.7
Bible reading	41.8
School prayer in homeroom	33.2
Released time for religious instruction	29.7
Lunchtime prayer	27.4
Chapel exercises	22.1
Hanukkah celebration	5.4
Bible classes	4.5

Source: Richard Dierenfield, *Religion in American Public Schools* (Washington, DC: Public Affairs Press, 1962), *passim*.

from the Bible in front of the class. David, Paul, Sarah, and Rachel Herring — the only Jews in their school — were forced to pray and write essays entitled, "Why Jesus Loves Me." School officials maintained that teachers must save children's souls if their parents did not. Protestant ministers led prayers at school football games, pep rallies, band concerts, 4-H meetings, and graduations. At a mandatory student assembly, a local minister condemned to hell anyone who did not accept Jesus Christ as savior. An evangelist preached to the students in a drug-education program and invited them to attend a Christian "pizza party" afterward. A missionary group distributed New Testament Bibles throughout the school. If a child dared to say, "No, thank you, I have one at home," or "No, thank you, I don't want one," the missionary would reply, "Why not? You need this. It will save your soul." When a federal judge prohibited these unwelcome religious activities as illegal, the governor urged public schools to ignore the decree.

Although these episodes in Alabama were extreme, such incidents occurred across the country. What is especially disturbing about this story is that the U.S. Supreme Court had prohibited such prayers and proselytizing thirty years earlier in the landmark *Engel* case.

Religious expression in public schools poses several knotty problems. In the First Amendment, the U.S. Constitution has a two-sided religion clause that recognizes religious liberty but bans religious establishment. The meaning of this clause has long been controversial, with the Christian majority emphasizing its right to have devotions in all U.S. public venues and members of minority religions demanding safeguards from the dominant religion. Aside from the constitutional questions arising from school prayer, there are practical considerations. The United States is the most religiously diverse nation in the world, with more than 1,500 different religious bodies and sects, including New Age cults, voodooists, Satanists, spiritualists, the Church of Scientology, and 75 varieties of Baptists. There are 360,000 churches, mosques, synagogues, and temples, and each sect believes it possesses more of the truth than the others.

The practices of one religious group are invariably not acceptable to another. Adopting one prayer or reading from one Bible in public schools means that the predominant group discriminates against the rest. It is — and long has been — a recipe for social division. Imagine these scenarios: Would Christians feel compelled to march into the hall when a Muslim prayer was recited over the school intercom? Would Protestants have to leave when Catholics wanted to petition the Blessed Virgin Mary? Would Jehovah's Witnesses have to walk out when Buddhists in Hawaii said their own particular prayers? Would Mormons have to depart if Jews recited their prayers? And on and on it would go.

The prayer controversy has been a critically important issue in U.S. history for several reasons. First, it reveals the dominance that Protestants have exercised over major institutions from government to education to culture. Second, because of its extraordinary longevity, the dispute over religion in public schools marks an exception — abortion being another — to the general pattern that U.S. politics resolves issues relatively quickly. Moreover, the simmering dispute persuaded the country's largest religious minority — Roman Catholics — to create a parallel school system, which eventually generated its own demands on the public purse for textbooks, transportation, and even teachers. Finally, the dispute led to a remarkable change in U.S. jurisprudence. The Warren Court determined that the long-standing practice of school prayer violated the First Amendment's establishment clause. Schools that had been founded to instill religious truths were now, the U.S. Supreme Court decided, to be inoculated from religious instruction and worship altogether. It was a remarkable turn of events.

CHAPTER I

"Forced Worship Stinks in God's Nostrils"

Roger Williams, an English minister who moved to Salem, Massachusetts, in 1631, impressed his congregation with his sweet temper. Underneath his pleasing personality was a penchant toward controversy, in large measure because he subscribed to a revolutionary idea: church and state belonged in separate spheres — the better to keep religion pure and the state honest. For Williams, religious truth was for each individual, not government officials, to determine. It is, he wrote, "against the testimony of Christ Jesus for the civil state to impose upon the souls of the people a religion. . . . Jesus never called for the sword of steel to help the sword of spirit." As such, each community of faith should pay its own bills, rather than expecting general taxes to do so. Because "forced worship stinks in God's nostrils," thundered Williams, there should be a "wall of separation, between the garden of the church and the wilderness of the world." Radical notions like these resulted in Williams's banishment, and it would take a long time before he would be seen as a prophet and not a heretic.

Aside from Roger Williams and William Penn, a Quaker who launched his own "Holy Experiment" in religious liberty, most English settlers believed that the colonies needed an established church because religious freedom was a chimera. All of history seemed to prove that social order, civic virtue, and truth itself depended on fealty to one privileged religion. For the Puritans of Massachusetts Bay, whom the English Crown had persecuted, the entire purpose of coming to the New World was to establish a Christian commonwealth based on God's Holy Bible. The rights of citizenship in the Bay Colony depended on a provable religious experience, which then qualified the believer for membership in the official church.

A government-sponsored church was thus built into most of the British colonies in America. Influenced by the established Congrega-

{ 5 }

tional Church, the colonial assemblies of New England required every household to have a Bible, established fines for irregular church attendance, prohibited "unnecessary walking" on Sunday, and limited the privilege of holding public office. In the southern colonies, the Church of England (Anglican Church) received tax revenues and could punish heretics and dissenters. Jurors, witnesses, and office-holders throughout British America were required to acknowledge Christianity, the divine inspiration of the Bible, and a belief in a literal heaven and hell.

Having established communities whose very purpose was to obey God's will, Protestants in New England trained their children to fear the Almighty. By custom and law, education at that time was a matter left primarily to the home, privately hired teachers, and religious societies. In 1647, the Massachusetts General Court paved the way for public education, passing a law that assessed taxes to employ "Protestant teachers of piety, religion, and morality." In towns of fifty families, an elementary school had to be established; in towns of a hundred families, a grammar school. Children participated in sectarian exercises in their classes, reciting the Lord's Prayer and reading from the King James Bible. For Protestants, the King James version was the "real" Bible, the literal "Word of God," and this mainstay of early American education was used most often to teach literacy, instill moral precepts, and prepare young men for the two learned professions of the time — the law and the ministry. In these ways, the local school complemented the work of the local church. No one objected because the townspeople were all, or nearly all, Protestant.

Gradually, a state church came to be regarded as unnecessary. The religious landscape changed profoundly in the eighteenth century in the wake of shifting immigration patterns, the revival known as the Great Awakening, and the emergence of the European Enlightenment. From the start, religious pluralism existed in every colony, and such diversity grew as time passed. Even where Congregationalism was dominant, that church was divided by rifts, and in the early nineteenth century, a sizable number of New Englanders followed the lead of William Ellery Channing of Boston and split off to form the Unitarian Church.

A wide variety of immigrants poured in from all corners of Europe, making the American colonies the most religiously diverse place on earth. The new settlers included Scottish Presbyterians, Welsh Baptists, Dutch Reformed, French Huguenots, and English Methodists, Quakers, and Shakers. The Germans came in many religious varieties, including Protestants (Amish, Dunkers, Hutterites, Lutherans, Mennonites, Moravians, and Schwenckfelders), Roman Catholics, and Jews. Naturally, these dissenting faiths resented the religious monopoly granted to their rivals, especially when they were taxed to support them. True Christianity, many dissenters believed, attracted followers by the force of Jesus' gospel, not the force of law. For Protestants in particular, getting to heaven rested on the transforming power of the Holy Spirit, not on the theological dogma of a state-controlled church.

The Awakening, inspired by Congregational minister Jonathan Edwards of Massachusetts and promoted by English divine George Whitefield, enlivened spiritually dead Protestant churches, spurred the growth of minor faiths, and helped create Methodism in America. Calvinist congregations of Presbyterianism and Baptism preached the New Birth with evangelical fervor, causing their numbers to increase quickly in the hinterlands of Pennsylvania, Virginia, and the Carolinas. One plain lesson of the Awakening was that people would flock to services when religion was red-hot, even without the police power of the state. It appeared that religious establishment was unnecessary after all.

The Awakening had the unintended effect of creating a choice of churches in many areas, prompting religions to compete for adherents in the marketplace — a process that resembled the trading of goods. Religious tolerance was not an ideal to be aspired to, but a reality that could not be ignored. It was Adam Smith, a staunch proponent of free trade, who suggested how religion could fit into American public life. Whereas most colonies sanctioned either one denomination or Protestantism in general, Smith proposed an open competition for all groups, including businesses, political factions, and religious sects. If groups had to compete, the larger society would benefit, he theorized. Religious leaders would devise more reasonable doctrines and thereby moderate the most divisive dogmas. Many Founding Fathers accepted this understanding of religion.

In the Enlightenment, English Whig thinkers, including John Trenchard and Thomas Gordon, promoted a radical equality in the press, politics, and conscience, and brooked no interference in any of these areas. Even pagans, they argued, should be protected from government injury. According to John Locke's social contract, everyone possessed natural or God-given rights, including the right to believe as one wished. This contract posited that an open society could not long exist in a state of nature, and so the people gave up some rights to a government of their choosing in order to live in peace. Fundamental rights, including freedom of conscience, remained in individual hands, beyond the reach of a coercive government. At the same time, Whigs distrusted the church as much as the state, and their views were laced with a strong strain of anticlericalism. Clerics, in the Whig view, were invariably arrogant and rapacious, so neither church nor state should control one's conscience.

All these developments meant that when Americans revolted against England — the mother country — they would seek political and ecclesiastical liberty. Indeed, many colonists could not fathom national independence without safeguarding the most essential liberty of all — freedom of the soul. As long as "royal brutes" like George III held sway, the colonists would never enjoy religious liberty. James Madison recognized this crucial point: "Torrents of blood have been spilt in the old world, by vain attempts of the secular arm to extinguish religious discord. . . . Time has at length revealed the true remedy." For Madison, that remedy was nothing less than complete religious liberty in a new nation. As religious historian Edwin Gaustad put it, "This was and is the essence of 'the American experiment.' "

Exactly what religious liberty meant in America was defined differently in nearly every state. The most notable contest over religion in the new country took place in the 1780s in Virginia, where Anglicanism was the official church. Baptists, who outnumbered Anglicans, protested laws that prevented Baptist clerics from obtaining licenses to preach, solemnizing marriages, and leading worship services during the daytime. Baptists, joined by Presbyterians and Lutherans, resented being taxed to support the Anglican Church and fined for failing to attend Anglican worship services.

The notion of religious disestablishment was chiefly the contribution of several Americans, including leading political thinkers such as Thomas Jefferson and James Madison, and devout churchgoers such as Samuel Davies, a Presbyterian minister and president of Princeton College, and two Baptist ministers — Isaac Backus of Connecticut and John Leland of Virginia. Their motivations in dethroning an official church were varied. Most obviously, they regarded the privileged status of the Anglican Church as a bitter legacy of British imperialism. They were convinced not only that formal ties between religion and government were unnecessary but that they degraded religion, harmed government, persecuted minorities, and obstructed individuals' search for truth. Rev. Backus explained, "Now who can hear Christ declare, that his kingdom is, not of this world, and yet believe that this blending of church and state together can be pleasing to him?"

Although Jefferson was not an orthodox Christian, the "Virginia Voltaire" was not antireligious or anti-Christian. Indeed, he believed that rights depended on one's belief in God and admired Jesus' gospel of love as "perfect and sublime." Jefferson nevertheless insisted on the freedom to pursue religion wherever his conscience or reason led. To that end, he wrote his own abbreviated version of the Bible, dispensing with the miracles he found incredulous. For Jefferson, "The legitimate powers of government extend only to such acts as are injurious to others. But it does me no injury for my neighbor to say there are twenty gods or no god. It neither picks my pocket nor breaks my leg." With so many different religious groups, Jefferson was convinced that it was practically impossible to prefer one among many.

Believing that tyranny appeared in several incarnations, including ecclesiastical, Jefferson called for the disestablishment of Virginia's Anglican Church. A state church, he thought, serves neither religion nor liberty; it makes "one half the world fools, and the other half hypocrites." Under such privilege, the clergy grew lazy or corrupt, and dissenters were taxed to support a religion they rejected. Not only that, dissenters risked fines for profanity, confiscation of children for allegedly being unfit parents, jail time for denying the Trinity, and even death for heresy. Determined to prevent dissenters from being consigned to second-class citizenship, Jefferson sought to protect all religions, including "the Jew and the Gentile, the Christian and Mahometan, the Hindoo, and infidel of every denomination." His minimum goal was to prevent the government from establishing an official religion and from favoring any religion or the religious over the nonreligious. The result, he was certain, would be true religious liberty.

As the bruising battle over religious freedom ensued, Patrick Henry introduced a bill in the Virginia General Assembly to renew tax levies for the Anglican Church. Alarmed by this turn of events,

James Madison, whose father was in the Anglican vestry, penned a classic statement of religious freedom. In his 1785 "Memorial and Remonstrance against Religious Assessments," Madison opposed a state church, noting that Christianity had been so privileged for 1,500 years. "What have been its fruits?" he asked rhetorically. "More or less in all places, pride and indolence in the Clergy, ignorance and servility in the laity, in both, superstition, bigotry and persecution." Madison argued that to prefer one religion to another would negate the American Revolution and "trespass on the rights of the minority." If government could choose among religions, he forecast a time when the privileged majority would become the aggrieved minority. To Madison, the "free exercise" of religion "according to the dictates of conscience" is "the gift of nature" and therefore entirely beyond the reach of government.

Madison's remonstrance helped persuade the Virginia Assembly to adopt Jefferson's Statute for Religious Freedom the following year. The statute removed the state's endorsement of the Anglican Church and ended what dissenters called a "long night of ecclesiastical bondage." It was the first statute in world history to declare that there was no religious view whose expression should in any way "diminish, enlarge, or affect" the "civil capacities" of the speaker or writer. In other words, all citizens had a natural right to pursue whatever religious thoughts they had without governmental interference or sanction. This revolutionary moment greatly influenced sister states and the federal government, and it marked the beginning, not the end, of the constant struggle for religious liberty.

The Founding Fathers on the whole were hardly hostile to religion, which they regarded as an indispensable aid to moral behavior and republican self-government. At the same time, the Founders believed that government should keep its hands off of religion, lest Europe's deadly sectarian strife be transported across the Atlantic. They therefore created a remarkably innovative government framework that secured "the blessings of liberty" in three forms — political, economic, and religious. Americans would put their trust in the rule of law, not the rule of God or his earthly representatives. Although the Declaration of Independence refers four times to a divine being (e.g., "Nature's God" and "Supreme Judge of the world"), the Constitution itself does not mention God, Jesus, or even religion at all, except to exclude Sundays from the period during which the president may veto legislation, to date the document as "in the Year of our Lord one thousand seven hundred and Eighty seven," and, most important, to bar religious tests for public office. In short, the Founding Fathers created the world's first secular government as the best way to minimize the religious tensions that had perpetually plagued Europe.

To win ratification of the new federal constitution, the Federalist supporters, including James Madison, promised to append a series of guarantees to protect individuals from arbitrary government action. Madison kept his promise, collating seventeen proposals from the states, even though he believed that the ever-increasing multiplicity of sects in America made improbable the establishment of any national religion. Madison opposed government preferment of religion in general, not just granting the establishment of a particular church. This thinking prevailed in the First Amendment because the Founding Fathers believed that government inevitably corrupted religion. There was general agreement that coerced religion was false religion. What is commonly overlooked is that the primary purpose of the Bill of Rights was to shield unpopular minorities from tyrannical majorities who might run roughshod over them, whether they be political protesters, accused criminals, or religious dissenters who object to organized school prayer.

In the Bill of Rights, the Founding Fathers could have established a particular church, as Massachusetts did, or favored the Christian religion, as South Carolina did. John Adams concluded that the Constitution should not address religion. He hoped that "Congress will never meddle with religion further than to say their own prayers, and to fast and to give thanks once a year." In the end, the Founders followed Virginia's example of permitting religions to compete for followers without state support. They simply refused to grant any power concerning religion to the new federal government because religion, in their view, was a divisive, not a unifying, force. Religious matters, the Founders believed, were best handled at the state level, in much the same way that Virginia had resolved its conflicting demands.

After considerable debate and redrafting, Congress finally approved, and the states ratified, the first sixteen words of what is now the First Amendment: "Congress shall make no law respecting an establishment of religion, or prohibiting the free exercise thereof."

This opening phrase was framed to guard a single freedom in two ways, and it is the only constitutional liberty to enjoy a double protection. In the name of religious liberty, the amendment barred Congress from helping religion (the establishment clause) *and* from hindering religion (the free exercise clause). Although the establishment clause has generated great controversy, its meaning at the time it was written was clear: the federal government has no power in religious matters, especially by preferring a single church or sect. The government, which is restricted to its enumerated powers, is not to assist any one religious group or to help religion generally, even if such aid could be given even-handedly; it is to avoid religion altogether. Because the First Amendment neither prescribes nor proscribes religion, the Founders believed that religion would not control politics and politics would not spoil religion.

In 1802, Thomas Jefferson volunteered his definition of the First Amendment. When Baptists in Danbury, Connecticut, asked him to set aside a national day of fasting to heal the wounds of the contentious election that made him president, he refused on constitutional grounds. In his response, Jefferson declared that the First Amendment had erected a "wall" — an impenetrable barrier — between church and state. Although a century and a half would pass before the U.S. Supreme Court embraced Jefferson's understanding of the First Amendment, this metaphor is commonly employed today to interpret the religion clauses.

At the same time, it was commonly believed that the First Amendment *protected* state establishments against congressional action. The amendment restricted the federal government in the area of religion just as the Constitution kept education, voting, and the police powers in local hands. As a result, state governments could act as they wished in the area of religion. Most states wrote into their new constitutions provisions for religious liberty and dissolved their official churches one by one, ending with Massachusetts in 1833. The idea that the Bill of Rights, as a whole or in part, applied to the states developed only gradually. As various issues came before it in the twentieth century, the Supreme Court used the due process clause of the Fourteenth Amendment to extend civil freedoms afforded to federal citizenship to state citizenship. This idea, known as the incorporation doctrine, was applied initially to freedom of speech, freedom of the press, and defendants in criminal cases. The establishment clause would not be applied to state action until after World War II.

The views of Thomas Jefferson and James Madison notwithstanding, the First Congress did enact some measures involving religion. The Congress that approved the First Amendment adopted a joint resolution to set aside a day of prayer and thanksgiving to God. President George Washington thereupon issued a proclamation calling for the American people to devote the day "to the services of that great and glorious Being who is the beneficent author of all the good that was, that is, or that will be." James Madison served on the joint congressional committee that set up the chaplain system for Congress and the military. Both Jefferson and Madison, as president, used tax money to support Protestant missionary work among Indians. The crier in the U.S. Supreme Court intoned then (and now), "God save the United States and this honorable Court." Such practices in an overwhelmingly Protestant country were evidently so integral to the culture that they were neither seen as controversial, nor deemed coercive. For the most part, however, Congress largely refrained from passing laws related to religion.

When church-state questions arose in the nineteenth century, the U.S. Supreme Court handled them without reference to the First Amendment because the Bill of Rights was regarded as applicable only to the federal government. The first case to reach the Court in this area arose out of the disestablishment of the Episcopal Church in Virginia. Subsequent church-state cases dealt with disputes over wills, charters, monopolies, contracts, church doctrine, conscientious objection to the draft, inoculations, parochial school aid, saluting the flag, and proselytism. Until the polygamy case after the Civil War, the U.S. Supreme Court never decided disputes that arose out of religious conflict on the basis of religion.

As for religion in public education, the matter did not reach the Supreme Court for more than 150 years. Indeed, public schools did not really exist until the 1830s, when a consensus emerged (at least in the North) that education could no longer be left to families. With the creation of a republic and the rise of the factory system, education would serve vital civic and commercial functions and needed a more formal setting. Religion would remain an indispensable part of this new schooling, and school prayers were common and unquestioned. The

King James Bible provided the basis for many class lessons, and the religious epigrams in *Webster's Speller* embodied Protestant views.

Many schools also used William McGuffey's *Eclectic Reader*, an enormously popular textbook that emphasized patriotism and moral values. McGuffey, a Presbyterian minister and former frontier schoolteacher, once explained why his reader contained religious excerpts: "The Christian religion is the religion of our country. From it are derived our notions on the character of God, on the great moral Governor of the universe. On its doctrines are founded the peculiarities of our free institutions. From no other source has the author drawn more conspicuously than from the sacred Scriptures. For all these extracts from the Bible I make no apology."

The McGuffey readers were adopted by Horace Mann, a formally trained attorney and the state superintendent of schools in Massachusetts. His motivation for using these books stemmed from an ugly childhood incident. On a Sunday morning in 1810, Horace's older brother Stephen drowned when he skipped church to go swimming. A heartless Rev. Nathaniel Emmons accused Stephen of being "criminally negligent in attending public worship." With the Bible as his authority, the Congregational minister pronounced the divine penalty — rotting in hell. The cutting words left an indelible scar that Horace never forgot. He rejected Emmons's God of vengeance in favor of a benign deity — the deity in McGuffey's readers — who allowed for human progress. The sermon so angered Mann that he vowed schools would not force children to follow a rigid religious party line.

Horace Mann simply did not see how one's behavior was affected by a belief in the divinity of Christ, bodily immersion at baptism, or the innate depravity of children. Mann's convictions were buttressed by the School Law of 1827, which prohibited sectarian religious instruction in public school classrooms in Massachusetts. The law ordered teachers to "impress on the minds of children . . . the principles of piety, justice, and sacred regard to truth," but forbade them to use any book "calculated to favor any particular religious sect or tenet." The practical solution to this dilemma, Mann thought, was to instill Christian principles through daily readings from the King James Bible and a carefully chosen textbook. Teachers could not comment in any way on the biblical passages they read.

Having provided for a pan-Protestant foundation in public education, Mann insisted that each denomination — whether orthodox Congregationalist, evangelical Baptist, or liberal Unitarian — "must be left to its own resources, for inculcating its own faith or creed." The real enemy of public education, Mann thought, was not competing Protestant sects but the Roman Catholic Church, which was allegedly intolerant and avowed that "men could not think for themselves." Mann repeatedly dismissed charges that the common schools were irreligious: "Everyone . . . knows that I am in favor of religious instruction in our schools, to the extremist verge to which it can be carried without invading those rights of conscience which are established by the laws of God, and guaranteed to us by the Constitution of the State."

Across the nation, the Massachusetts template for religious instruction was implemented sporadically in the 1800s. Daily devotions were often held only when the classroom had visitors or the local minister stopped by. The annual reports of the New York State superintendent of public instruction reveal that the Bible was used in the public schools of 28 percent of towns in 1827, a figure that declined steadily to 11 percent in 1840, the last year for which records were kept. From 1839 forward, New York state superintendents of public education declared that "prayers cannot form any part of the school exercises . . . if had at all, they should be had before the . . . hour of commencing school in the morning." State education officials in the antebellum period understood that the cost of sectarianism in public education was too high. Public schools would never be universally accepted as long as religious minorities were made to feel unwelcome.

But this understanding did not preclude religious exercises *in toto*. New York State superintendents ruled in disputes that came before them that religious exercises during school hours were not in themselves illegal. They were illegal only when someone objected. As a result, school districts continued or adopted several kinds of religious exercises, including Bible reading without comment, recitation of nondenominational Christian prayers, and singing popular hymns. Because pupils used the Bible as a reader and a speller, they heard scripture far more often than they sang hymns or recited prayers and creeds; but even the Bible was not universally used. In the period after the Civil War, about half of New York's public school districts with 75 percent of the state's total school enrollment had religious exercises.

This pattern was observable elsewhere. In St. Louis, Missouri, Bible reading was not permitted when the first public school opened in 1840. In Watertown, Wisconsin, the local board removed the Bible from the curriculum in 1858, to the consternation of the state superintendent of public instruction. Except for the smallest district, the Bible was not read in Louisiana public schools before the Civil War. In the West, Bible reading was against the law in Washington and Idaho, not permitted in a single school in Nevada, and read in few schools in the other western states.

As early as the mid-nineteenth century, the pattern of Bible reading had become clear, with the practice most common in the Northeast, followed closely by the South, less common in the Midwest, and hardly present in the West. Smaller cities and towns were more likely to have Bible reading than large ones. The U.S. commissioner of education reported that, except for a few New England states, "there is no considerable area where use [of the Bible] can be said to be uniform."

In part, this variation in Bible reading grew out of profound social changes. A wave of religious enthusiasm in the early nineteenth century — known as the Second Great Awakening — resulted in new sects popping up on the fertile American soil, including the Disciples of Christ, Seventh-Day Adventists, and Church of Jesus Christ of Latter-Day Saints (the Mormons). Later that century, the Church of Christ, Scientist (Christian Science) formed. The Mormons and Christian Scientists supplemented the King James Bible with their own bibles. Moreover, existing Protestant sects divided almost as easily as cells replicating in the human body. The Methodist Church, for example, divided forty times, giving rise to the African Methodist Episcopal Church, Free Methodist Church, Southern Methodist Church, Wesleyan Church, and others. The result was that control of the public schools became increasingly difficult for any one denomination.

The nation's religious tapestry became ever more intricate as immigration soared. Between 1830 and 1870, the number of Roman Catholics in the United States more than quadrupled to 4 million. Many of them fled Ireland and Germany to escape religious persecution, political turmoil, poverty, and, in the case of the Irish, mass starvation. Because the Irish were dirt poor, they took the cheapest passage across the Atlantic, settling at least initially in the Northeast, where Bible reading was commonplace. Protestant denominations grew, too, but no single Protestant denomination approached the Catholic Church in membership. Combined, the total number of Methodists and Baptists — the two largest Protestant bodies — fell considerably short of the number of Catholics. The longstanding rivalry, animosity, and bloodshed between Protestants and Catholics meant that a showdown over Bible reading in U.S. public schools was a foregone conclusion.

Much of the impetus to keep religion in public schools can be traced directly to anti-Catholicism. Such prejudice was deeply ingrained in U.S. history and had its origins in the Protestant Reformation in Germany. There were important theological, doctrinal, and ritualistic differences that divided these two heavyweight variants of Christianity. Convinced that God's word was fully expressed in the Bible, Martin Luther and other Protestant reformers rejected the Roman Catholic Church's reliance on tradition. Another central difference was that Protestants believed that salvation came not from deeds but from faith alone. Catholics are particularly devoted to Mary, "the Mother of God," and images of her abound in Catholic churches. A large pantheon of saints offers Catholics inspiration for a godly life on earth. For most Protestants, Mary is not venerated, and sainthood is a designation reserved for God Almighty. The Catholic Mass relies on symbols and rituals; the Protestant "worship service" emphasizes preaching from a biblical text. Whereas Roman Catholics observe seven sacraments, including marriage and unction, Protestants recognize only the two that Jesus performed — baptism and the Lord's Supper. For Catholics, the Eucharist means that the elements of bread and wine are supernaturally transformed into the body and blood of Jesus; for most Protestants, the Lord's Supper is symbolic of Christ's sacrifice.

Even God's holy word is a point of great contention. For Roman Catholics, tradition counts as much as scripture; for Protestants, the Bible is the centerpiece of spiritual guidance. For Catholics, the Douay-Rheims Bible (1582) — an English translation of the Latin Vulgate — consists of seventy-three books, including such Apocrypha works as Esdras and Tobias and extensive commentary. The Protestant King James Version (1611) rejected these writings and therefore contains sixty-six books. Moreover, the Catholic Bible, like the daily Mass, was then in Latin, while Protestants read their Bible and held services in their native tongues. Protestants found such doctrinal differences deeply disturbing and concluded that the Roman Catholic Church had become hopelessly corrupt.

Protestants also thought Catholic immigrants were incapable of assimilation and threatened U.S. institutions. Catholics were viewed as part of the world's largest subversive organization — the Roman Catholic Church — whose objective was not the salvation of lost souls but the constant aggrandizement of a worldly pope. The pope, it was said, had dispatched a tidal wave of Catholic immigrants to overrun the United States, a prospect that seemed nearer with the arrival of every boatload of Irish and Germans. Protestants also felt that Catholics could not be good Americans because Catholicism was a top-down religion in which faithful Catholics followed the teachings of the Vatican and the complicated hierarchy that stretched all the way to the parish priest. The United States, Protestants believed, worked the other way around. Democracy required independent minds that put the good of the country ahead of self-interest. Even more repellent were persistent (and untrue) rumors of sexual depravity involving supposedly celibate priests and nuns. Their illicit offspring, the story went, were murdered and buried beneath the floors of convents.

Not only were Roman Catholic immigrants suspected of being political subversives and followers of a bastardized form of Christianity, Protestants blamed them for unemployment and an increase in public drunkenness, pauperism, and crime. To resist the multitudinous threats that immigrants apparently posed to the United States, Protestants formed various nativist fraternities, such as the Order of United Americans, and political organizations, including the American Republican and Native American Parties. Strongest in the nation's Northeast, the most popular of these groups was the Know Nothings, which attracted 1 million supporters by the mid-1850s. Among the nativist demands were that immigrants be prevented from citizenship and voting until they had resided in the United States for twenty-one years, that Catholics be proscribed from public office, that the sale of liquor be restricted, and that in the public schools only Protestants be hired as teachers and that the King James Bible be read daily.

As much as nativists wanted to define Americanism by religion, if not by ethnicity and race, the increasing diversity of the population made such attempts problematic at best. An institution other than a national church would have to provide the glue binding the nation as the nineteenth century progressed. That institution was public education. As Yale University historian Sidney Mead put it, "The public schools in the United States took over one of the basic responsibilities that traditionally was always assumed by an established church. In this sense the public school system of the United States *is* its established church." By transforming Catholic immigrant children into loyal Americans, Protestants regarded the public school as an indispensable bulwark.

Protestant hegemony in public education left religious minorities few options. Catholics and Jews could (a) enroll their children in the public school system, which was saturated with Protestant Christianity, (b) create a parochial school system, which was costly, if not prohibitively so, or (c) stand and fight sectarianism in the public schools. Catholics took the lead to challenge Protestant-controlled schools because they were more numerous and felt a greater claim to the Christian faith. For a long time, German Jews stayed out of the line of fire because of their strong belief in public education as the vehicle for assimilation and opportunity. Even when compromised, Jews were reluctant to draw attention to themselves because of their small numbers until the late nineteenth century and because they did not want to be the Protestants' next target.

In line with their church's teachings, Roman Catholic parents resented Protestant prayers and Bible reading as well as offensive textbooks in the public schools. One textbook passage warned that if Irish immigration continued, the United States would become "the common sewer of Ireland"; another suggested that children make their own religious choices. Additional assigned readings labeled the pope as the "anti-Christ" and accused the allegedly superstitious and depraved Roman Catholic Church ("the Whore of Babylon") of conspiring with Satan to obscure scriptural truth. Catholic students read textbooks that were contemptuous of their faith in every class except mathematics.

Repelled by bigoted textbooks, desirous of teaching their faith openly, and fearful of "mixed schools" where Protestants would fraternize with their children, Catholics established costly parochial schools. It was the Catholic drive for government funding of these schools that inflamed public opinion more than any other religious issue in the nineteenth century. In Europe, state support of private schools was commonplace and noncontroversial; money was doled out to both Protestant and Catholic schools on a per-student basis. Such funding was unthinkable in the United States. In 1818, Connecticut became the first state to bar public funds for religious education, and other states followed its lead.

Legislators in nearly every state with a sizable immigrant population fought over funding for Catholic schools or removing the King James Bible from public schools. The first major such dispute arose in the 1830s in New York City. A private organization, the Free School Society (later called the Public School Society), was responsible for allocating tax monies to the city's schools. Under its definition of sectarianism, the society, whose trustees were all Protestant, refused funding requests from Baptist, Methodist, and Presbyterian schools because they promoted religious ideas and instituted religious practices unique to one denomination. The fiery Catholic bishop John Hughes, an Irish immigrant who loved his adopted country, accused the society of rank discrimination and denounced public schools for using a Protestant Bible and stuffing their libraries with "sectarian works against us."

Bishop Hughes insisted there was only one acceptable alternative — public funding of the eight run-down, overcrowded Catholic schools. If Catholic schools went unfunded, he argued, a Roman Catholic parent faced "double taxation for the education of his child — one to the misinterpreted law of the land, and another to his conscience." Hughes insisted that he was not asking for tax money to support the Catholic religion. "But," he declaimed, "we are unwilling to pay taxes for the purpose of destroying our religion in the minds of our children." At the same time, Catholic leaders opposed the very idea of common schools with their largely secular curriculum, which, in their view, bred "the sectarianism of infidelity." Religion and education were, from the Catholic view, inseparable.

Shocked by these demands, Public School Society trustees offered to expunge from classroom texts passages that Roman Catholics deemed offensive. "Dagger John" Hughes was in no mood to compromise, so on its own the society excised some offending passages by stamping them with ink, gluing pages together, or removing books altogether. Meanwhile, Protestant clergy and the city's newspapers denounced "popery" and called on politicians to deny Catholic school funding. The target of vandalism and death threats, Bishop Hughes was condemned as a Jesuit (which he was not) who opposed Americanism and democratic government.

The campaign of calumnies failed because of the intercession of New York's Whig governor, William Seward, a lifelong religious skeptic. In siding with Bishop Hughes, Seward pandered to Irish Democratic voters, but he genuinely believed that education should be universally available. His leadership produced a solution built on local control. The state legislature barred funding of schools that practiced open sectarianism, while at the same time declaring that Bible reading (without commentary) was not a sectarian activity. Most important, voters would elect their own school boards to fund local schools as they saw fit. Despite winning control of public schools in Catholic neighborhoods, Hughes seemingly tossed away the fruits of victory, urging his congregants to flee to a separate school system, expensive though it would be. To create room for so many students, Hughes founded 100 Catholic schools before he died, including St. John's College (later Fordham University), and was celebrated as "the father of Catholic education in America."

The fight over religion in the public schools reached a more frightening conclusion in Philadelphia — the City of Brotherly Love — where a Bible war erupted in 1844. Francis Kenrick, a dignified Dublin-born bishop, asked that anti-Catholic books be removed and that Roman Catholic children either be permitted to read the Douay Bible — the only English translation approved by the Catholic Church — or be excused from reading the King James version. Rumors spread like wildfire that "Catholics were trying to drive the Bible from the schools." The board offered assurances that Catholic students could be excused, but the students continued to be humiliated, beaten severely, and expelled. The *Catholic Herald* described one incident in which a Catholic child refused to read the King James Bible. Her public schoolteacher asked, "Why do you grow pale?" The child answered, "I'm delicate ma'am, and afraid of being whipped." "And would you bear a whipping rather than read the Bible?" the teacher demanded to know. "Yes, ma'am," the child sobbed, to which the teacher replied, "Sit down, you little fool."

The Philadelphia School Board finally agreed to let children read from any unannotated Bible, which excluded the Douay Version with its extensive commentary. This minor concession infuriated the American Protestant Association, a nativist organization that was convinced that Catholics were scheming to capture the souls of Protestant children. Anti-Catholic rallies turned ugly, with fistfights leading to rock throwing and then to murderous gunfire. The *Native American* sounded an alarm against a foreign invader: "The bloody hand of the Pope has stretched itself forth to our destruction. We now call on our fellow-citizens, who regard free institutions, whether they be native or adopted, to arm."

Rallying behind a tattered American flag and waving anti-Catholic banners, nativists terrorized the Irish neighborhood in Kensington, at one point firing cannon blasts of nails and broken glass. The city's worst riots left in their wake eighteen people dead and destroyed by fire fifty homes, a Catholic church, and a convent founded by Mother Elizabeth Seton. The rioting stopped only when the militia appeared and the bishop closed all his churches. Catholic leaders concluded that they should abandon the public school system in favor of a parallel parochial system. Failure to do so would produce Catholic children who were either apostates to or apathetic about their religion. The memory of this violent episode would long haunt the U.S. Supreme Court, and played a part in determining the school prayer and Bible reading cases of the 1960s.

Partly as a result of such violent attacks and increased Catholic and Jewish immigration, a truce of sorts was achieved in the 1840s. Leo Pfeffer, the preeminent student of U.S. religious liberty, put it this way: The "Bible yes, sectarianism no." In practice, this meant that public schoolteachers and students would read from the King James Bible, but would do so without comments from school officials. That silence passed for neutrality, but it was an uneasy truce.

Protestants remained convinced that the public school system was best for the United States, though sectarianism had no place within that system. The common school was God's chosen instrument for instilling religion and Americanizing the youth. In the mid-nineteenth century, Horace Bushnell, a well-known Congregational minister in Connecticut, pontificated: "Those who exclude themselves [from the common schools] are not Americans." The Rev. Daniel Dorchester, a prominent New England Methodist minister, thought that all children should be required to attend public schools to maintain the health of the republic. Put another way, the common school combined the powerful emotions of patriotism and religious conviction. Criticism or failure to support that institution was often regarded as a sign of disloyalty.

Given such attitudes, Roman Catholics remained on the margins of American life. Incidents proliferated of Catholic children compelled to read the King James Bible in public schools, causing the Catholic Church to address the matter head-on. Led by Francis Kenrick, now archbishop of Baltimore and apostolic delegate, U.S. Catholic bishops held their First Plenary Council in 1852. The council noted with consternation that Catholic children who questioned Bible reading were condemned as "enemies of the Bible and of free institutions." Inevitably, the council noted, Catholic children become "ashamed of their faith." The council reminded Catholic children of their obligation not to read the Protestant Bible in public schools. Not surprisingly, more conflict over Bible reading soon surfaced.

John Bapst, a Swiss Jesuit, was dispatched in 1848 to Ellsworth, Maine, where his assignment was to elevate the community's moral standard and promote Catholicism to the Abenaki tribe. In town, he organized several temperance societies, evangelized to increase church membership, and founded a parochial school for Catholic children. What really rankled town Protestants was Fr. Bapst's advice to Catholic students who still attended public school not to read from the King James Bible or recite the Lord's Prayer.

Fifteen-year-old Bridget Donahoe followed her priest's directive and was expelled. After Bridget enrolled in a private school, her father sued the State of Maine for tuition reimbursement. The court ruled that the King James Bible was nonsectarian, that the Donahoes' real aim was to remove that Bible from the public schools, and that the issue at hand was not religious freedom but the board's proper authority to discipline disobedient students. A member of the school committee declared, "We are determined to protestantize the Catholic children; they shall read the Protestant Bible or be dismissed from the schools; and should we find them loafing around the wharves, we will clap them into jail." The only way to change this state of affairs, the court held, was for Catholics to elect a pro-Catholic school board.

Before long, Fr. Bapst was singled out by the Know Nothings, a nativist group known formally as the Order of the Star-Spangled Banner. In June 1851, Bapst was attacked in the press and his home was torched. As the fury gathered momentum, a band of masked men seized the priest, stripped, tarred, and feathered him, and rode him out of town on a rail. He never fully recovered. The perpetrators of this near-lynching were widely known, but no one was arrested. Maine's highest court ruled that Bible reading was "no more an interference with religious belief, than would reading the mythology of Greece or Rome be regarded as interfering with religious belief or an affirmance of the pagan creeds."

In March 1859, another egregious episode involving a stubborn Catholic child occurred, this time in Boston, Massachusetts. The state legislature, which included many supporters of the Know-Nothing movement, required public school students to recite the Ten Commandments each day from the King James Bible. Sophia Shepard, a teacher at the Eliot School for boys, insisted that all her students recite the commandments individually, which put Roman Catholics on the spot because the Protestant second commandment cautioned against the worship of any "graven image."

Fr. Bernardine Wiget urged Catholic children at St. Mary's Church not to recite any Protestant prayers or scripture, lest they succumb to "infidelity and heresy." From the altar itself, Wiget threatened to identify anyone who relented. One of his parishioners was eleven-year-old Thomas Whall [*sic*], who willfully disobeyed the law. As it happened, Assistant Principal McLaurin Cooke witnessed the defiance and told the class: "Here's a boy that refuses to repeat the Ten Commandments, and I will whip him till he yields if it takes all afternoon." Wielding a three-foot-long rattan stick, Cooke required only a half hour to change Tom's mind. Tom's classmates shouted at him not to give in, but the pain and blood were too much. Even after the sadistic beating, 400 Catholic students remained defiant, ripping the Protestant Ten Commandments out of their readers rather than recite them, resulting in their mass expulsion. As a victim of torture, Tom received tributes, presents, and a gold medal from admiring Catholics around the country.

When Tom Whall's father sued the assistant principal for assault, H. F. Durant, Cooke's attorney, warned the court that the Vatican was behind the suit. Durant pointed out that Wiget was a priest from Switzerland — a Jesuit no less — who regularly corrupted the minds of young Irish children in secret meetings conducted in his church's basement. Such actions were doubtless seditious. "The real objection" raised by the Whalls, Durant contended, "is to the Bible itself, for, while that is read daily in our schools, America can never be Catholic." Swayed by Durant's logic, the judge dismissed the charges against Cooke, maintaining that Bible reading without comment "is no interference with religious liberty." Any student who refused to recite the Protestant Ten Commandments undermined public education, "the granite foundation on which our republican form of government rests." With these high stakes in mind, school officials would beat Roman Catholic children until they saw the light.

CHAPTER 2

"Christ Loves All But the Hypocrites"

The survival of the Union after the Civil War offered proof that the United States was the new Zion, and religious sensibilities heightened as a result. To confirm this tie between God and government, Congress coined the motto, "In God We Trust," and stamped it on the nation's currency. Pressure mounted to infuse public education with more religion, lest children become morally reprobate and deadweights on the body politic. The questions were what kind of religion and how much of it. In 1869, the National Teacher's Association, which became the National Education Association, resolved: "The Bible should not only be studied, venerated, and honored as a classic for all ages . . . but devotionally read, and its precepts inculcated in all the common schools of the land." Where Bible reading proved impossible because of apathy or opposition, proponents of devotions turned to school prayer, which, they were convinced, could be written without explicit reference to a particular religious tradition. It was entirely possible, one Long Island school commissioner maintained, to have religious education without "sectarianism and bigotry."

Demands for Bible reading and school prayer arose in large measure because the public school curriculum was becoming ever more secular. As a compromise of sorts, many public schools set aside a few minutes for reading the Bible before formal instruction began. "Chapel exercises," as they were often called, were attractive for several reasons. From a practical point of view, devotions quieted students who had worked up a sweat getting to a distant school and marked a transition to formal instruction. For a few minutes, the teacher invoked the authority of the Ruler of the Universe to maintain order, which was a prime indicator of a teacher's effectiveness. Moreover, religious exercises were ideally suited to the pedagogical revolution that was taking place. Formerly, pupils in one-room

schoolhouses studied at their own pace, but graded scho
instructors to teach students in groups. Devotions gave stu
tice in working together. Most important, students would le
ity from hearing God's revealed word. It was widely assu
morality and good citizenship went hand in hand to fortify w
be called Protestant republicanism.

Disorienting socioeconomic changes after the Civil War reinforced
these educational imperatives for religious exercises. Record numbers
of Roman Catholics, Jews, and Russian, Ukrainian, and Greek Orthodox Christians immigrated to the United States. They were too
readily blamed for all manner of ills, including poverty, corruption,
disease, and violent crime. As city populations swelled, local governments found it impossible to absorb the new inhabitants easily. Pre-
dictably, the economy careened from boom to bust, tossing large
numbers of native-born workers from their jobs, and immigrants
seemed the obvious cause of the dislocation. Christianity itself faced
a profound spiritual crisis after Charles Darwin's theory of evolution
was published in 1859. God seemed to have been rendered superflu-
ous, replaced by a mechanical process that randomly selected earthly
occurrences. For a small but growing number of Americans, the Bible's
claim of being the literal record of God's supernatural actions seemed
to be all too implausible. According to a census official in 1893, the
number of atheists had grown to 8 percent of the U.S. population.

For many Protestants, such as social gospeler Josiah Strong, these
unsettling changes could be ameliorated by having public schoolteachers read the King James Bible without comment to their students. Whether proponents of Bible reading regarded the "Good
Book" as God's revealed word, a moral compass, or great literature,
they agreed with a late nineteenth century New York superintendent
of education: "The influence of the Bible upon the mind of a child, if
daily read in his hearing, cannot but be inspiring, and the unconscious
influence of familiarity with its teachings, by all analogy, would certainly tend to the development of good moral character." More profoundly, by setting eternal truths before schoolchildren, Americanism,
as well as Protestantism, would be preserved. With the stakes so high
and the remedy so simple, about half, and perhaps as many as three-
fourths, of all public school districts in New York State required
teachers or principals to read the Bible to their students.

Of course, not everyone agreed with this formula for individual and social redemption. U.S. Education Commissioner William Harris opposed devotions in public schools as educationally inappropriate because academic instruction and religious instruction required different responses from students. As he observed, schoolwork requires critical thinking and worship demands unquestioning faith. Jews opposed pan-Protestant devotions on religious grounds, and Freethinkers and Spiritualists objected intrinsically to the idea of traditional religious exercises. Even some Protestants opposed routine school devotions, either because they would have "no ethical value whatever" or because they would violate individual rights of conscience.

Doctrinal and personal considerations led Roman Catholics to be adamantly against religious exercises. Sometimes, Catholic children were expelled from public schools for refusing to participate in the exercises. Sometimes, physical abuse was meted out to the recalcitrant. In Cayuga County, New York, Julia O'Neil complained that her son John had been tortured in the winter of 1874 for remaining silent during the exercises. Celia Gutchess, a public schoolteacher, had directed her brother (a school district trustee) and a hired hand to drag John outside, where they scratched his face until "the blood flowed down his cheeks." Fortunately, the evidence suggests that such shocking episodes were rare because local officials intervened to fashion compromises before religious conflict got out of hand.

Such nods to non-denominationalism impressed the Roman Catholic Church as mere window dressing. Throughout the late nineteenth century, the church denounced public schools and demanded tax support of Catholic institutions. In a typical comment, Bishop Stephen Ryan of Buffalo, New York, remarked, "Public schools are either godless or sectarian; by law they are godless, in fact, they are mostly sectarian." Because public schools were unacceptable to Catholics, the Second Plenary Council of Baltimore (1866) urged priests to redouble their efforts to provide a religious education for Catholic children. New York's *Catholic World* wrote flatly, "The children of Catholics must be trained up in the Catholic faith, in the Catholic Church, to be good exemplary Catholics, or they will grow up bad citizens, the pests of society." A generation after the Catholic Church had begun contesting Protestant control of public education, the church remained insistent that compromise in this area was impossible.

As time passed, the squabbling over school devotions ended up in court, rather than in violence. A watershed event in this long-simmering dispute occurred in Cincinnati, Ohio, the Queen City of the West, where public schools had required reading from the King James Bible since opening their doors in 1829. In 1842, Bishop (later Archbishop) John Baptist Purcell, then serving as a city school examiner, finally won the right for Roman Catholic parents to have their children excused from the practice. Purcell was greatly influenced by Bishop John Hughes, his fellow seminarian, life-long friend, and frequent correspondent, who had just waged his own battle to oust anti-Catholic textbooks in New York's common schools. Ten years later, Purcell convinced the Cincinnati school board to permit students to read "such version of the sacred scriptures as their parents or guardians prefer." In 1869, Cincinnati's Catholic leaders upped the ante: The rapidly growing, but increasingly expensive, Catholic schools could be merged with the public school system, provided all city schools removed religious instruction and Bible reading.

This request ignited conflict in what was one of the most religiously heterogeneous cities in the United States. Convinced that Catholics were scheming to destroy public education, Protestant ministers in Cincinnati linked Catholicism to the "black flag of atheism" and warned that the republic was imperiled by moral decay and political intrigue. City newspapers reprinted Thomas Nast's virulently anti-Catholic cartoons and Bishop Hughes's statement that the public school system should "go where it came from — the devil."

As the controversy grew heated, other groups, including Jews, Quakers, Unitarians, and Universalists, also complained about sectarianism in the public schools. Although 20 percent of Jewish children attended Jewish day schools, most went to the public schools, where they were confronted with the Protestant Bible, the Lord's Prayer, and Christian hymns. Two local Reform rabbis — Isaac Mayer Wise and Max Lilienthal — proposed that if the public schools were to read from a Bible at all they should set aside translations and rely on the original Hebrew and Greek. Confident that their proposal would never be adopted, the rabbis thought a better course was to remove the Bible altogether and have "nonsectarian" education. The rabbis argued forcefully that public schools should promote patriotism instead of religion. In this way, Judaism would be denationalized, and Jews in the New World could finally feel that "I am a man like every other." Thus, for the first time, the Catholic chorus against religious exercises in public schools was joined by several other dissenting voices. The result would be a solution that neither the Roman Catholic Church nor the Protestant majority sought.

In an attempt to quiet the controversy without raising taxes, the Cincinnati School Board deliberated over several options, including excusing children who objected to Bible reading and permitting the use of other sacred texts. Ultimately, the board, whose membership reflected the city's religious diversity, concluded that divisiveness was the inevitable result of having any devotions in public schools. It therefore excluded Bible reading, hymn singing, and religious instruction from the classroom. The board's pragmatic and unprecedented decision flabbergasted Protestants. Rumors flew of sinister papal plots by "Romanists" against public education and the nation itself. A headline in the nativist *Cincinnati Gazette* screamed: "Jesuitical Scheme on Foot." A mob mentality rapidly reached the boiling point, and thousands of hotheaded Protestants signed petitions and demanded the return of the Bible to public schools.

When the petitions proved fruitless, thirty-seven irate Protestants sued the school board and triumphed at first. In November 1869, the Superior Court of Cincinnati ruled that the board had overstepped its authority because Ohio's state constitution required the teaching of "Holy Scriptures" in public schools and because Christianity was "the prevailing religion in the State." In a ringing dissent, Judge Alphonso Taft — who was later appointed U.S. attorney general and whose son, William Howard Taft, became president and U.S. Supreme Court chief justice — observed that neither Catholics nor Jews accepted the King James Bible. Judge Taft, a Unitarian who rejected the divinity of Jesus, laid out the ideal of religious freedom: "The government is neutral, and, while protecting all [religious sects], it prefers none, and it disparages none."

When the Cincinnati School Board appealed, the Supreme Court of Ohio sided with the board, maintaining that religion was a part of life that should remain "outside the true and legitimate province of government. . . . The only fair and impartial method . . . is to let each sect give its own instructions." Even a minimal core of religion in public schools was inappropriate. This was the beginning of the end of Bible reading in public schools, and a century later the U.S. Supreme Court would cite Taft's reasoning for a secular state. The Catholic schools in Cincinnati never again sought to join the public system, but in the short term, the distrust that Protestants and Catholics felt toward each other deepened considerably.

Surprisingly little outcry followed the court decision to prohibit Bible reading from Cincinnati public schools. Many Catholics saw the ruling as proof that the public schools were indeed godless and remained convinced that parochial schools were more suitable for their children. It may have been that public anger in the city had become exhausted or that the schools simply retained much of their religious flavor in spite of the ruling. Banning the Bible was one thing; actually removing religion from the curriculum was something else altogether. As late as 1887, E. E. White, Cincinnati's superintendent of schools, admitted in a speech to the National Education Association that the school day still contained "sacred song" and "the literature of Christendom," which were led by "faithful and fearless Christian teachers." He saw nothing illegal in what his schools permitted. In White's estimation, "the only way to teach children to revere both the school and society is by teaching them about God."

School officials from across the county had a similar understanding of the establishment clause. As long as no one was required to attend or contribute financially to a particular church, religious liberty was not compromised. The Cincinnati Bible War thus produced a stalemate: public schools would scale back religious activity, including banning the Protestant Bible, and Catholic schools would not receive public monies. The Protestant majority, in other words, invoked a policy of being "soft on prayer, tough on money" when it came to religion in public schools. This pattern would be repeated in other cities, including Chicago, Illinois, and Buffalo, New York City, and Rochester, New York, where Roman Catholics wielded increasing power that reflected their growing populations.

The outcome of the Cincinnati Bible War hardly allayed Protestant antipathy toward the Roman Catholic Church. Noting that the church was based in Italy, was authoritarian in its governing structure, and had once opposed slave abolition, leading ministers, editors, and intellectuals charged the institution with being "hostile to every fundamental principle of the United States constitution and of modern civilization." In their estimation, a strong Catholic presence would cause reform to wither, freedom to die, and scientific progress to come to a crawl. Anti-Catholic sentiment in the United States swelled in 1870, when the Catholic Church pronounced the doctrine of infallibility — the notion that on matters of faith and morals the pope spoke without human error. For Protestants, the Bible alone was supreme, and they accepted the Apostle Paul's statement to the Romans that "all have sinned, and come short of the glory of God."

With anti-Catholic feelings so pronounced and Union plans for Reconstruction turning sour, Republican politicians saw a golden opportunity to broaden their party's appeal and thereby hold on to the reins of power. President Ulysses S. Grant, who attended Methodist Church services with his wife, issued a clarion call in 1875 to Civil War veterans to draw a new line in the sand, not between North and South, but at the schoolhouse door. The enemy this time, he charged, would be "sectarian, pagan, or atheistic" influence, by which he meant Catholicism. In the most emotional and most publicized speech of his career, Grant implored Americans to "leave the matter of religion . . . to the family altar, the church, and the private school supported entirely by private contributions. Keep the church and State forever separate." To fail to do so, he intimated, would mean that the war to save the Union had been waged in vain. The *Chicago Tribune* reported that the speech "set the nation agog."

Former speaker of the House James Blaine, a Scots-Irish Presbyterian from Maine with presidential aspirations, saw in Grant's stirring address the makings of a winning campaign issue. Known for his great personal magnetism and skillful political maneuvering, the Republican "Plumed Knight" warned of "Roman Catholic aggression" and introduced an amendment to prohibit state funds to support religious education. The measure sailed through the House of Representatives, but was narrowly defeated in the Senate, where Democrats with large Catholic constituencies blocked it. Some senators thought that the Constitution prohibited the federal government from acting on what was a state matter.

Though Congress reconsidered the Blaine Amendment for more than sixty years, it never passed. Congress did compel states admitted to the Union after 1876 to constitutionally prohibit public funds from being spent on sectarian schools or on "sectarian instruction" in public schools, an ambiguous phrase that left the door open for nondenominational religious exercises. Eventually, thirty-seven states adopted mini-Blaine Amendments in one form or another, reassuring Protestants that government could not be used to aid the growing network of Catholic schools. Despite their foundation in anti-Catholicism, the Blaine Amendments represented an early manifestation of an ideology of church-state separation that remains well within the constitutional mainstream.

It would be easy to conclude from Republican Party rhetoric, the inflammatory cartoons of Thomas Nast, and the occasional horrifying incident in public schools that constant religious warfare between Protestants and Roman Catholics prevailed in the post–Civil War period. The latest scholarship suggests that was untrue. In New York State, for example, half of all district schools conducted some form of opening religious exercises, usually simple Bible reading, but rarely did such exercises provoke major disputes. Between 1865 and 1905, the state superintendent received no complaints about religious instruction from 80 percent of the school districts. Of the remaining 20 percent, only 1 out of 1,000 complaints involved religion.

Why were devotions less controversial — at least in New York — after the Civil War than before? Religious minorities in New York increasingly tolerated what they regarded as an unpleasant beginning of the school day. This was so as long as the devotions did not go too far. Although the state maintained overall control of the public school system, local school districts mitigated disputes in several different ways. In various places, school officials banned religious exercises, required devotions to take place before school instruction began, allowed teachers and school administrators to work out compromises in required religious exercises, permitted the use of the Douay Bible, recruited teachers who would not proselytize their students, hired Roman Catholic teachers, devised relatively homogeneous districts in which one religious group predominated, absorbed parochial schools into public school districts, and permitted religious groups to use school buildings after hours. Even when devotions had a sharper sectarian edge, students often paid the exercises little mind, which school officials freely admitted. Nor did school itself dominate the lives of children as it does today. Public schools a century ago experienced low daily attendance rates and operated for short terms.

The desire for minimizing such conflict over religion in New York State stemmed from multiple motives. Besides altruism and a constitutional tradition of freedom of religion, financial considerations were crucial. The more students in public schools the lower taxes everyone paid and the more jobs existed for administrators, teachers, janitors, and suppliers. There was always the threat that the state might intervene, creating a financial drain on a district. Even the appeals process itself encouraged local officials to manage conflict before it escalated.

The very existence of an alternative school system to public education siphoned off some frustration. Although Pope Pius IX's 1864 encyclical, *Syllabus of Errors*, condemned the very idea of public education by the state and Roman Catholic bishops threatened to excommunicate Catholic parents who sent their children to public schools, Catholics were not of one mind about public schools. Indeed, more Catholic children attended public schools in New York State than enrolled in parish schools. Some liberal Catholic priests refused to open parish schools, encouraging Catholic children to attend public schools instead. Catholic parents defended parochial education, but knew that the academic quality of public schools was invariably superior. Moreover, some Catholics valued assimilation into U.S. society over ethnic solidarity and their religion, and assimilation was best achieved in public schools.

The conflict over school devotions was not managed as well in other states as it was in New York. Between 1890 and 1930, Roman Catholics brought suit in several major cases. One such case arose in Wisconsin, where public school teachers had read from the King James Bible ever since the state superintendent of public instruction had included it in his list of recommended textbooks in 1858. The practice had been uncontroversial until school attendance became compulsory in the 1880s. A group of German Catholic parents in Edgerton brought suit against the school board to proscribe the reading of the Protestant Bible, which they viewed as an incomplete and incorrect translation. They also believed that the Catholic Church was the only "infallible" interpreter of the scriptures and feared that "indiscriminate" reading of the Bible by schoolteachers could lead to "dangerous errors," including heresy and irreligion.

Because the Edgerton public school was tax-supported, the Bible readings arguably amounted to an illegal use of state funds to support a place of worship. The Catholic parents noted that not only did the state constitution prohibit sectarian instruction in the public schools, but the state legislature had enacted a law in 1883 barring textbooks that would "have a tendency to inculcate sectarian ideas." Their attorney, Henry Desmond, concluded, "In effect, the school board says: 'Do not permit the Catholics to save their souls in their own way. Appoint us as a guardian for their conscience.' They say our version of the Bible is not good for them; but we know better. . . . If you would not have Catholics force the Catholic Bible and beliefs and conscience upon you, then you should not force the Protestant Bible and beliefs and conscience upon them. That is the true meaning of non-sectarian schools."

In response, the Edgerton School Board noted that the sacred passages taken from the King James Bible — Psalms, Proverbs, the four Gospels, and the Pauline epistles — were also contained in the Catholic Douay Bible, that the teachers did not comment on the passages, and that students could be excused from the readings. The board flatly rejected the Catholic notion that priests needed to explain the Bible, asserting, "Every person has the right to read the Bible and interpret it for himself."

In *State ex rel. Weiss et al. v. District Board* (1890), the Wisconsin State Supreme Court struck down Bible reading as unconstitutional. The court noted that certain passages read at the school proclaimed belief in predestination, "punishment of the wicked after death," and the divinity of Jesus of Nazareth — doctrines that were not universally accepted by religious sects. The court did, however, permit the use of textbooks based on the Bible or containing extracts from the Bible in order to "inculcate good morals." The *Weiss* decision drew national attention and would be referred to by other courts as time passed. The *New York Independent* embraced the ruling, pointing out that a Protestant parent would have "good cause for complaint" if the school had mandated the Douay Bible, Qur'an, or Book of Mormon.

The fight over Bible reading and school prayer revived in the early twentieth century, when public schools came under increasing pressure to teach more than "reading, 'riting, and 'rithmetic." Nearly 60 percent of schoolchildren in the nation's largest cities were Catholic and Jewish immigrants, and public education was intended to Americanize them in a variety of ways. Public schools provided instruction only in English, adopted history and civics textbooks that inculcated patriotism, and required recitation of the Pledge of Allegiance. Prodded by the National Reform Association (NRA) — a precursor to today's religious right organizations — defensive state legislatures in the Northeast, Midwest, and South once more permitted or required brief spoken petitions, such as the Lord's Prayer, and Bible reading in the public schools. Such authorization came by statute, court action, rulings by state attorneys general, or the law's silence. Protestants regarded Catholic parochial schools as sectarian, but were convinced that Protestant prayers and Bibles in the public schools were not. Before the NRA became involved, only Massachusetts had a law on the books requiring Bible reading in public schools.

Devotions thus returned as a regular feature of the public school day. In Maine, teachers opened their Bibles to read the Ten Commandments, the Psalms of David, the Proverbs of Solomon, the Sermon on the Mount, and the Lord's Prayer. To promote "Christian virtue," elementary schoolteachers in Florida were to read the Bible to their students and teach them that moral values stem from a belief in God. In Arkansas, the law required teachers to recite a prayer in class every day or face a $25 fine for a first offense and possible dismissal for a second offense. Alabama public schoolteachers filed reports proving that they had read from the Bible daily; any school district not in compliance risked losing its state funding. Delaware public schoolteachers had to recite five Bible verses or face revocation of their teaching credentials after repeated violations of that law. Public schools in Miami, Florida; Philadelphia, Pennsylvania; and the State of California permitted the distribution of Gideon Bibles, an abridgement of the King James Bible that includes the New Testament and the Psalms and Proverbs. Protestant evangelists entered Vermont's public schools to present entire classes on the Bible.

Roman Catholics resisted such laws — sometimes successfully, but more often not. Where Catholics predominated, some public schools permitted the Douay Bible. Courts in five states — Nebraska, Illinois, Louisiana, Washington, and South Dakota — followed Wisconsin's lead by banning Bible reading, but other state courts let local school districts decide what to do. In *Ring v. Board of Education of District 24* (1910), the Illinois Supreme Court banned devotions that were intended to promote a moral code and school camaraderie: "The law knows no distinction between the Christian and the Pagan, the Protestant and the Catholic. All are citizens. Their civil rights are precisely equal. . . . There can be no distinction based on religion." Although there were few such decisions between the Civil War and World War I, state courts began to perceive the United States as a secular, rather than a Christian, nation. The ultimate implications would be profound, including a redefinition of church-state relations and the removal of organized religion from public schools. Reflecting the new attitude, former president Theodore Roosevelt, an outspoken Protestant layman, recognized that in the interest of "absolutely nonsectarian public schools," it was "not our business to have the Protestant Bible or the Catholic Vulgate or the Talmud read in these schools."

Like Roman Catholics, Jewish immigrants resented Protestant-controlled public schools. But Jews had experienced far more serious problems in their countries of origin, including genocide. Moreover, in the United States, Sunday-closing laws seemed more immediately disturbing. It meant that Jewish businesses could not compete economically because they closed on Saturday for their Sabbath and could not open on Sunday, the Christian Sabbath. As a result, Jewish proprietors and Jewish workers lost a day's profits and a day's pay. So, in the new U.S. environment, individual Jews at first swallowed their objections to sectarianism in the public schools and sent their children to be educated there. Survival, assimilation, and success became the Jewish watchwords in the new land, and there was no better vehicle for success than learning English in the public school.

The "December Dilemma" finally pushed Jews to take action. Most U.S. public schools held programs in December to celebrate the birth of Jesus, the Christian messiah. These programs were replete with crèches, Santa Claus, evergreen trees, the singing of carols, the hanging of mistletoe, and gift-giving. Students in many schools spent more time on planning, rehearsing, and performing Christmas programs than on any other activity during the school year.

An egregious example of sectarianism in a public school occurred in Brooklyn, New York. In an assembly held in late 1905, elementary school principal Frank Harding admonished his predominantly Jewish students: "Now, boys and girls, at this time of the year especially, I want you all to have the feeling of Christ in you. Have more pleasure in giving than in taking; be like Christ — that is how I want you to be." When thirteen-year-old Augusta Herbert suggested that such teaching was "more appropriate in a Sunday School or a church," Harding replied, "Christ loves all but the hypocrites and the hypocrites are those who do not believe in him." Fed-up parents complained, noting a long pattern of such religious programming, including recital of the Lord's Prayer, and they demanded that the school board dismiss Harding. The parents pointedly reminded the board that Jews do not accept the notion that any human being is "Lord" and resent Jesus' characterization that those who pray in synagogues are "hypocrites."

When the Brooklyn school board exonerated Harding, Jewish newspaper editors exhorted Jewish parents to keep their children away from school on the Monday before Christmas in 1906. In response, 20,000 pupils, one-third of the local school population, stayed home. School officials capitulated only in part, permitting seasonal decorations, including Christmas trees, but prohibiting hymns mentioning "Christ" or "Christmas," assignments dealing with religious themes, and reading from any religious book except the King James Bible. A year later, the school board conceded that Christmas trees and Santa Claus were "very much in evidence everywhere" and that "Hebrew children" even impersonated Santa, but, the board claimed, implausibly, "to these children Santa Claus stands only for the spirit of good cheer and happiness and has no other significance." In sum, the board convinced itself that the revamped Christmas celebration did not offend anyone.

Such incidents forced the Jewish community to mobilize to defend its religion. Jewish organizations, including the Central Conference of American Rabbis (founded in 1889), the Union of Orthodox Jewish Congregations in America (1898), the American Jewish Committee (1906), and the American Jewish Congress (1918), strongly objected to public schools requiring Protestant prayers and hymns and the use of the King James Bible. In 1906, the Central Conference published a bold and widely distributed pamphlet, "Why the Bible Should Not Be Read in the Public Schools," which detailed cases in which religious minorities had triumphed in court. A few years later, the Central Conference called for an end to Christmas and Easter observances in public schools. The pamphlet and the resolution marked the beginning of a long Jewish campaign to educate the U.S. public about the harm wrought by sectarianism in the classroom.

One way to reduce tension over religious devotions in public schools and, simultaneously, to increase the time spent on religious instruction was the purportedly neutral practice of "cooperative weekday religious education." This scheme, which came to be known as "released time for religious instruction," permitted elementary public schoolchildren to be absent from regular classes on Wednesday afternoon to attend religion classes in their own churches or synagogues. That missed time amounted to 8 percent of regular instruction. On its face, the idea was appealing: it would increase religious knowledge, reduce juvenile delinquency, and apparently preserve separation of church and state. Protestants, in particular, were concerned about the lack of religious education for their children, given the widespread closing of Protestant church schools and the inadequacy of Sunday schools and devotions in public schools.

Released time was popularized in Indiana beginning in 1914. William Wirt, a John Dewey student at the University of Chicago, was hired to create a school system for the new city of Gary, a factory town for the U.S. Steel Corporation. His Gary Plan, also called the "duplicate school plan" and the "work-study-play school," was designed to implement a progressive educational philosophy. Wirt offered first-rate facilities, a longer school day and year, and an advanced curriculum to educate the whole child, all at a bargain price. The key to this innovative plan was to make full use of school facilities, especially by moving students from teacher to teacher and by having students spend the lion's share of the day on the playground and in the swimming pool, auditorium, and laboratories, and in vocational workshops devoted to domestic science, carpentry, plumbing, electricity, and printing. Such maximum use of facilities meant that twice as many students could attend the "platoon school." A ministerial group convinced Wirt to add released time, which would involve faith communities and free up additional classroom space.

The Inter-Church Conference on Federation, which represented thirty Protestant denominations with 17 million members, threw its weight behind released time, making it a viable experiment in religious education — one that persists to this day. Although the program was widely imitated, it did not appeal to atheists, Jews, Missouri Synod Lutherans, Unitarians, and, at first, to Roman Catholics. As time passed, however, Catholic participation jumped to 80 percent or more in larger cities. The surface calm regarding released time reflected the general satisfaction that the programs could legitimately instill a local community's moral values.

The same concern for religious literacy that led to released time for elementary school pupils also led to Bible classes for high school students. The idea arose in North Dakota in 1912, when the State Department of Public Instruction worked hand-in-glove with the North Dakota Council of Religious Education, a ministerial association. Because the classes could not be taught by public schoolteachers on school property during regular school hours, the ministerial council organized the classes, supplied the instructors, and distributed the reading materials, and the state set the standards and conducted the examinations. Each student who successfully completed a Bible course received one elective credit toward the required total of fifteen or sixteen. By 1927, twenty-five states, including New York, awarded high school credit for Bible courses.

A turning point in the fight for religious liberty came during the Great Depression and World War II. Prior to that period, there had been practically no federal case law involving the First Amendment's religion clauses. School prayer was not yet on the U.S. Supreme Court's radar screen and would remain invisible for another generation. But as these larger national emergencies heightened patriotic feeling, religious dissenters found themselves under attack. When they sued for relief, the Court began to shift its primary focus from protecting property to protecting individuals. This line of thinking was developed in part by Harlan Fiske Stone, an Episcopalian from New Hampshire, who as U.S. attorney general under Calvin Coolidge helped clean up the Teapot Dome scandal.

Repulsed by news reports of the Nazis blackballing Jewish physicians and a southern lynch mob gouging out a black man's eyes with an ice pick, Justice Stone penned the most famous footnote in the U.S. Supreme Court's history. In footnote 4 of *U.S. v. Carolene Products* (1938), an otherwise unremarkable case involving interstate shipments of adulterated milk, Stone creatively fashioned the "double standard" doctrine, meaning that the Court should subject legislation to different standards of scrutiny. In particular, Stone thought the judiciary should carefully scrutinize government claims that it had a compelling interest that justified infringements upon individual rights, especially the rights of minorities. The doctrine planted the seed of a new jurisprudence called "preferred freedoms," which emphasized human rights over property rights, and marked the beginning of the modern Court. Henceforth, the Supreme Court itself would be the refuge for the oppressed, a development that the American Civil Liberties Union (ACLU), American Jewish Congress, and the National Association for the Advancement of Colored People (NAACP) quickly grasped.

The ACLU, which formed in 1920 to protest government abuses, took the lead in defending the free exercise rights of an unpopular minority — Jehovah's Witnesses. The Witnesses disturbed many communities with their apocalyptic message and persistent proselytizing, prompting frustrated authorities to enact licensing fees and restrictions on leafleting and littering. The first such case arose from a 1938 dispute in New Haven, Connecticut. Newton Cantwell and his sons — Jehovah's Witnesses all — had accosted pedestrians in an Irish and Italian neighborhood by playing a record on a portable phonograph that pilloried the "harlot" Roman Catholic Church as "the wickedest organization of liars, murderers and gangsters that has ever cursed the planet." Unsurprisingly, the aggressive campaign to evangelize Catholics was received poorly, and the police arrested the Cantwells for breaching the peace and failing to obtain a license to distribute literature.

Writing for a unanimous Court in the landmark case of *Cantwell v. Connecticut* (1940), Justice Owen Roberts, an Episcopalian appointed by Herbert Hoover, sided with the Jehovah's Witnesses, holding that, however annoying the Cantwells had been in distributing church literature, the authorities had illegally denied their freedom of religion and free speech. Seeing the free exercise clause as involving competing principles, Roberts held that religious behavior could be restricted only if it posed "a clear and present danger to a substantial interest of the State." For the first time, the Court ruled explicitly that the states are bound by the First Amendment's free exercise clause through the Fourteenth Amendment. This finding enabled religious minorities to pursue a flood of litigation against the states.

Two weeks after *Cantwell*, a second Witness case inadvertently laid the basis for an even broader interpretation of the First Amendment. Walter Gobitas (his last name was misspelled in court papers as "Gobitis") was a cheerful Pennsylvania grocer who had abandoned the Roman Catholicism of his Lithuanian parents to join the faith of his wife's grandparents—Jehovah's Witnesses. His new spiritual leader, Joseph Rutherford, had been sickened by wholesale Nazi persecution and execution of German "Bible Students"—as Witnesses were then called—for refusing to shout "*Heil, Hitler!*" and join the raised-palm salute. Noticing a disturbing similarity between the Hitler salute and the U.S. flag salute as it was then practiced, Rutherford praised a third-grade Massachusetts boy who was arrested for not paying tribute to "the Devil's emblem." Rutherford urged the 40,000 Witnesses in the United States to do likewise because the Ten Commandments require believers not to have any other gods before Jehovah. This meant that the Witnesses could not honor a national flag that they considered a "graven image." Before long, the Gobitas children—Lillian and Billy—stayed glued to their school seats when the Pledge of Allegiance was recited, thus becoming the targets of painful taunts and rock throwing as they walked through town. Billy, who was once beaten and thrown into the gutter, explained to school officials why he did not salute the flag: "I love my country [but] I love God more and I must obey his commandments." The school finally expelled Lillian and Billy for insubordination.

The U.S. Supreme Court turned a deaf ear to the Gobitas children and made the dismissal permanent. In *Minersville School District v. Gobitis* (1940), the Court decided, eight to one, that schoolchildren could be expelled for not saluting the flag, even if they were motivated by religious beliefs. Chief Justice Charles Evans Hughes fully realized the controversial nature of the case and assigned the opinion to Felix Frankfurter, a Vienna-born "agnostic" Jew whom Hughes hoped would rein in the more liberal, activist judges appointed by Franklin D. Roosevelt—Hugo Black, William O. Douglas, and Frank Murphy. Frankfurter, who subscribed to a legal doctrine known as judicial restraint, was delighted with the opportunity to outline the Court's proper role in the new political era.

Writing for the Court, Frankfurter declared that religious belief "does not relieve the citizen from the discharge of political responsibilities," particularly as the clouds of all-out war approached. Under such dire circumstances, Frankfurter held that the need for national cohesion, as defined by democratically elected bodies, always trumped narrow sectarian religious beliefs. As a proud immigrant who regularly whistled "Stars and Stripes Forever," Frankfurter regarded Old Glory as "the symbol of our national unity, transcending all internal differences" over religion and politics.

Throughout his brilliant career as a Harvard law professor, an adviser to President Franklin D. Roosevelt (FDR), and a Supreme Court justice, Frankfurter always believed that cultural assimilation, particularly through the common experiences of the public school classroom, including the flag salute, was critical to the success of the American experiment. There could be no exceptions to the flag salute, in part to prevent the virus of dissent from sapping patriotism. But for the Gobitas family, patriotism came in a distant second to honoring God, and the Gobitas children never again attended public school. Frankfurter urged future petitioners to "fight out" their battles with local officials at the ballot box and urged his colleagues to respect the judgments of elected officials, even if the laws seemed "harsh" or "foolish."

Frankfurter's fervent patriotism and belief in judicial self-restraint make his *Gobitis* opinion understandable. But its conclusion seems hard to reconcile with Frankfurter's defense, as a crusading attorney, of Sacco and Vanzetti, the notorious anarchists, and his role in cofounding the ACLU. Frankfurter's law clerk was so upset by Frankfurter's "terrible mistake" in *Gobitis* that he broke the Court's sacrosanct rule of confidentiality. Even the three liberals — Hugo Black, who would become a staunch separationist; the eccentric and often irascible William O. Douglas; and FDR's former attorney general, Frank Murphy — went along with the majority because they were "naive," as Douglas put it, and because "Felix Frankfurter was our hero" in their early days on the Court. Moreover, none of the liberals wanted to defy the august Charles Evans Hughes, who favored the school board's position.

Although chauvinists lauded the U.S. Supreme Court for safeguarding the revered flag, the *Gobitis* decision was roundly condemned. The *St. Louis Post-Dispatch* characterized it as "a surrender to popular hysteria." The *New Republic*, a progressive magazine that Frankfurter helped to establish, compared the Court to a Nazi tribunal and mocked

Frankfurter for "heroically saving America from a couple of school-children whose devotion to Jehovah would have been compromised by a salute to the flag." Liberals across the land criticized the decision, not least because it precipitated a wave of attacks that included kidnapping, assault, arson, and even castration against Jehovah's Witnesses from Maine to Texas. One southern sheriff told a reporter why Witnesses were being run out of town: "They're traitors, the Supreme Court says. Ain't you heard?"

At the urging of ACLU Executive Director Roger Baldwin, the American Bar Association, and Justice Harlan Fiske Stone, the U.S. Supreme Court reversed *Gobitis* three years later in *West Virginia State Board of Education v. Barnette* (1943). Besides the general disgust with *Gobitis*, the Court's personnel had changed remarkably since then, as FDR had replaced Chief Justice Hughes with Stone, added Attorney General Robert Jackson to fill Stone's seat, and elevated U.S. Circuit Court Judge Wiley Rutledge to replace Justice James Byrnes, who retired after one unhappy term to serve as the nation's economic czar during World War II.

In a ruling announced on Flag Day 1943, the Supreme Court struck down West Virginia's statute requiring the salute to the flag because such refusal posed no immediate danger to society. Jackson, who attended law school for just one year and who had recommended Frankfurter's appointment to the Court, systematically demolished every argument made by the former Harvard professor in *Gobitis*. For Jackson, measures affecting the precious freedoms of religion, speech, press, and assembly had to pass stricter scrutiny than, say, economic restrictions. In eloquent language, Jackson, who was Episcopalian, defined religious freedom: "If there is any fixed star in our constitutional constellation, it is that no official, high or petty, can prescribe what shall be orthodox in politics, nationalism, religion, or other matters of opinion or force citizens to confess by word or act their faith therein." Jackson rebutted Frankfurter's argument that disputes should be settled by elections: "The very purpose of a Bill of Rights was to withdraw certain subjects from the vicissitudes of political controversy, to place them beyond the reach of majorities and officials."

In the *Barnette* case, the U.S. Supreme Court apologized for the mistreatment that Witnesses endured and emphasized individual rights, thus anticipating the revolution in civil liberties wrought after

World War II. The opinion was greeted with general relief and widespread applause, but Frankfurter felt betrayed by it. He believed that civil liberties were limited by what a reasonable majority of the U.S. public was willing to concede. Because Frankfurter was not an absolutist on freedom of speech or religion, the Court's liberal wing gravitated to Hugo Black, whom Frankfurter deemed an unsophisticated man from the Deep South, incapable of understanding the subtleties of the First Amendment. Black, however, would lead the way in protecting the civil liberties of religious minorities. After *Barnette*, atheists and religious minorities, including Jews and Unitarians, would demand their rights to religious freedom in the one forum that protected such liberties — the U.S. Supreme Court.

CHAPTER 3

"Good Fences Make Good Neighbors"

Until the end of World War II, the U.S. Supreme Court had not applied the establishment clause to the states. That era would come to an end in the seminal case of *Everson v. Board of Education of Ewing Township* (1947). The dispute involved a New Jersey law that allowed school districts to pay for transporting students to and from "any schoolhouse." Under the statute, Ewing Township officials chose to reimburse the parents of twenty-one children for the expense ($354.74) of traveling on public buses to four Catholic schools. At the time, sixteen other states and the District of Columbia provided free transportation for students attending public and nonpublic schools under similar statutes. Arch Everson objected to the Ewing bus reimbursement plan as a form of religious establishment and filed suit to stop it. He was executive director of the New Jersey Taxpayers Association and a member of the Junior Order of United American Mechanics, a century-old nativist group known for its anti-Catholic views and ties to the Ku Klux Klan.

Everson was decided by the U.S. Supreme Court by the slenderest of margins (five to four) as the justices battled over an incipient area of the law. The swing vote in *Everson* belonged to Frank Murphy, the Court's sole Roman Catholic and one of the most liberal justices ever to serve on that bench. Murphy described his belief system as faith in both the "Goddess of Reason and the Sermon on the Mount." Although he once told a White House adviser that he kept religion and politics in "air-tight compartments," Murphy nonetheless believed that God's "higher law" should inform constitutional interpretation. When some people, evidently including fellow justices, thought Murphy should disqualify himself because of his religion, Murphy told a friend, "Well, I'm damned if I'll kick myself out. I'm either equipped to be a justice or I'm not. And I think I'll tell them to go to hell."

Although Murphy believed that the separation principle was "essential" to the health of the country and his church, he was so ambivalent about *Everson* that he wondered whether he should abstain. He prayed that God would supply the answer.

As Murphy waited for divine guidance, Felix Frankfurter hectored "The Saint" to dissent from Hugo Black's majority opinion. In a "Dear Frank" letter, Frankfurter urged Murphy to ignore "flattery," "false friends" (i.e., Black and Douglas), and "temporary fame" to uphold the "great American doctrine" of separation of church and state. Appealing to Murphy's patriotism and loyalty to his Catholic faith, Frankfurter urged Murphy to vote his conscience: "You have a chance to do for your country and your Church such as [has] never come to you before — and may never again. . . . No one knows better than you what *Everson* is about. Tell the world — and shame the devil." Frankfurter also leaned on Robert Jackson, who had returned from prosecuting Nazis in Nuremberg, Germany, and Wiley Rutledge, a warm-hearted Baptist preacher's son and FDR's last Court appointee, to shore up their dissenting opinions. Hugo Black caught wind of the backstage maneuvering and sharpened his defense of the First Amendment.

In the end, Frankfurter's lobbying did no good, as Murphy provided the margin of victory to bus private school students at public expense. Recalling a time when "bigots" burned Catholic convents, Murphy wanted to "err on the side of freedom of religion." An enraged Frankfurter lambasted Murphy as a second-rate mind who put loyalty to his church ahead of his country.

In his majority opinion, Hugo Black, a longtime anti-Catholic who had once belonged to the Ku Klux Klan, resuscitated and defined the First Amendment's establishment clause. In so doing, Black became the Court's civil-libertarian conscience and reaffirmed a separationist view of the First Amendment that had initially been embraced by Chief Justice Morrison Waite in *Reynolds v. United States* (1879), a Mormon polygamy case involving George Reynolds, Brigham Young's secretary. In this nineteenth-century case, Waite looked to Thomas Jefferson for guidance, since he regarded Jefferson's Virginia Statute for Religious Freedom as practically a part of the legislative history of the First Amendment. Waite, an Episcopalian, also accepted Jefferson's "wall of separation" metaphor as an appropriate interpretation of the First

Amendment. By applying the First Amendment to the Utah territory, the Waite Court transformed the doctrine of federalism and the Constitution itself. In comparing the "odious" practice of polygamy to human sacrifice, the Waite Court let its prejudices and those of the nation as a whole override the protections of the First Amendment. As a result of the decision, Reynolds served two years at hard labor and paid a $5,000 fine for his polygamy.

Almost every religion case decided by the U.S. Supreme Court in the past half-century has been affected by Hugo Black's schizophrenic decision in *Everson*. Its most memorable turn of phrase came from Jefferson, who interpreted the establishment clause as "building a wall of separation between church and State," a phrase that appears nowhere in the Constitution or the Bill of Rights. Using Jefferson's metaphor, Black declared that certain government actions were absolutely proscribed by this division: "The 'establishment of religion' clause of the First Amendment means at least this: Neither a state nor the Federal Government can set up a church. Neither can pass laws which aid one religion, aid all religions, or prefer one religion over another." For Black, religious establishment did not depend on the extent of government support: "No tax in any amount, large or small, can be levied to support any religious activities or institutions, whatever they may be called, or whatever form they may adopt to teach or practice religion." Jefferson's architectural metaphor, as employed by Black, would come to have the same hold on the American imagination as Winston Churchill's "Iron Curtain" reference to the Soviet Union's relentless grip on Eastern Europe.

For Black, the First Amendment meant exactly what it says: "Congress shall make no law" concerning freedom of religion, speech, and the press. Individual rights, not government needs, come first, and government cannot pass any law on these subjects, regardless of the particular justification for it. The Founding Fathers, Black asserted, were both wise and patriotic in prohibiting Congress from passing such laws: "They knew what history was behind them; they were familiar with the sad and useless tragedies of countless people who had had their tongues plucked out, their ears cut off or their hands chopped off, or even worse things done to them because they dared to speak or write their opinions." Such torture was at the forefront of Black's mind because his ancestors in Ireland had faced execution before fleeing to the United States. To prevent such abuse, Black argued, "There are 'absolutes' in our Bill of Rights, and they were put there on purpose by men who knew what words meant, and meant their prohibitions to be absolutes." Despite his absolutist position concerning church and state — later expressed so forcefully in the *Engel* decision — Black never changed his mind about his *Everson* opinion. The school-bus decision, Frankfurter said acidly, revealed Black's penchant "to utter noble sentiments and depart from them in practice."

Black's constitutional convictions were reinforced by his evolving religious beliefs. Although Black was raised in a devout Southern Baptist home, taught a popular Sunday school class for twenty years, and entertained visitors to his home with renditions of old Protestant hymns, he had long since drifted into agnosticism and doubted there was an afterlife. "I can't exactly believe and I can't exactly not believe," he concluded. He never forgot how harmful and humiliating religion could be, especially when a local congregation publicly expelled his father and two uncles for imbibing alcohol. Black found a spiritual home of sorts at All Souls Unitarian Church in Washington, D.C., particularly because he liked the ministers. Ultimately, he placed his trust in the golden rule of treating "the other fella the way you want him to treat you" and what he famously described as his "constitutional faith." Like a Bible-toting preacher, Hugo Black always carried a copy of his holy writ — the Constitution.

With the *Everson* decision, the "wall" metaphor was now firmly grafted onto the language of the First Amendment. Instead of pointing out that public education did not exist when the Constitution was written, Black advanced a revolutionary interpretation of the First Amendment. He described the wall as "high and impregnable" and applied the metaphor for the first time to all levels of government. He thereby somewhat exaggerated the separationist views of Jefferson and Madison, excluded from consideration the views of the other Founders, failed to recognize the extent of religious establishment that existed throughout U.S. history, and overshadowed the equally important guarantee of the free exercise of religion. Moreover, Black and the other separationists on the Court maintained that the social effects of religion were as divisive in the mid-twentieth century as they were in the colonial period when Quakers were hanged and blasphemers had their tongues chopped off.

Oddly, Hugo Black then adopted a balancing approach in *Everson*, rather than vigorously defending a sharp division between church and state. Although Black maintained that the Court "could not approve the slightest breach" in the wall of separation, he declared that New Jersey had not surmounted that wall in this instance. Relying on the child-benefit theory outlined in a 1930 Louisiana case permitting state-paid textbooks for religious schools, Black upheld the New Jersey reimbursement plan as a "reasonable" means of promoting the general welfare, not a particular religion. For Black, the state's law had a secular purpose — to provide benefits for all students regardless of their religious affiliation. The general purpose of safely transporting schoolchildren constituted incidental aid, meaning no aid, in Black's view. It was incidental that the schoolchildren of Ewing Township were being driven to Catholic schools on buses paid for by public funds. He observed that the government spent taxes to protect parochial schools against fire and crime; bus transportation to parochial schools, he reasoned, was essentially the same thing. Black held that the First Amendment "requires the state to be a neutral in its relations with groups of religious believers and non-believers; it does not require the state to be their adversary."

Several justices had problems with the *Everson* majority decision. Stanley Reed, a nominal Protestant and FDR's former solicitor general, sided with the majority, but he objected to the "wall" metaphor, insisting that decisions should be based on law, not an ambiguous figure of speech. The First Amendment, according to Reed, was "aimed only at a state church," not government aid given to all religions. Wiley Rutledge, who abandoned his father's Baptist faith for Christian humanism, followed Black's historical argument to reach a diametrically different conclusion. Rutledge held that the price of religious liberty was that believers could not receive government assistance. He warned, "Every religious institution in the country will be reaching into the hopper if we sustain this" practice, particularly Roman Catholics. Robert Jackson noted that public schools were largely the product of Protestantism, and that to permit bus reimbursement might well reignite deep-seated religious quarrels. Better, he thought, to preserve social harmony by not reimbursing Catholic parents for their children's bus expenses. Stunned by Black's astonishing judicial pirouette, Jackson was reminded of Lord Byron's poem of unrequited love. Byron's feckless Julia whispered to her lover Don Juan, "I will ne'er consent," and then consented. That, Jackson believed, was exactly what Hugo Black had done.

Despite the divided Court, all of the justices on the *Everson* Court agreed on two vital points. For the first time, the U.S. Supreme Court declared that the Fourteenth Amendment extended the First Amendment's establishment clause to the states, in what is called the "incorporation doctrine." But the Founding Fathers intended the First Amendment to give wide latitude to the states in the area of religion, and the writers of the Fourteenth Amendment gave no indication that they intended to incorporate the religion clauses of the First Amendment. Indeed, the Fourteenth Amendment says not a word about religion. The Court also agreed that the Founders intended to build a wall between church and state, though justices have quarreled over the meaning of the establishment clause in dozens of church-state cases since World War II. These disputes over religious establishment, along with cases involving abortion, have generated particularly passionate opposition to Supreme Court decisions in the modern era. *Everson* remains the starting point for this contentious and ongoing debate.

There was considerable fallout from the *Everson* decision. Despite the ruling's support of parochial school aid, Roman Catholics criticized its "false history" and "fallacious reasoning," which endorsed a separationist view of the First Amendment. To counter the pervasive threat of secularism, Catholics pressed state legislatures for even more aid for parochial schools and asked school boards for more released-time programs for religious instruction. Baptists and Methodists staunchly opposed such requests and accused the U.S. Supreme Court of "turning back the hands of the clock" on church and state.

In January 1948, some clergy and laypeople formed a lobbying group called Protestants and Other Americans United for Separation of Church and State (POAU) to hold the line against apparently never-ending Catholic demands for government assistance. The organization, which was led by Glenn Archer, a university law school dean and a former legislative director for the National Education Association (NEA), issued a manifesto designed to prevent further breaches in the wall separating church and state. Archer warned that parochial school funding would "mark the beginning of the breakdown of church and state, which will ultimately lead to social domination and thought control." The Roman Catholic Church accused members of POAU of being anti-Catholic bigots.

The heat from the Court's decision gradually dissipated, and it became clear that *Everson's* real significance was Black's pointed definition of religious establishment, which boded ill for government sponsorship of, or participation in, religious practices. By using the First Amendment to review state action, the *Everson* case set the stage for the U.S. Supreme Court to consider a host of questions concerning religion and public education.

The first church-state matter the Court addressed after *Everson* concerned released time for religious instruction. Religion classes, which were intended to raise religious literacy and to eliminate juvenile delinquency, were sometimes held in the public schools, or, much more often, in nearby churches or church buildings. Such instruction supplemented religious education provided by Protestant and Jewish Sunday schools. Roman Catholic leaders warmly supported the released-time program, even though many of their children attended full-time parish schools in which Catholic theology suffused the curricula. Some Jewish students joined Christian education classes in the public schools, but the vast majority stayed away, engendering hostility toward Jews. Protestant teachers pressured Jewish students to attend the classes with remarks like these: "Why don't you want to listen to these pretty Bible stories? We just talked today about King David; you know he was a Jew."

Released-time programs proved popular. At their zenith in the mid-1940s, religion classes enrolled up to 2 million students, or 10 percent of the public school population, in 2,200 communities in forty-six states. Suddenly, the program came under sharp attack in Illinois, one of ten states where religion classes on released time were held in public school buildings. In 1945, Vashti McCollum, a humanist mother of three living in Champaign, rebelled against religious instruction in the public school attended by her son James Terry. Vashti's grandfather was a Presbyterian elder, and she was baptized in the Lutheran Church, but her father, Arthur Cromwell, gravitated to rationalism and publicly condemned religious worship as "a chronic disease of the imagination contracted in childhood."

The Champaign religion classes for fourth through ninth grades met in regular school classrooms on Wednesdays for less than an hour and were conducted by instructors selected and paid for by the inter-faith Council on Religious Education. Among other activities, the children made posters of Jesus' bodily resurrection. The public schools approved of the instructors, checked student attendance, and supervised the religious instruction classes, which enrolled 850 Protestants, 20 Roman Catholics, and no Jews (after the first year). The rabbi stopped teaching his class when Jewish students were subjected to anti-Semitic slurs. The students who did not attend religious instruction were required to go elsewhere in the building to pursue "meaningful secular studies."

To reach her goal of 100 percent participation, Terry McCollum's fifth-grade teacher pressured him to join. When he refused, the teacher banished him to a tiny room next to the teachers' toilet and then to the hall, where he was teased and given a steady diet of "black eyes, bloody noses, and welts." Terry often came home crying, prompting Vashti McCollum to investigate the classes to learn more about them. The Rev. Clifford Northcott, the Methodist minister who started the program, angrily told her that he would fight to retain the program even if it was unconstitutional.

Vashti McCollum was determined to prove just that. For McCollum, whose first name came from a defiant queen in the Old Testament, the Bible was an archaic and singularly unsuited text for children to read because it contained stories filled with "myth, filth, murder, war, and hate." With the encouragement of Philip Schug, the area's Unitarian minister, the financial backing of Jewish businesses in Chicago, and an attorney recommended by the American Civil Liberties Union (ACLU), this "harebrained, impetuous female crusader," as McCollum called herself, sued to stop the classes.

Rushing to her defense with an amicus brief was Leo Pfeffer, chief counsel of the American Jewish Congress. Pfeffer, the son of an Orthodox rabbi from Austria-Hungary, had attended public school on New York's Lower East Side, where he was subjected to readings from the King James Bible. When Pfeffer's school considered adopting released time for religious education, his parents abruptly transferred him to a yeshiva. Unlike the American Jewish Committee and the Anti-Defamation League, Pfeffer, the attorney, was convinced that legal reform was the best way to root out religion in the public schools, even if such litigation on behalf of an outspoken atheist reawakened anti-Semitism. Over the course of his long career, Pfeffer submitted eighty-five briefs to the U.S. Supreme Court and argued fifteen cases there, winning twelve of them. After losing in the local circuit court, Vashti McCollum dismissed her ACLU attorney and retained Walter Dodd, a distinguished former Yale law professor.

In what became a sickening pattern, the plaintiff in the establishment clause case endured escalating abuse. A newspaper columnist accused Vashti McCollum of "throwing spitballs at God," and of being "an emissary of Satan, a Communist, and a fiend in human form." Thus stigmatized, she was pelted with rotten tomatoes, her home was vandalized, and her cat was stolen. The postal carrier delivered hundreds of hate letters, one of which read, "You slimy bastard, may your filthy rotten soul roast in hell." The heated response cost McCollum her job as an adjunct instructor in physical education at the University of Illinois. To escape the abuse, the McCollums finally sent Terry to live with his maternal grandparents in Rochester, New York, where he attended a supportive but expensive private school until the family's funds were depleted a year and a half later.

Vashti McCollum endured three years of abuse before final vindication. In *Illinois ex rel. McCollum v. Board of Education* (1948), the U.S. Supreme Court, in an eight to one vote, used the establishment clause to strike down a state law for the first time. After considerable feuding between Hugo Black, who wrote the opinion, and Felix Frankfurter and Robert Jackson, who had deep reservations, the Court prohibited religious instruction in tax-supported public schools as an unconstitutional aid to religious groups. Just a year after *Everson*, Black abandoned his balancing approach concerning church and state and converted to Wiley Rutledge's absolutist position. Black now wrote: "Here not only are the State's tax-supported public school buildings used for the dissemination of religious doctrines. The State also affords sectarian groups an invaluable aid in that it helps to provide pupils for their religious classes through use of the State's compulsory public school machinery. This is not separation of Church and State." His opinion left unresolved the legality of released-time programs generally.

Black's authority in the *McCollum* case was his own opinion in the *Everson* case, something that Frankfurter could not abide. Frankfurter regarded *Everson* as a terrible mistake — "mischief breeding," he wrote his colleagues — and hoped to consign it to oblivion. He called the other three dissenters from the *Everson* case — Robert Jackson, Wiley Rutledge, and Harold Burton (a leading Unitarian and the former Republican senator from Ohio who replaced Owen Roberts) — into his chambers and asked that they not join in Black's draft unless it omitted any reference to *Everson*. He also sent Stanley Reed a newspaper clipping that contained an emotional letter describing how Christian activities in a public school adversely affected a young Jewish boy. "Please read this and then reread it," Frankfurter implored Reed, in order to understand how released-time programs violated a basic tenet of democracy. Reed remained unconvinced because he did not see how any student's religious liberty was being infringed upon.

As the memos flew back and forth among the brethren, Black fired back that he would not support any opinion that did not use *Everson*. Although Frank Murphy, a pious Roman Catholic, had joined Black's majority opinion in *Everson*, Murphy was still conflicted over it and prepared a separate opinion in *McCollum*. When Black saw the opinion, he "just blew up and objected violently to [Murphy's] filing it." Black finally tweaked his own draft enough to satisfy Burton, Rutledge, and Murphy.

Even though he agreed with the result in *McCollum*, Frankfurter privately called Black "malignant" for not repudiating *Everson*. Drawing from Pfeffer's amicus brief, Frankfurter wrote a moving concurrence that violated his core beliefs in federalism and judicial restraint. Frankfurter felt compelled to write because he viewed public schools as an Americanizing force that contributed mightily to social "cohesion." Throughout his life, he remembered how he had been influenced by Miss Hogan, a stern disciplinarian of Irish descent, who taught her students to become patriotic, English-speaking Americans. To permit religious instruction in the schools, Frankfurter reasoned, would undermine, if not destroy, the "most powerful agency for promoting cohesion among a heterogeneous democratic people. The public school must keep scrupulously free from entanglement in the strife of sects." Schools, he wrote, could only be kept from such conflict if the establishment clause were rigorously enforced: "Separation means separation, not something less." Praising the public school as "the symbol of our democracy," Frankfurter advised that in church-state matters " 'good fences make good neighbors.' "

McCollum came just as U.S. society was becoming more openly religious and the Supreme Court was adopting a new church-state jurisprudence that hewed to an ever-stricter line dividing church and state. As such, the decision was highly controversial. Some Jews acclaimed the decision as the "Magna Carta of the secular school system," but many Christians labeled it as irresponsible. The Court stood accused of misinterpreting the First Amendment and reading secularism into the Constitution, thereby curtailing the people's religious liberty. For Roman Catholics, the *McCollum* decision was devastating, and Vashti McCollum was accused of pulling down the public school system — "the symbol of our democracy" — in a "Sampson-like" manner. The Catholic press ran headline after headline against it: "God Is Out! Atheism Wins in Court Fight." "Keep Out, God." "McCollum Decision Makes First Amendment 'Historic Relic.'" The *Catholic Chronicle* of Toledo, Ohio, editorialized against this "madness": "A degenerate disease has been eating away at the highest tribunal's legal philosophy ever since Oliver Wendell Holmes brought the infection to the bench. . . . The most charitable thing we can say is that they have gone out of their legal minds."

The U.S. Supreme Court justices were presumed to be unwitting dupes of international communism. Attorney General J. Howard McGrath, a Roman Catholic, attacked Hugo Black before the National Catholic Educational Association, accusing the justice of distorting the First Amendment's meaning. "If anything," the nation's chief law enforcement officer said, "the state and church must not have any fence between them." Erwin Corwin, a distinguished constitutional scholar at Princeton University, charged the Court with becoming a busybody national school board. Democratic Congressmember Samuel Hobbs of Alabama, a Presbyterian, declared that the decision was calculated "to destroy every mark that characterizes this a Nation dedicated to God and to freedom of worship." He introduced a joint resolution to repeal the Fourteenth Amendment, so that *McCollum* would not make the United States "a pagan Nation." Black chuckled as he read the criticism by politicians with whom he was friends because, his law clerk remembered, Black "knew which ones were using the Court as a whipping boy in their election campaigns." These attacks notwithstanding, released-time programs never recovered their previous popularity.

The *McCollum* ruling left unresolved the question of whether other public school programs for religious instruction could be permissible. Unlike Champaign's released-time program, which allowed religious instruction in public school classrooms, New York City's program took place away from school grounds and did not involve any direct public expense. At first, it proved highly controversial. Initial attempts to introduce it in New York City schools in 1917 led to riots in public hearings, causing a delay in its implementation. In 1923, the Greater New York Coordinating Committee on Released Time of Jews, Protestants, and Roman Catholics—a twelve-person, interfaith body—ultimately won approval for released time. The committee persuaded city school officials that religion was an antidote to atheism, immorality, social fragmentation (delinquency, divorce, and prejudice), totalitarianism, and eternal damnation. A spokesperson for the released-time committee said that parents were afraid that longer school days, increased homework, and "the momentum of secularism" were "pushing religion and the church into the backwaters of life." Program supporters also hoped to increase church membership. Some Jews backed the program because religious holidays, including their own, would be considered excused absences. On the whole, however, Jewish organizations preferred dismissed time (shortening the school day), but they capitulated to maintain Christian goodwill.

In 1940, New York Governor Herbert Lehman, a Jew, signed the Coudert-McLaughlin Religious Instruction Bill, dismissing concerns over the released time it sanctioned as "groundless." The measure was enacted over the vigorous opposition of teacher unions, which condemned it as "thoroughly vicious" and the "opening wedge" for further inroads by religious sects. Under the law, the released-time program in New York City grew from 3,000 elementary school pupils in 1941 to 105,467 (19.2 percent of the school population) a decade later. Of the children enrolled in religion courses, 80 percent were Roman Catholic, 13 percent were Protestant, and 5 percent were Jewish, primarily orthodox. School officials verified parents' permission slips and checked student attendance, though evidently not closely enough. One principal estimated that the truancy rate for the released-time program was 40 percent. Too often, the program bred dishonesty and delinquency instead of moral behavior. Even so, William Jansen, the superintendent of schools, believed that New York City schools were minimally involved in such abuses and announced that *McCollum* would not produce any changes in the city's released-time program.

Encouraged by the *McCollum* decision, Joseph Lewis, the crusading president of Freethinkers of America, filed a lawsuit against "this pernicious practice of corrupting our . . . children with the virus of religious prejudice." The self-educated son of an Alabama Jewish merchant, Lewis argued that if public schools were not an indispensable part of the success of released time, students "would play baseball instead" of attending religion classes held after school let out. Lewis's ACLU attorney argued that taking time from the school day amounted to a "bait to get the child to church." It was clear, however, that Lewis's lawsuit against released time would be fruitless, as was his first such lawsuit in 1927, because he neither resided in New York City nor had any children in its schools.

Civil liberties groups persuaded Lewis to withdraw his latest complaint on the condition that they file another test case. Before long, two new plaintiffs from Brooklyn stepped forward to stop the state's released-time program for religious instruction. The ACLU had been casting about for "a good solid white Protestant plaintiff" with a child in the public schools, and Tessim Zorach, an active Episcopalian, a successful food broker, and son of a well-known sculptor, fit the bill. Jewish groups were, as usual, divided about the wisdom of having a Jewish co-plaintiff, but in the end, the American Jewish Congress recruited Esta Gluck, who was president of her parent-teacher association, belonged to the local synagogue, and sent her children to Hebrew school in the afternoons. In a disturbing affidavit, Gluck alleged that her daughter's public schoolteacher had made an unusually cruel remark to a student who was not enrolled in released time. One day, the student had a queasy stomach, but the teacher commented that the sick child's face was more repulsive than the vomit.

Despite Leo Pfeffer's initial reluctance about the released-time case, he designed the legal strategy, gathered evidence, prepared the case for trial, and raised funds to litigate it. His brief contended that the released-time program violated the Constitution by using "tax-supported state schools to help religious groups propagate their faiths." The result was considerable "pressure and coercion upon parents and children."

The *Zorach* lawsuit was not publicly well received, as the Cold War intensified patriotic and religious feelings. For the majority culture, the suit became symbolic of a larger contest between atheism and Americanism, between secular Jews of dubious loyalty and godly, patriotic Christians. Monsignor John Middleton, secretary of education for the New York Archdiocese, accused Reform rabbis of "encouraging the secularism that is already eating away the heart of American life." Middleton rejected the demand that the majority culture should "closet the historical Christ and obliterate the memory of His existence because the few are displeased."

In dismissing the *Zorach* suit, New York Supreme Court Justice Anthony DiGiovanna upheld the released-time program, stressing that separation of church and state did not mean "freedom from religion." If the religious instruction program were prohibited, DiGiovanna decided, that would be a "step in the direction of . . . totalitarian and Communistic philosophies . . . wherein atheism and suppression of all religions are preferred to freedom of the individual to seek religious instruction and worship." The New York Court of Appeals also sanctioned the program, concluding, "The constitution does not demand that every friendly gesture between church and state shall be discountenanced. This so-called 'wall of separation' may be built so high and so broad as to impair both state and church."

In the wake of rising public controversy and two defeats in New York courts, Jewish defense organizations wanted to avoid sparking a Jewish-Christian confrontation and refused to allow Pfeffer to join the ACLU in arguing *Zorach* before the U.S. Supreme Court. Even without Pfeffer's capable assistance, the Court seemed likely to pull back from *McCollum*. Not only was the Court sensitive to negative reaction to its first released-time decision, but the Court's personnel had changed considerably since 1948 when *McCollum* had been decided. President Harry Truman appointed three political cronies — Fred Vinson, Tom Clark, and Sherman Minton — who were more conservative than the justices they replaced, especially Frank Murphy and Wiley Rutledge, who died suddenly in their fifties. These new justices helped the Court produce the first accommodationist decision in its history.

Writing for the six-to-three majority in *Zorach v. Clauson* (1952), William O. Douglas baffled constitutional scholars in upholding New York's released-time program. Douglas, a former Yale law professor and the son of a Presbyterian minister, had not "the slightest doubt that the First Amendment reflects the philosophy that Church and State should be separated," but it "does not say that in every and all respects there shall be a separation of Church and State." If the wall was impermeable, he thought, government and religion would be "aliens to each other — hostile, suspicious, and even unfriendly." Douglas suggested that the proper function of government in the area of religion was cooperation, not neutrality. In this case, Douglas averred, the public schools did no more than "accommodate their schedules to a program of outside religious instruction." In Douglas's estimation, New York City's program simply extended the practice of excusing students for their respective religious holidays.

Although he reaffirmed the *McCollum* decision, Douglas concluded that the Bill of Rights could not be interpreted as possessing "a philosophy of hostility to religion." After all, he noted, "We are a religious people whose institutions presuppose a Supreme Being. . . . When the state encourages religious instruction or cooperates with religious authorities by adjusting the schedule of public events to sectarian needs, it follows the best of our traditions." Douglas's aphorism has been quoted ever since to rationalize government support of religion. The *Zorach* case was the U.S. Supreme Court's last word on religion in the schools for a decade.

There were three revealing dissents to the *Zorach* ruling. Hugo Black, who was once a father figure to Douglas, was astounded by Douglas's apostasy. Black saw no difference between the Illinois program invalidated in the *McCollum* decision and the one in New York upheld in *Zorach*. The State of New York, Black said bluntly, was "manipulating its compulsory education laws to help religious sects get pupils. This is not separation but combination of Church and State." Felix Frankfurter accused the majority of ignoring the heart of *McCollum:* "There is all the difference in the world between letting the children out of school and letting some of them out of school into religion classes." He chastised supporters of released-time programs for their "surprising want of confidence in the inherent power of the various faiths to draw children to outside sectarian classes — an attitude that hardly reflects the faith of the greatest religious spirits." Robert Jackson, who sent his children to parochial schools despite a distaste for the "silly emotional stuff" in religion, accused Douglas of having "warped and twisted" the wall of separation, apparently to appeal to Roman Catholics and thereby pave the way for a presidential bid later that year. For Jackson, the school "serves as a temporary jail for a pupil who will not go to Church." He warned, "The day that this country ceases to be free for irreligion it will cease to be free for religion — except for the sect that can win political power."

The public reaction to *Zorach* was mixed, though more positive than negative. Dennis Hurley, New York City's corporation counsel, said the decision restored a " 'common sense' approach to church-state relationships." The editor of the Catholic diocesan newspaper of Buffalo, New York, was gratified: "The United States Supreme Court may have put a brake on an aggressive and growing campaign for secularism in this country." Although the secularists had only been "temporarily halted," the editor thought, "the pause could provide a breathing spell during which Catholics, Protestants, and Jews who believe in the American way could regroup their forces for the defense of democracy."

Others were scathing in their criticism. Jewish organizations were devastated by *Zorach*, which they saw as a giant step backward from *McCollum*. Joseph Lewis of the Freethinkers of America called the decision "a triumph for religious superstition and . . . a fatal blow to religious freedom because to make one pay for the religious instruction of another, whose religious beliefs he does not subscribe to, is tyranny." One New Jersey man who described himself as a "self-ordained priest of the United Mushroom Worshippers of America" penned a heavily satirical letter to Douglas, thanking the justice for providing "THE ONLY TRUE CHURCH" a golden opportunity to enlarge its membership by "capturing the young, plastic minds of the schoolchildren" through released time. As the Court considered later establishment clause cases, *Zorach* would be rendered a constitutional anachronism.

And what of released-time programs after *Zorach*? Although more students enrolled in religion classes than ever before, the percentage of participating students declined from the zenith reached during World War II. Several factors explain this continual decline. One-third of the programs in the 1950s violated the law by holding religion classes in public schools, and this fact turned off many law-abiding people. Public school administrators generally opposed the programs all along. Protestant groups regarded the classes as theological gruel that ineffectively transmitted religious precepts. Other options seemed more desirable, including enhancing religious schools, devising shared-time programs, or teaching "about" religion or ethics in public schools.

Yet another sign that the U.S. Supreme Court wanted to make amends over *McCollum* came when it ducked a New Jersey Bible reading case while deciding *Zorach*. Since 1903, the State of New Jersey had permitted the recital of the Lord's Prayer and had required public schoolteachers, as part of their daily routine, to read at least five verses from the Old Testament. In a test case, the ACLU represented two freethinkers — Donald Doremus and Anna Klein — against the Hawthorne Board of Education and the State of New Jersey. As officers in the United Secularists of America, one of the nation's newest rationalist organizations, they maintained that the state forced schoolchildren to attend — and their parents to pay taxes to underwrite — what were essentially Protestant exercises. But the New Jersey Supreme Court ignored *Everson* and *McCollum* and upheld the statutes. Incredibly, Justice Clarence Case maintained that the Lord's Prayer was nonsectarian because "Christ was a Jew and He was speaking to Jews." Even more shocking, Case dismissed the objections of all other groups because they were "numerically small and, in point of impact on our national life, negligible."

When Doremus considered appealing the decision, Leo Pfeffer of the American Jewish Congress strongly advised against it, warning that the monumental gains made in *McCollum* might well be washed away entirely. Pfeffer was convinced that the U.S. Supreme Court would uphold the "innocuous type" of Bible reading in New Jersey because it could not withstand "the tremendous propaganda led by the Catholic Church which has been unleashed" against *McCollum*. The fault for this missed opportunity, Pfeffer claimed, belonged to the American Jewish Committee, a rival group that boasted of its expertise in public relations but had done little to educate the U.S. public about the wisdom of keeping church and state separate. Taking matters into his own hands, Pfeffer flew Vashti McCollum to New York City to dissuade the *Doremus* plaintiffs in person. (Evolving circumstances made such a meeting pointless, and it never occurred.) When the appeal proceeded anyway, Pfeffer calculated that filing an amicus brief was preferable to silence. He was unable to convince any other religious organization — Jewish or Protestant — to join him.

For all of Pfeffer's "extreme pessimism" concerning *Doremus*, the U.S. Supreme Court dismissed the case because the plaintiffs had either graduated from school or suffered no particular injury. The trifling expenditures involved in Bible reading and the Lord's Prayer had evidently not increased taxes. The High Court had no intention of marching straight into the briar patch, as it had in the *McCollum* decision.

Nor was the U.S. Supreme Court willing to hear another New Jersey case involving religion in public education. In *Tudor v. Board of Education* (1954), the dispute concerned the distribution of Bibles to students in public elementary schools. Citing a seventy-year-old state law authorizing Bible reading in public schools, public school officials in Rutherford allowed Gideons International, a nonprofit association of Protestant business owners based in Illinois, to give away their 35¢, pocket-sized New Testaments (King James Version), which included the Psalms and Proverbs. The Gideons, whose purpose was "to win men and women for the Lord Jesus Christ," had recently launched a national campaign to distribute their Bibles in all public school classrooms as well as in every hotel room. The Gideons assured the Rutherford School Board that furnishing "the Word of God" was "the answer to the problem of juvenile delinquency." New Jersey school superintendent Guy Hilleboe called the Bible-distribution plan a "100 percent democratic process" that would aid a student "to better understand himself and others around him," all for the total cost to the district of $5 for consent slips. More than one-fourth of the 2,200 students returned permission slips signed by their parents.

A local rabbi and a priest, representing Jewish and Catholic parents, hired Leo Pfeffer to challenge Rutherford's practice. Pfeffer and the school district tried to resolve their differences before going to trial, but Pfeffer rejected the Gideons' argument that the Jewish Holocaust had occurred because the Nazis had repudiated the Bible. Although Catholic canon law forbade Roman Catholics from accepting the King James Version, Jacob Stam, the school district's attorney, maintained that the Bible was a nonsectarian book with unique authority and value. No child, Stam pointed out, was forced to take the Bible or read from it at any time or in any way. Stam concluded that the First Amendment "certainly does not say there shall be a separation of the Bible and the state."

Pfeffer prevailed in the New Jersey Supreme Court, which decided that the Gideon Bible was indeed sectarian and therefore prohibited its distribution in the public schools. The state court, including William Brennan, who would soon join the U.S. Supreme Court, distinguished between Bible reading in public schools, which it had just upheld, and Bible distribution, a "vice" that went far beyond the mere accommodation of religion permitted under *Zorach*. The ruling recalled the testimony of prominent rabbis who testified that the Gideon Bible "is in profound conflict" with the basic principles of Judaism, and psychologists and educators who called the distribution "divisive."

The *Tudor* decision was roundly condemned by conservative Christians. Southern Baptist evangelist Billy Graham spoke for many when he said that the decision made "a tremendous contribution to the Communist cause." He asserted, "We are a Christian nation, but if this kind of thing keeps up, we'll soon have to rule [out] Bibles from our courtrooms and inauguration ceremonies because it is a 'sectarian' book." Conservative Christians like Graham were generally suspicious of political involvement and were, in any case, unorganized. They would remain so until the late 1970s. Without organizational vehicles, they counted on legislators and judges to preserve the religious status quo.

When the nation's High Court refused to hear the *Tudor* appeal, it sent a powerful, though indirect, signal that Bible distribution in public schools was illegal. As a result, school boards in Boston, Massachusetts; Detroit, Michigan; Reno, Nevada; Akron and Youngstown, Ohio; and other cities refused to allow the distribution of Gideon Bibles. Some communities, including East Baton Rouge, Louisiana, claimed to be unfamiliar with the *Tudor* ruling and permitted the Bibles to be passed out. The practice continued into the 1980s in public schools in South Carolina, for example.

These cases came during the height of the Cold War in the early 1950s, when the Soviet Union and Eastern Europe competed with the United States to expand their nuclear arsenals. For many Americans, the best defense against Soviet aggression was not political, economic, or even military mobilization, but open expression of religious conviction. A Gallup poll reported that 96 percent of Americans declared their belief in God, and formal religious affiliation reached an all-time high of 64 percent. Of those belonging to a faith community, Protestants accounted for 68 percent, Catholics accounted for 23 percent, and Jews constituted only 4 percent. As a sign of the importance they attached to religion, Americans spent twice as much on churches as on hospitals.

U.S. institutions proclaimed their religiosity to win battles at home and abroad. In addition to school prayer and Bible reading, there were numerous efforts to further inculcate civil religion in U.S. public life. In 1952, Congress required the president to proclaim a "National Day of Prayer," which encouraged all Americans to pray at the same time in their own ways. Although a belated convert to organized religion's strengths, President Dwight Eisenhower opened cabinet meetings with prayer, consulted with evangelist Billy Graham, held prayer breakfasts, delivered homey exhortations at press conferences, and encouraged Americans to attend worship services regularly. He told the country, "Recognition of the Supreme Being is the first, the most basic expression of Americanism. Without God, there could be no American form of government, nor any American way of life." In that spirit, Congress adopted "In God We Trust" as the national motto and incorporated the phrase "under God" into the Pledge of Allegiance.

Popular culture reflected this turn to religion. The best-selling books included the new Revised Standard Version of the Bible, Rev. Norman Vincent Peale's *The Power of Positive Thinking*, and Bishop Fulton Sheen's *Life Is Worth Living* and *The Greatest Faith Ever Known*. Ministers, bishops, popes, and rabbis all graced the cover of *Time* magazine. Radio airwaves played "It Is No Secret What God Can Do," movie houses screened *The Ten Commandments*, and a toy company produced a doll whose knees could be bent in a "praying position."

The turn to religiosity did not unite Americans except in their desire to identify the United States as their chosen land and to resist communism from abroad. As theologian Will Herberg observed, postwar religion supplanted national origin, language, and culture as the prime means of distinguishing oneself from others, especially in new suburbs where social boundaries were still fluid. Protestant and Jewish children attended public schools, and Catholics retreated to parochial schools. Each major group withdrew to its own enclaves, including country clubs and fraternal organizations such as the Masonic Lodge (Protestant), Knights of Columbus (Catholic), or Temple Brotherhood (Jewish). Even when Protestants, Catholics, and Jews did belong to the same groups, close friendships across religious lines were infrequent and invariably less trusting than those that developed within the same faith. Christians and Jews still felt uncomfortable around each other, a fact that was reflected in the continuing reluctance to marry outside one's faith.

Given the Cold War unease that pervaded U.S. society, educators searched for new ways to teach moral and spiritual values. So great was this desire that prayer and Bible reading became part of the school day in districts where such practices had been unknown or rare. Nationally, 41 percent of public schools had Bible reading, and one-third of them required morning devotions. There was considerable regional variation in the prevalence of these exercises. In the South and East, more than 80 percent of elementary schoolteachers said morning prayers; in the Midwest, that figure was 38 percent; and in the West, just 14 percent. Although the courts had barred classroom devotions in the schools of California, Illinois, Louisiana, Nebraska, South Dakota, Washington, and Wisconsin, few Americans believed that the First Amendment to the U.S. Constitution prohibited these rituals.

Such practices were clearly sectarian, though many officials and parents missed this crucial point. Indeed, many Christians believed that these divine petitions were interdenominational and were therefore fully consonant with the country's Judeo-Christian heritage. The unrecognized truth was that the country was overwhelmingly Protestant and that Protestants controlled most political institutions, including the local school boards that adopted required prayers. The version of the Lord's Prayer that was recited, the version of the Ten Commandments that was posted on classroom walls, the version of the Bible that teachers read from, and the manner of praying and reading from that Bible were all transparently Protestant. Most Jews, as a small national minority, tolerated them; some Jews did not. Underneath the surface calm was an explosion waiting to happen. Its name was *Engel v. Vitale*.

CHAPTER 4

"The One-Size-Fits-All Prayer"

In November 1951, in the midst of the Korean War, a rising juvenile crime wave, and disturbing charges of corruption and disloyalty in high places, the New York Board of Regents unanimously adopted the nation's first government-prepared prayer for public schools. Religious practices such as spoken prayer and Bible reading were offered in many of the state's schools, but the state board wanted a uniform exercise as part of its program in moral and spiritual training that included the salute to the flag. It may also have been prompted by the rejection of the Lord's Prayer in New York City public schools.

Postulating that Americans have always been religious, the regents believed that such a program would ensure that schoolchildren would acquire "respect for lawful authority and obedience to law." By "teaching our children, as set forth in the Declaration of Independence, that Almighty God is their Creator," the regents thought students would gain the "best security" possible in that turbulent time. Reflecting the religious composition of New York State — 50 percent Catholic, 25 percent Jewish, 20 percent Protestant, and 5 percent unidentified — a team of ministers, priests, and rabbis spent months contriving a twenty-two-word prayer that left out any explicit Christian reference: "Almighty God, we acknowledge our dependence upon Thee, and we beg Thy blessings upon us, our parents, our teachers, and our country."

On the surface, this official "nondenominational" prayer, which was designed to be religiously correct, seemed innocuous enough, and the regents expected that most people of "goodwill" would support it. The thirteen-member board, which included five attorneys and the wife of the Gannett newspaper chain owner, announced in a press release that it was fully aware of the establishment clause and believed that the new prayer was "clearly constitutional" even though it promoted sectarian notions of monotheism, supernatural creation, and divine response to petitions. The regents introduced their generic prayer to local school districts and recommended but did not require them to use it. If local school officials decided to have their students recite any prayer in their opening exercises, it had to be this one.

The regents' prayer received strong support from establishment figures in New York. Governor Thomas Dewey, an Episcopalian, quickly endorsed the idea as an essential means of defeating "the slave world of godless communism." The New York Association of Judges of Children's Courts "heartily endorsed" the regents' prayer because of "the importance of religious training in the formation of moral character in the early life of the child." The New York Association of Secondary School Principals and the Directors of the New York School Boards Association urged local boards to adopt the prayer to combat "the vicious menace of all narcotics and alcohol." Maximilian Moss, a prominent attorney, leading Jewish philanthropist, president of the New York City Board of Education, and future state supreme court justice, called the prayer a "refreshing answer" to charges that public schools were ungodly. Most Protestant leaders, including Norman Vincent Peale, pastor of Manhattan's famed Marble Collegiate Church, and Ralph Sockman, the Methodist chaplain of New York University and a featured speaker on the "National Radio Pulpit," backed the prayer.

The Roman Catholic Church was especially supportive of the regents' prayer because of its conviction that education needed a religious foundation. Bishop William Scully of Albany and Monsignor John Middleton, education secretary of the New York Archdiocese, spoke out in its favor. So did *The Tablet*, the official organ of the Brooklyn Catholic Diocese, which decried "Godlessness" in public schools. John Brosnan, an estate attorney who promoted Catholic causes and chaired the New York Board of Regents, told the Friendly Sons of St. Patrick, "The only criticism [of the prayer] came from those who do not believe in God."

In fact, God-fearing critics of the regents' prayer abounded. *Christian Century*, a liberal Protestant magazine, deemed the practice ineffectual because the government-prescribed prayer was "likely to deteriorate quickly into an empty formality with little, if any, spiritual significance." Because Christ's name had "deliberately been omitted to mollify non-Christian elements," some Protestant ministers asserted that the devotion was not a prayer but "an abomination and a blasphemy." Nonreligious groups, such as the New York Teachers Guild and Citizens Union, a nonpartisan watchdog group founded to fight Tammany Hall, also concluded the prayer had no place in the public schools. The United Parents Association, which claimed to speak for 235,000 parents of New York City pupils, declared flatly that prayers should not be recited by children who "do not even understand the words."

Major Jewish organizations, including the American Jewish Congress, the Synagogue Council of America, and the New York Board of Rabbis, labeled the regents' prayer "a serious infringement" of the "cherished tradition of separation of church and state." As such, these Jewish groups declared, the prayer was another ill-advised attempt to equate belief in God with good citizenship. Potentially more serious, the prayer threatened to open the door to other, more far-reaching, kinds of sectarianism.

The board of the New York Society of Ethical Culture, a humanist group, criticized the new prayer in a letter to the *New York Times*. Not only did the prayer run afoul of the New York State constitution and the *McCollum* case against religious instruction in public schools, it purportedly violated common sense because supernaturalism was "morally and intellectually unacceptable." Better, the humanist board wrote, to rely on "the latent power for reason and good in men themselves." Although the regents had urged a unity of spirit during the Cold War, the board believed that the prayer would sow "bitterness and conflict." Moreover, the prayer would "threaten the integrity of the public school," which, the board declared, "is almost necessarily a secular institution" in a democracy. It is in the school that children must be regarded as Americans, "not as Protestants or Catholics or Jews or Ethical Culturists or infidels." The board's letter concluded: "It is a cardinal principle in American life that questions of religion should not be decided by ballot, that even a single child of non-religious parents in a school that is otherwise composed of pupils from religious homes should not be coerced in matters of religion."

The American Civil Liberties Union (ACLU) and its New York affiliate, which had just formed, immediately questioned the regents' prayer and urged the New York City Board of Education to hold public hearings before adopting it. In a letter to School Board President Maximilian Moss, ACLU Executive Director Patrick Murphy Malin, a Swarthmore economist who helped the organization grow exponentially, and the Rev. John Paul Jones, who chaired the New York chapter of the ACLU, emphasized that religion and public education belonged in separate spheres. Citing the *Everson* and *McCollum* decisions, Malin and Jones insisted, "The teaching of our spiritual heritage, through prayer and special programs, is the function of religious leaders and of parents and not the proper function of public school teachers." President Moss, who also served on the Greater New York Coordinating Committee on Released Time, knew full well that the regents' prayer would be highly controversial, and he had already predicted that "a public hearing will be held before we take any action."

The combined pressure from these separatist groups had the desired effect. After stormy hearings, a compromise developed in which the offending government prayer was removed from the public schools of the state's largest city. Protestants and Catholics proposed that schoolchildren sing, rather than recite, the fourth stanza of "America" (also known as "My Country, 'Tis of Thee"): "Our fathers' God, to Thee, Author of liberty, To Thee we sing; Long may our land be bright With freedom's holy light; Protect us by Thy might, Great God, our King." The Board of Rabbis insisted, however, that the first stanza be sung along with the fourth, as a patriotic hymn. The school board decided that New York City's public schoolchildren would begin each day by listening to a teacher read a scriptural passage without commenting on it, reciting the Pledge of Allegiance, and singing both the first and fourth stanzas of "America." So the regents' prayer was prohibited in New York City, but the compromise seemed to favor Christians, who announced that the recital of the fourth stanza was a prayer.

Even more disconcerting from a Jewish perspective, New York City retained the regents' program on moral and spiritual values. To Jews, this program was an insidious scheme to introduce religion "into every phase of school life and in effect makes the public teacher a full time religious missionary." It was bad enough, they said, when the state provided released time for religious instruction and then wrote its own prayer for students to recite. Now the state, with the strong support of the Roman Catholic Church, wanted to infuse religion into every part of the school day and to interfere with religious instruction by religious bodies.

Before long, the New York Board of Regents felt compelled to revisit the school prayer issue. The board was particularly concerned about the rise of juvenile delinquency. Between 1948 and 1953, the number of youngsters charged with crimes nationwide increased by 45 percent, climbing to an annual total of 1 million delinquents. For every juvenile hauled into court, an estimated five others had not been caught. Many of these delinquents were part of frightening gangs that controlled large sections of downtowns across the state and sported colorful names such as Dragons, Cobras, and Jesters. Using all manner of weapons, including handguns, knives, brass knuckles, and Molotov cocktails, the gangs fired into crowds, stole automobiles, vandalized public buildings, firebombed nightclubs, assaulted women, and terrorized schools. The young criminals often showed no remorse. One thug laughed as he confessed to a bloody assault: "I stabbed him with a bread knife. You know, I was drunk, so I just stabbed him. He was screaming like a dog." Such senseless violence by "our vicious young hoodlums," as *Newsweek* called them, provoked much soul-searching in the mainstream United States.

In 1955, the New York Board of Regents addressed such serious concerns in its "Statement on Moral and Spiritual Training in Schools," which argued that the regents' prayer might serve as an antidote to such delinquency in the public schools. The board cited U.S. history, especially the spiritual foundation of the country, to justify the prayer. In so doing, the board denied that it illegally promoted formal religion in the public schools. The regents admonished teachers that they were to "always be mindful of the fundamental doctrine of the separation of church and state and careful at all times to avoid any and all sectarian or religious instructions."

According to press reports, only 17 percent of the state's 900 school districts adopted the regents' prayer by 1955. These districts were mainly in smaller upstate communities where Protestants, with occasional Catholic support, exerted sufficient influence. Some larger cities, including Binghamton, Endicott, Hornell, Rochester, Syracuse, Troy, Utica, and Yonkers, also adopted the prayer. School districts elsewhere regarded the prayer as a "hot potato" and steered clear of it because of vigorous opposition. On Long Island, however, six of the sixty-one school districts adopted "this act of reverence to God" along with the Pledge of Allegiance. One of the six districts was Herricks

(Union Free School District Number Nine), which was created in 1813 and located in the town of North Hempstead in Nassau County, 20 miles southeast of Manhattan. (The 4 square-mile school district was served by the New Hyde Park Post Office, and the case is usually identified as having occurred in New Hyde Park.)

When the Herricks School Board adopted the regents' prayer, it set off a chain of events that would lead to the greatest outcry against a U.S. Supreme Court decision in a century. John Brosnan, chair of the regents, had no inkling of what was to come: "We didn't have the slightest idea the prayer we wrote would prove so controversial. . . . At one time, one rabbi said he didn't see how anybody could take offense."

Even as some Long Island school officials adopted various religious practices, the island was changing in important ways. After World War II, a large number of Jewish families of Eastern European descent, including the five plaintiffs in the *Engel* case (Steven Engel, Monroe Lerner, Daniel Lichtenstein, Lenore Lyons, and Lawrence Roth), flocked to Nassau County from New York City. Many of the new suburbanites were managers, salespeople, stockbrokers, physicians, accountants, and attorneys in search of more land and better education for their children. Lenore Lyons moved from Queens because she detested her tiny cockroach-infested apartment. She had half-jokingly planned to paint the kitchen black so the disgusting insects would be invisible, but when her family's fortunes improved, it was easier to buy a house in the suburbs. Along with improved living conditions came rising expectations for the schools the children would attend. Steven Engel recalls that in his neighborhood "there was a genius in every house. . . . Almost every other house had over-achievers" whose parents had large libraries. In a nutshell, these strivers wanted a bigger slice of the American dream.

Thanks to rising wages and the G.I. Bill of Rights, which made it much easier for veterans to buy homes, as well as the extension of the Long Island Expressway, Nassau County was transformed almost overnight from a potato-farming community into the nation's largest suburb, with its population doubling to 1.4 million. In the late 1930s, there had been 18,000 Jews in Nassau County, including Eddie Cantor and the Marx Brothers, who had summer homes in Great Neck; twenty years later, there were 330,000 Jews in the county. By 1959, 23.2 percent of Nassau County residents affiliated with Roman

Catholic churches, 17.7 percent with Protestant churches, and 15.8 percent with Jewish synagogues.

Jews had first come to Long Island in the colonial period, with large numbers arriving in the late nineteenth century. Anti-Semitism swelled alongside the influx of immigrants. In the 1920s, the Ku Klux Klan burned crosses in several communities, upset over alleged Jewish control of advertising. Job discrimination forced Jews to scramble for work as itinerant peddlers, tree trimmers, cigar rollers, and garment workers — anything to get by. Upon reaching adolescence, Jewish children lost Christian playmates and were excluded from neighborhood activities. Jewish students were kept out of New York medical schools and engineering colleges and from Long Island country clubs and beaches. In 1934, the Friends of New Germany established its headquarters in a New Hyde Park hotel called the Brauhof. Inspired by Adolf Hitler, this white supremacist group organized long parades of automobiles festooned with swastikas that passed through seven towns in Nassau County. In Yaphank, a small town in neighboring Suffolk County, the German-American Bund established Camp Siegfried in 1937. The Bund paid tributes to the Nazi hierarchy in the camp's signs — Hitler Street, Goering Street, and Goebbels Street.

In Nassau County, the obvious signs of anti-Semitism receded as Jews moved in, but, as one lifelong resident recalled, the Herricks School District remained "a very, very conservative community." To a considerable extent, the tenor of that community was set by the many different Christian churches that could be found in Herricks, including Dutch Reformed, Episcopal, Lutheran, Methodist, and Roman Catholic. As a religious revival swept the country after World War II, many towns and churches in Nassau (and across the United States) favored melding patriotism and religion to defeat the Soviet Union abroad and overcome disloyalty and moral degeneracy at home. The indispensable institution in this regard was public education. A morning ritual consisting of a salute to the flag and a prayer to the Almighty could train millions of young, God-fearing, patriotic "soldiers" to "fight" the Cold War. Although school officials claimed these devotions were nondenominational, they invariably bore a Protestant stamp.

At the same time, American-born Jews opened a new chapter in their history by renewing their resistance to sectarianism in public schools. By mid-century, Jews were more confident, more prosperous, and more assertive than ever before. Many no longer had to struggle for survival and had no firsthand knowledge of Eastern European ghettoes and Christian state schools. Many Jews had fought in World War II, and like African Americans, their wartime experience encouraged their insistence on equality. The creation of the modern State of Israel filled many U.S. Jews with pride and counteracted feelings of inferiority that persisted within their community. In short, U.S. Jews had come of age and would no longer remain silent about infringement upon their rights and those of their children in public schools. They would turn to the ACLU and Jewish organizations — the American Jewish Congress, the American Jewish Committee, and the Anti-Defamation League of B'nai B'rith — for defense against school prayer, released time for religious instruction, and Christological observances of Christmas. This help came in the form of educational campaigns, lobbying of officials, and, increasingly, lawsuits.

The rapid influx of new residents into Long Island resulted in serious overcrowding of schools at the time the regents' prayer was adopted. Before the new wave arrived, the only schools in the Herricks School District served kindergarten through eighth grade — Park Avenue, which opened in 1930, and Herricks, which opened in 1949. As the population mushroomed to include 12,500 families in forty-six neighborhoods by the late 1950s, the need for more classrooms became acute, and four elementary schools were built after World War II — Searingtown, Wickshire, Denton Avenue, and Center Street. Enrollment in Searingtown School grew from 413 pupils in 1952 to 689 in 1958, peaking at 956 in 1965. Before long, a junior high school was needed, and ninth grade was added to the original K–8 school. The growing population dictated the need for two junior high schools, but the proposal was defeated for years, resulting in twice as many students in Herricks Junior High as the building was designed for. Officials instituted double shifts, rented classrooms in other buildings, and sent students to three neighboring districts. Even after the Herricks schools opened, the district kept scrambling for space to accommodate its 4,294 students.

The rush to build schools in Herricks was so great that the pupils had to walk across planks to get into unfinished buildings. Students could buy sandwiches, milk, and ice cream, but with no cafeteria, the lunches had to be eaten in classrooms. Nor was there an art classroom, so a cart with art supplies was wheeled from room to room. Portable chairs had to be brought into the multipurpose auditorium, which doubled as a gymnasium. The rooms themselves were not redesigned. Teenagers studying home economics and industrial arts trooped into former kindergarten classrooms. Teachers had to write at the top of blackboards so that their older (and taller) students could see.

Most Herricks taxpayers, especially Roman Catholic parents whose children attended financially strapped parochial schools, opposed spending money on new public school "palaces," particularly when the new expenditure seemed a luxury. A proposed $350,000 bond issue to build a school swimming pool seemed especially wasteful. The *New Hyde Park Courier* characterized the swimming pool as "tax-icide" and hoped that the special referendum would sink this "wasteful extravagance" to keep taxes from becoming "ridiculously high." Although Lester Peck, the principal (equivalent to superintendent) of the Herricks School District, endorsed the proposed swimming pool as a community asset, the pool referendum was defeated by a five-to-one margin.

Because there was no local industry to share the school property tax bill, the Herricks School District endured austerity budgets and long delays in building construction. The budget shortfalls meant that students who could not pay for supplies for art, shop, or home economics simply sat in the classroom without taking part in the classes themselves. These budget setbacks greatly frustrated the new arrivals, who quickly approached the board to change its direction. When Julia Lerner moved into the district in 1953, she recalled, "I don't think we were in the door five minutes when someone arrived to get somebody on the school board who had a brain." Weeks of meetings followed between up-in-arms neighbors and prospective school board members. The struggle over public school spending soon produced a campaign dripping with what one scholar at the time termed "anti-Semitism, anti-newcomerism, and anti-wealth," particularly against "Gold Coast Jews."

In January 1958, voters in Herricks, after three tries, finally endorsed a $445,000 bond issue to purchase land for more school construction. This was on top of a $7.5 million bond issue that already had been authorized for building or expanding schools. The Herricks School District had the county's highest tax rate, climbing 50 percent in four years. Part of the construction funding went to the junior high, which expanded its library and added shop facilities, an art room, science labs, and a music suite. So sensitive was the subject of school spending that, when the new high school finally opened in the fall with a sunken library, courtyard eating area, and the state's first foreign language laboratory, district officials pronounced it "beautiful," but felt constrained to declare, "It's functional as well. You won't find a lot of frills — no mahogany or marble." Such statements did not pacify Catholic parents who resented the new bond issues. One Herricks teacher remembered hearing many of these parents comment bitterly: "Oh, the Jews want that in school, so they'll get it."

Once built, Herricks High School — often called "The Hill" because of its elevated location — was excellent by several measures. Principal Thomas Langley, a former Colby College football player, recruited all over the country to assemble a first-rate faculty, members of which were attracted by high salaries and Langley's vision of creating an innovative, top-flight school from scratch. Teachers held degrees from such premier educational institutions as the University of Chicago, Harvard, Johns Hopkins, and Yale. The all-white high school offered a wide variety of activities in which students could participate, including science, math, literary, and foreign language clubs; sports teams and cheerleading squads; music and dance groups; vocational groups; leadership and service organizations; drama and film groups; a public affairs symposium; and an honors society. Some students thought Langley was trying to cast Herricks in the image of neighboring Garden City, a "snooty" school district from which Langley had come. To promote school involvement, several sets of parents, including Daniel and Ruth Lichtenstein, served as official boosters.

The talented faculty, abundant extracurricular opportunities, and parental involvement paid dividends. Of the 300 graduating high school seniors in 1963, 9 received National Merit commendations, 38 won New York Board of Regents scholarships, and others were accepted into excellent universities, including Columbia, Cornell, Northwestern, Temple, and Virginia.

Even more divisive than rising school tax levies in Nassau County was the mixture of religion and public education. In May 1958, Henry Toy, Jr., president of the National Citizens' Council for Better Schools, wrote a column that appeared in the *Long Island Advocate*, describing the coming conflict in local schools. He was in a position to speak authoritatively because the council, which began after World War II at the suggestion of Harvard President James Conant, had 18,000 local committees reporting to it. Toy remarked, "There's a topic boiling underneath the surface these days that I'd like to see brought out into the open." He observed that conflicts concerning religion and education took many forms, including released time for religious education, public funds for bus transportation to private schools, the posting of the Ten Commandments, and prayers before lunch in cafeterias. School prayer was an especially controversial issue because Jews from Brooklyn and Manhattan who moved to the Herricks School District had never been required to say the regents' prayer in New York City. Based on what he had seen, Toy warned, "It's a highly explosive topic in many communities and predictions are that it's going to explode one of these days."

Even as Toy issued his warning, religious conflict had been brewing for two years in the New Hyde Park School District (Number Five), which adjoined Herricks (Number Nine). In 1956, New Hyde Park decided to fight the twin evils of communism and juvenile delinquency by posting an "interdenominational" version of the Ten Commandments in every public school classroom. The driving force for this move was Emil Bobek, an attorney with two school-age children, a member of the Episcopalian Church, and the commander of the local American Legion post. The Parents-Taxpayers League (PTL), the American Legion's Back to God Committee, and the *New Hyde Park Courier* endorsed the decision to post the Ten Commandments. PTL president Stanley Purgar explained that members of his group, although from varied faiths, supported displaying the Decalogue because they believed in the principle of "separation of church and state, but not the separation of God and state."

The New Hyde Park School Board's decision to post the Ten Commandments proved controversial in an election year. The local vice president of B'nai B'rith condemned this "invidious attempt to inject religion into the schools." Letter writers to local newspapers posed several objections to the posting. H. V. Stone worried that without protective covers the Ten Commandments would be desecrated with graffiti that would "shock the decency of people." He also thought the posting would lead to inappropriate conversations between bewildered youngsters and their teachers. How, he wondered, would teachers explain the commandments not to commit adultery or "covet thy neighbor's wife"? If there had to be postings, he suggested substituting the Golden Rule, the Boy Scout oath, or some other inspirational saying. Helen Fittipaldi, another letter writer, condemned supporters of the Decalogue as "the same group that has been hurling about irresponsible charges of communism for several years." She recalled that these super-patriots had two years earlier carried out a "Salem witch-hunt" to remove controversial books from the public library. Despite the vocal opposition of some, two New Hyde Park trustees who backed the posting were elected, and the one candidate who opposed it lost his bid for office. If students asked questions about the Decalogue, teachers were not to answer but to give out small cards containing the sentence: "Please take the question up with your clergyman [*sic*]."

New York Education Commissioner James Allen, a humorless, unflappable, and high-strung official, watched the developing controversy closely. But Allen, a Presbyterian elder, delayed his decision on posting the Ten Commandments until after the New Hyde Park School Board elections. In June 1957, Allen ruled against the posting because it stirred up "divisiveness" and "ill feeling." The commissioner criticized the school board for arbitrarily blending the three versions of the Ten Commandments into a single version, thereby creating and establishing a "new religion" in the district. Allen declared, "It is the fundamental law of the land (State and Federal Constitutions) that religion shall not be taught in the public schools because of the right of all people to restrict their children to their own religious beliefs. Religious instruction is proscribed and it is no defense that it is merely nonsectarian. The teaching of religious tenets violates the doctrine of the separation of Church and State." Allen noted that schoolchildren could be excused in order to have religious instruction at their own worship centers, thus providing an ideal opportunity for discussion of the Ten Commandments.

The New Hyde Park School Board regarded Allen's decision as "a most dangerous precedent" because some persons or groups might "deliberately create a controversy which could again conceivably nullify the action of an autonomous, duly elected, representative body." Board President Frank Picciano, a dentist who had once said prayers in Brooklyn's public schools, told reporters, "The board hasn't given up yet!" Privately, Picciano believed that Allen was "anti-Catholic." In September, the New Hyde Park School Board asked the New York Board of Regents to review Allen's ruling against posting the Decalogue. When the regents decided that they had no authority to review Allen's decision, Picciano commented, "I regret deeply that the schoolchildren of our community will be deprived of the opportunity of being reminded daily of the greatest moral code given to all mankind [*sic*] by God himself."

The New Hyde Park School Board increased the stakes the following year. In November 1958, the board barred discussion of Hanukkah and the singing of Hanukkah songs during December. The new policy stated, "While Chanukah is a religious and historical fact, it has no supercedence [*sic*] over countless other religious and historical events and should not be celebrated during the Christmas season." Local Jewish leaders called the decision "outrageous and discriminatory." The rift between local Christians, Jews, and nontheists widened dramatically after Thanksgiving vacation. The high school was bedecked with Christmas decorations, and an elementary school glee club in choir robes sang, " 'Twas the Night before Christmas" and "Angels We Have Heard on High." As the Christmas celebration continued, Jews and Christians traded accusations of bigotry, unwarranted control, and illegality. Picciano denied any prejudice on the board's part and charged New York City newspapers with having blown the story "out of all proportion." For years, Picciano's Jewish dental patients stopped going to his office, and he was convinced that the Anti-Defamation League spied on him.

The trouble in the New Hyde Park School District served as a prelude to the conflict in Herricks. Herricks public school officials had long provided for religion, especially by requiring students to sing Christmas carols in December, instituting released time for religious instruction off school grounds, and inviting clergy to say invocations at graduation and building dedications; but school prayer would be more difficult to mandate. At a school board meeting on January 8, 1952, District Principal Lester Peck reported that the New York Board of Regents had five weeks earlier recommended its "little prayer" at the opening of the school day. The tenth lineal descendant of Roger Williams, Peck was a taciturn forty-six-year-old man from Mongaup Valley in upstate New York, where he began teaching in a one-room schoolhouse. By the time Peck informed the Herricks School Board about the regents' prayer, he had spent twenty years in the district while earning two degrees from New York University and rising from history teacher to a position equivalent to superintendent. Peck was, his son George recalled, a "very religious man" who belonged to the Methodist Church, but felt the prayer had "no educational value."

The Herricks School Board was uncertain what to do about the regents' prayer, though it could not be ignored. The board evidently took no action on the prayer when it was first introduced. Another meeting was held later that month, and the board received word that the Holy Name Society of Notre Dame Church endorsed the regents' prayer. Two weeks later, the board convened again and heard a resolution from the Ethical Culture Society of West Hempstead opposing the prayer. Because of the sensitive nature of the matter, the board president implored the members to "give very careful consideration" to the prayer before adopting any policy. The board did not act on the matter for three years.

Herricks School Board Vice President Mary Harte believed that the regents' prayer would help strengthen the moral fiber of the Herricks School District's growing towns and villages of Albertson, Manhasset Hills, New Hyde Park, Roslyn Heights, Searingtown, and Williston Park. Harte was director of the parent-teacher association, a successful entrepreneur, and a longtime resident of Williston Park, an older, all-white, blue-collar Catholic neighborhood, where she raised three children. As a devout Roman Catholic, she listened to her priest, the Rev. Alfred Loewe of the Church of St. Aidan, who urged her to promote religion in the public schools because many parents could no longer afford parochial education.

In July 1956, the regents' prayer again came up for discussion. Herbert Balin, the Herricks School Board's (nonvoting) attorney and a refugee from Nazi Germany, told Harte, "Mary, I don't think it's legal." Harte replied, dismissively, "Okay, Herb, fine," and then called for a vote. The board rejected the prayer by a three-to-two vote. Undeterred, the strong-minded Harte reintroduced the regents' prayer at a special board meeting the following year. Once more Balin counseled against it, and the motion died for lack of a "second." The prayer was not adopted easily because, as the *New Hyde Park Courier* observed, the five-member school board meeting had long been the arena of heated debates between old-timers (largely blue-collar Catholics) and newcomers (largely better-educated, professional Jews).

Mary Harte's luck — as well as that of religious minorities in the Herricks District — would change when school elections allowed Roman Catholics to take control. Besides Harte, the other Catholics on the five-member board included attorney William Vitale, Jr., and homemaker Anne Birch, a past president of the parent-teacher association. Richard Saunders, a tax attorney, did not belong to a church, but was married to a Catholic. Only Philip Fried, another attorney, was Jewish. At a special school board meeting on July 8, 1958 — the seventh meeting on the subject — the board finally endorsed the regents' prayer by a four-to-one vote and fired its attorney, Herbert Balin. It held three more meetings that summer to hammer out details of saying the prayer: the prayer would precede the Pledge of Allegiance; no school official could tell students how to pray or comment on who did not pray; and there would be an excusal provision. No community opinion polls were taken by the board, but Lester Peck, the district principal, reported that the regents' prayer was already being used in the Nassau County towns of Bethpage, Carle Place, Glen Cove, Levittown, New Hyde Park, and Port Washington. He added that other prayers were said regularly in the public schools of Garden City, Great Neck, Manhasset, Mineola, and Roslyn.

Privately, Peck was embarrassed by the prayer but ordered his staff to comply with the school board's directive. Magill Shipman, a junior high school English, social studies, and math teacher, attended the meeting with his wife, Jeannette, who also taught in the district. When they returned home, Shipman looked squarely at his wife and predicted that trouble would soon arise from "the Jewish population," which "was absolutely dead against it." Shipman had come from upstate New York, attended a one-room schoolhouse, read with a kerosene lamp until he graduated from high school, and earned honors from Potsdam State University. Along the way, he had not encountered Jews until he came to Long Island, but soon came to believe that Jews were "the driving force for education." Although he knew that Jews reflexively voted for larger school budgets, he was certain that they would not accept the regents' prayer. In this largely conservative district, the school board ignored such doubts.

Peck dutifully reported the school board's action in a letter to district parents, advising them that they could have their children excused from saying the regents' prayer. Although there was considerable public support for the prayer, school records reveal that twenty-eight families requested their thirty-nine children be excused from the exercise. Some parents who requested excusal thanked school officials for "the privilege of making this choice." Most of them opted to have their children remain in the class but keep silent as the teacher recited the prayer. A few parents left to their children the choice of what to do.

In letters to the board, these parents explained why they opposed the regents' prayer. Their reasons ranged from constitutional objections to social stigmatism to spiritual emptiness. R. J. Farber told an elementary school principal, "The recitation of an organized prayer in a public school is contrary to the American tradition of complete separation of church and state." He therefore wanted his son, Andrew, to remain silent in his classroom while the regents' prayer was recited. Rhoda Fusey was concerned that social pressure would coerce her second-grade daughter, Stefanie, to say the prayer. Fusey wanted Stefanie to remain silent in the room during the prayer because she already had "fine spiritual and moral values which she has learned at home and at our place of worship." Herbert Ostreicher, a dentist, objected to "indoctrinating children with a prescribed and precise way of praying to God each morning. I have endeavored to teach my children (Jane and David) a closer, more flexible relationship with God. I have doubts as to whether the public school classroom at all times offers the proper atmosphere of dignity for so reverent an act as prayer." At the same time, Ostreicher did not want his children to be "pawns of pressure groups or legal adversaries," so he let his children decide for themselves.

The Rev. Charles Lee of the Hillside Methodist Church described the exercise as "a mockery of the idea of prayer" and "an insult to our spiritual integrity. . . . Prayer is not a trivial matter of twenty seconds, nor a magic formula of words. We think you and the board are making a serious mistake in pressing this issue." Lee instructed his daughter to say her own silent prayer during the school's opening exercises.

At least one set of parents investigated the school board policy more fully before deciding upon a course of action. Robert and Leone Baum, whose son, Douglas, attended Mrs. Duffett's kindergarten class at the

Center Street School in Williston Park, explained their thinking to the board: "Although we believe deeply in the private and personal concept of religion, it has been very difficult for us to reach a decision on this issue, as we are not sure of all the facts." Three matters concerned the Baums. "First, and most important, Douglas tells us that he recites two prayers, one at the start of the day, and one before eating. One of these is the Board of Regents prayer. What is the other prayer? Secondly, the children have been taught to clasp their hands. We are Jewish, and do not clasp our hands when we pray. Jewish males pray with covered heads. Would it be proper to send Doug to school with a yarmulke for this purpose? Third, if we request that he be silent during the recital of the prayer, how will this be handled by his teacher? If we request that he leave the room, where will he be sent? Will there be proper supervision for him?" After the principal and Mrs. Duffett politely answered their questions in person, the Baums requested that their son remain silent in the classroom during the prayer.

Compliance with the prayer directive proved somewhat problematic, and so it varied from school to school. High School Principal Thomas Langley met with his staff and explained the school board's expectations, but he left the matter in the teachers' hands. Some teachers grumbled initially about saying the regents' prayer, but most complied. Michael Carbone, a popular art teacher, recalled, "There was no effort to squelch it or not engage in it or to fight it off." As a lapsed Catholic, Carbone "was not happy about [the prayer], but I didn't advertise it" except to his closest friends. Nevertheless, Carbone "accepted it as my responsibility that everybody would stand as required. The minute it's over, it's done, and it's none of my business" what anyone thought about it. Although the prayer was short, a few teachers had trouble remembering it. The head football coach, who was a devout Catholic, bowed his head, as was customary, but to avoid an embarrassing memory lapse in front of his math class, he glanced down at his desk drawer where he had written out the prayer. Other teachers refused to cooperate. Scot Finegan, a first-year social studies teacher who abandoned his Catholic faith, never supported the prayer: "I always had doubts about it because what was a Pagan [like me] doing leading a prayer to a bunch of Druids." Catholic students reported Finegan to their new priest — the Rev. Charles Bermingham of St. Aidan's — who was a "real pain" to the young instructor.

The regents' prayer elicited different reactions among Herricks High students. Judith Lichtenstein remarked that the rapidity and predictability of the devotion "made a farce" out of the prayer: "Many students laughed or mumbled the prayer by rote." Others stopped saying the prayer when they realized they "could get away with it." Still others were angered by the prayer but felt they had no choice but to recite it. Several Herricks alumni could readily repeat the prayer nearly a half-century later. For David Rubin, that "stupid" prayer is burned in his memory because he had to say it so often. His home-room teacher "chose a victim" each morning to lead the prayer, and was upset when students declined to do so.

Barbara Kantowitz, a Conservative Jew from Brooklyn, remembers her visceral shock at prayer time: "I couldn't understand why they would do this. I was totally unprepared." She came home to her parents and told them Herricks was "a parochial school." Her parents left to her the decision of whether to say the prayer. Sometimes she half-heartedly recited the words, but most of the time she "just stood" and "didn't say anything." Kantowitz informally surveyed fifteen Herricks High School juniors and discovered that eight students refused to say the prayer. Some Jewish students remained silent at the urging of Rabbi Andrew Robbins of Temple Emanuel, a Reform congregation in New Hyde Park.

In the junior high, Principal Wilbur Olmstead told teachers straight out that they were to recite the prayer in front of their students. In the faculty lounge, new math teacher Frederick Pedersen asked his veteran colleagues what they were doing about the prayer and was told, "Oh, we're just silent." When Pedersen responded, "I thought we were supposed to read the prayer," his older colleagues said coolly, "Well, some do, some don't." Later on, Pedersen, who was Presbyterian, came to believe that at least some of these teachers were bluffing. Not having tenure, most young instructors such as Pedersen followed the administration's directive to the letter. To ensure cooperation in reciting the prayer, Pedersen used reverse psychology on his students: "You know, the mere fact that you don't have to say this would be a good reason to say it." Whether Pedersen's students said the prayer because it was required, because they felt peer pressure, or because they were fooled into saying it, none of them resisted it by remaining silent or leaving the classroom.

The task of enforcing the school board's decision to implement the regents' prayer fell to Magill Shipman, newly promoted to junior high assistant principal. Shipman was a "very conscientious administrator" and "tough disciplinarian," who roamed the halls of his school to make sure that teachers complied. Shipman recalled that teachers "didn't like it," but said it was "rare" that a teacher did not say the prayer. When Shipman caught a defiant teacher, he or she was reprimanded in Shipman's office. On occasion, teachers reported that a student was "causing a problem" during the regents' prayer. Shipman called the disobedient child's parents into his office and offered two options. Either the child could remain silent in his or her seat or go into the hallway until the rest of the class finished reciting the prayer. From an administrative point of view, this strategy minimized the problems in implementing the prayer. Shipman admittedly had an Irish temper and once knocked a Jewish boy to the ground who told him to "go to hell," but the assistant principal claimed he acted circumspectly in enforcing the prayer with which he disagreed.

Eventually the community learned that the regents' prayer was not going well. At a school board meeting, a taxpayer reported visiting several classrooms where he observed "a lack of respect and reverence" during the prayer's recital. District Principal Peck received a letter from a parent who was an attorney complaining that teachers conducted prayer time in different, and sometimes seriously objectionable, ways. Peck asked school principals to investigate "how this prayer is being said in each classroom" and circulated a memorandum reminding the faculty that the school board mandated the prayer. Serious consequences, Peck intimated, would descend on teachers who defied the board's edict: "Failure to do this could be considered insubordination" resulting in dismissal. Insubordinate teachers represented a minor impediment to reciting the regents' prayer; a small group of parents intent on preserving religious liberty would ultimately terminate the government prayer itself.

CHAPTER 5

"The Day I Stopped Believing in God"

The now-forgotten force behind the *Engel* case and the ouster of government-sponsored school prayer was Lawrence Roth. Roth's story offers considerable insight into the life of an ostensibly ordinary American who defended his family's civil liberties through years of legal action. His involvement caused his family — and others who joined him — considerable emotional stress and nearly cost him his life. Simply put, Roth's courage and dogged determination to claim his First Amendment rights changed U.S. constitutional law and society.

Lawrence Roth was born in Fort Wayne, Indiana, on May 9, 1914, to Michael and Ethel Kline Roth, Hungarian Jews who had immigrated to the United States at the turn of the century. When the Roths arrived, there were 1.5 million Jews (2 percent of the U.S. population). Fort Wayne stood at the convergence of two rivers and was conveniently located near three industrial behemoths — Chicago, Detroit, and Pittsburgh. Thanks to such geographic advantages, Fort Wayne's economy flourished and beckoned many Eastern and Southern Europeans to work in heavy industry. Its massive foundries were the world's largest makers of railroad axles and washing machines. The rapidly growing city billed itself as a community "where almost everyone owned his own home."

For all of its opportunity, Fort Wayne was not the Promised Land for Michael Roth. Like many other immigrants, he changed jobs and residences frequently. In one of his first jobs, he worked as a smelter, but his employer — the Fort Wayne Smelter Company — soon failed. At least once he was listed in the census as unemployed. After a few years, the Roths gave up on Fort Wayne and moved to Turtle Creek, Pennsylvania, a small industrial town of 8,100 inhabitants, 10 miles southeast of Pittsburgh. Turtle Creek had nearly doubled its population in a decade because it was near the center of an industrial revolution that was reshaping the nation and the world. The area boasted the world's largest electric plant (Westinghouse) and largest railroad (Pennsylvania), and produced more steel (U.S. Steel Corporation) and moved more goods than anywhere else in the country. In 1920, the radio industry was born in Turtle Creek, as KDKA broadcast the presidential election returns between Warren G. Harding and James Cox.

It was in Turtle Creek that a young Lawrence Roth rejected his Jewish birthright — indeed all religion — after a scarring childhood incident. Precisely what happened cannot be determined, but this tragedy is crucially important in explaining why government-sponsored school prayer would one day be outlawed. According to a family story, on September 26, 1924, a group of young men chased Roth's beloved older brother, sixteen-year-old Sidney, shouting, "Get the Jew! Get the Jew!" When the lynchers finally tackled Sidney, they apparently threw him into an automobile and began driving around town. As the family story goes, they pushed him from the moving car into a roadside pole, causing his death. Although newspaper accounts recorded frequent fatal car crashes, this attack occurred during a period of considerable anti-Semitism. The Pennsylvania Ku Klux Klan was one of the largest in the nation, and in the same year that Sidney died, a local klavern held a huge cross-burning and induction ceremony that could be seen for hours across the valley.

The one surviving newspaper article paints a different story. The *Pittsburgh Post-Gazette* reported that Sidney Roth was riding on the running board of an automobile driven by Andrew Urane — probably a fellow teenager — when "the accident occurred." This published account suggests that Sidney took a terrible chance by holding onto the outside of the car. When the driver lost control of the vehicle and slammed into a telephone pole, Sidney was crushed to death, but no one else suffered so much as a scratch. Whatever the truth of the matter, the Roth family believed then and now that Sidney was the victim of a hate crime.

Lawrence, then ten years old, was in school when his brother died. When a wailing ambulance raced by his classroom, Lawrence was sharpening his pencil next to a window, but he had no inkling of what had happened. After school let out, Lawrence returned home to find his dead brother stretched out on the parlor floor. It was a sickening sight that he never forgot. "He was my hero," Lawrence remembered later. "The day I stopped believing in God was the day my brother was killed." Lawrence concluded that any just deity would have prevented the senseless death. When he had sons of his own, Roth repeated the horrifying story to them. It was this episode that triggered his desire to oust organized school prayer thirty-four years later.

Like his brother, Lawrence attended Union High School, graduating in 1930. As he pursued a college-preparatory curriculum, he was active in extracurricular activities. Most curiously, given the apparent hate crime that cost his brother's life, Lawrence participated in Hi-Y Club, whose purpose was "to promote a higher standard of good Christian character in the boys of the school and thereby to promote a higher ideal of moral and spiritual life among them." Perhaps he thought he would do his part to change the community in which he lived; perhaps Hi-Y was so popular that he felt he had to join it. The caption beneath Lawrence's yearbook photograph reports that he was intent on a career in advertising — the king of business in the Roaring Twenties. Lawrence was on the yearbook's advertising staff and clerked for a clothing store. At his own commencement exercises on May 28, Lawrence likely heard an invocation and a benediction delivered by two Christian clergymen, including a Presbyterian minister.

Roth's high school yearbook referred to him thus: "With such a head, we can see Roth in the headlines already." Little did he suspect that the headlines he would generate would come not from his business acumen but from his views of constitutional law. When he became nationally known in midlife, Lawrence Roth would experience persecution and become largely reclusive. He had not wanted the headlines at all.

The 1930 class motto was "Set your sails forward," and that was what Lawrence did after graduation. For two semesters during the Great Depression, Lawrence studied business administration part-time, first at Duquesne University, a Catholic institution, then at the University of Pittsburgh. As he came of age, Roth moved to New York City and married Frances Harris, who shared his radical politics and unconventional religious philosophy. They settled down in Manhattan's Chelsea District, where Roth and a business partner opened a middling manufacturing concern — Acor Plastic Covers Corporation.

As their personal fortunes improved, the Roths had two sons — Daniel and Joseph.

In the mid-1950s, the Roths sought a better life and joined the exodus from New York City, moving first to Bayside, Queens, and then to the middle-class community of Roslyn Heights in Nassau County. Their sons much preferred the constant swirl of activity on the streets of Queens, but their mother, a psychiatric social worker aide, disliked their "goldfish bowl" existence in that borough. In Roslyn Heights, the Roths paid $17,000 for a modest three-bedroom, one-bathroom, two-story frame house at 17 Deepdale Parkway in the Brower's Hill subdivision, which had been completed shortly after World War II. Son Daniel recalled the new neighborhood as "pleasant" and "safe," but "kind of boring. There was nothing extraordinary about it one way or the other." Outside his neighborhood, Daniel was disturbed to discover "pockets of really deep, deep reactionary fervor."

At a time when McCarthyism still hung in the air, neighbors described the Roths as "different" from the rest of the community — intellectual, bohemian, pacifist, and "very liberal." According to their sons, the Roths "were really devout Reds" with a "theological reverence" for communism. Like many intellectuals, artists, African Americans, and other Jews, the Roths were undoubtedly enamored of communism's egalitarian ideology and vision of a just society. So committed was Lawrence Roth to this vision that he hosted Communist Party meetings in his home and, his family reports, ran unsuccessfully for political office under a radical party ticket. Never one to settle for idle talk, Roth actively promoted a more equitable society, first as a labor union organizer, then as a staunch civil rights activist for the Congress of Racial Equality and, in a personal capacity, for Martin Luther King, Jr. Given his family's Eastern European origins, his father's job as an industrial laborer, his own experience growing up in the Great Depression, and the leftist groups in New York City that he must have known about or joined, Lawrence Roth's radicalism was not altogether unusual. When not crusading for justice, the mild-mannered, self-effacing Roth enjoyed reading Shakespeare's plays and listening to recordings of African tribal music.

Frances Roth shared her husband's radical politics, strongly supported the Committee for a Sane Nuclear Policy (SANE), and was passionate about the value of education. For unknown reasons, Frances had been expelled from a Manhattan high school and never graduated. According to her older son Daniel, this sobering experience led his mother to "always aggressively compensate" for this hole in her background: "She did fashion herself part of the vanguard, the intelligentsia."

Roth's older son Daniel, "the scholar, the artiste in the family," according to his younger brother, likewise was intrigued by intellectual pursuits. A self-described "beatnik" who was "culturally curious" and whose tastes were "a bit off-center," Daniel was forever reading books, writing poetry, and listening to alternative music. For years, he attended a leftist summer camp near the Catskills, where he mixed easily with different races and creeds and sang folk songs with Pete Seeger. One former camper remembered Camp Hurley as a place where the children "could see the ideas [their] parents taught [them] put into practice." Daniel proudly remembered his camp experience as "the best years of my life."

Lawrence Roth enrolled his sons in the Herricks School District, which was largely Roman Catholic (Irish and Italian) and increasingly Jewish. The senior Roth took a strong interest in his children's education because, as a college drop-out, he wanted them "to go to better universities." He became active in a newly formed Committee for Better Schools and monitored classroom developments. To his chagrin, Roth learned that Joe's third-grade teacher displayed a statue of Jesus in her room and threatened miscreant children with divine discipline: "If you were bad, she would say, you would be punished by Christ." Roth had not moved to the suburbs to have his children subjected to religious persecution. Religion, he maintained, "is such a personal matter, such a private matter. One's relationship to the creative process is not something that can be thrown down a bunch of unwilling, unsuspecting, and unknowing children." Coerced prayer, he remarked, "distorts . . . the meaning of the creative process of which we are a part."

This was not the only instance of religion in the Herricks School District. Besides invocations by clergy and released time for religious instruction, all seven elementary and secondary schools in the district had a Christmas program. At Herricks Junior High, which allowed Christmas trees in the cafeteria and Christmas parties in classrooms, one Christmas concert of that period included Johann Sebastian Bach's "Jesu, Joy of Man's Desiring," "The Christmas Suite" by Harold Walters, and several Christmas carols, along with Yiddish, Jewish, and Chasidic folks songs — a strained, but not uncommon, effort at ecumenism. The high school newspaper featured the Christmas season prominently. One December, the newspaper included two cartoons, both featuring Santa Claus. The theme of the school's annual holiday hop was "Christmas in Switzerland," and students decorated the cafeteria to look like a Swiss chalet and organized gift-giving parties between students and teachers. The sophomores accepted a challenge from *Newsday* to "play Santa Claus" and help needy neighbors. Although there were a few references to Hanukkah and a few more to "Season's Greetings" in the student newspaper, most holiday wishes were for "Christmas."

Already annoyed by school sponsorship of religion, Lawrence Roth's ire grew in early August 1958, when he learned from the district's newsletter that the Herricks School Board had adopted the regents' prayer. "My immediate reaction," Roth said of the regents' prayer, "was that the state and the school board had no right to impose religion or prayers on the schoolchildren. My basic feeling was that if the state could tell us what to pray and when to pray and how to pray, that there was no stopping. . . . And I felt that something had to be done about it. It just couldn't stand the way it was." Roth explained, "We were heartily in favor of prayer, but we believed it belonged in church and in the home. We believe that religious training is the prerogative of parents and not the duty of the state." The goal of challenging the regents' prayer proved to be enormously difficult because the school board was insensitive to religious pluralism.

The forty-four-year-old Roth was clearly frustrated but unsure what to do. He spoke about the regents' prayer to a Catholic neighbor who commuted with him to New York City on the 7:03 morning train. Because Roth was largely ignorant of the First Amendment, his neighbor suggested that Roth contact the American Civil Liberties Union (ACLU) for assistance. Roth telephoned the Manhattan offices of the ACLU's local affiliate, the New York Civil Liberties Union (NYCLU), and conferred with its executive director, George Rundquist, a soft-spoken, dignified, and well-educated man who had worked for the American Friends Service Committee during World War II.

For years, Rundquist had received telephone calls about the regents' prayer, but "none wanted to serve as a plaintiff. No one wants to get involved in a religious conflict." Rundquist suggested that Roth come by to discuss the matter further in person. Rundquist gave Roth an unvarnished and uncannily accurate assessment of the costs of involvement: "You will be hated and despised by most of your neighbors, and your children will have to face the scorn of many of their classmates. But if you are willing to endure all of this, I'll query our board of directors." "I'm willing," Roth answered without hesitation. Roth was unaware that no New Yorker had ever successfully used the courts to challenge religious exercises in the public schools of the Empire State.

On September 9, 1958, the NYCLU discussed Roth's complaint at its regular luncheon meeting in a downtown hotel. Some members thought legislative action made more sense than what would be a $9,000 lawsuit against the Herricks School Board, but a majority voted to assist Roth. Rundquist asked thirty-four-year-old board member William Butler of the young Manhattan law firm of Butler, Jablow, and Geller to represent Roth pro bono. Butler replied, "I consider this prayer ruling a dangerous threat to freedom of religion. That is why I will take the case." Within ten minutes, Butler phoned his new client. During his fourteen years as NYCLU executive director, Rundquist won victories against police brutality and government loyalty oaths, but the eventual prohibition of the regents' prayer would be his most significant achievement, spurring membership growth and enlarging the coffers of the national organization.

William Butler, educated at Harvard and New York University, was in many ways a logical choice to handle the *Engel* case. After being injured in the Normandy invasion of World War II, Butler met and soon married a volunteer nurse named Jane Hays. His new father-in-law was the brilliant attorney Arthur Garfield Hays, a "confirmed skeptic" of German Jewish descent. Hays was influenced by his grandfathers, both of whom had served as president of a synagogue in Rochester, New York, but one became an agnostic under the influence of Robert Ingersoll and the other became a spiritualist. A cofounder of the ACLU and a former chair of the New York Progressive Party, Hays led a double life, exacting hefty legal fees from Wall Street and Broadway figures, then defending society's underdogs for free. By his own admission, Hays believed in individualism, "hate[d] to see people pushed around," and was a "nut" on the Bill of Rights.

As the ACLU's general counsel for forty-five years, Hays participated in several epic legal battles of the early twentieth century, including the Scopes "monkey" trial, the Ossian Sweet and Sacco-Vanzetti murder cases, the Scottsboro boys rape case, and the *Gobitis* flag-salute case. He had also represented the Freethinkers in their suit against New York City's released-time program. It was this example that profoundly influenced Hays's son-in-law, and Butler would carve out his own distinguished career on behalf of human rights, particularly through the United Nations and the International Commission of Jurists. No doubt Hays's recommendation clinched Butler's appointment as the NYCLU staff counsel fresh out of law school. Having worked closely with ACLU Executive Director Roger Baldwin, Butler had little doubt about the illegality of the regents' prayer, which he considered "a dangerous threat to freedom of religion."

It was Butler's religious upbringing, not his family ties, which led to this historic assignment. All four of his grandparents had immigrated to the United States from Ireland, and three of his uncles were priests. "When the case came up," Butler recalled, the NYCLU "decided that the lawyer could not be a Jew. He must be a Catholic, that is, someone taking the attitude that he is DEFENDING prayer and religious freedom, not attacking it. And they looked down at the end of the table and saw a nice Irish-Catholic boy — William Butler." Although Butler had his children baptized, he had in fact ceased being a practicing Catholic since he was a youngster and had become an agnostic.

Butler wondered whether he should take the case because he was "a conservative corporate lawyer . . . not a civil liberties lawyer." He admitted candidly, "I never wanted to be an expert on separation of church and state." And he never took another church-state case after *Engel*. Butler and his law firm did, however, have experience in successfully defending persecuted minorities in the McCarthy era. He had just filed an amicus brief in *Kent v. Dulles* (1958), a case that involved Rockwell Kent, an artist with leftist ties who was denied a passport because he refused to swear he was not a communist. In a victory for the ACLU, the U.S. Supreme Court ruled that the secretary of state does not have the power to curb "freedom of movement" for political reasons.

Butler was assisted by his scholarly partner, Stanley Geller, a Gregory Peck look-alike whom Butler dubbed "a Jewish Abraham Lincoln." Although Geller was an ACLU dues–paying member, he "didn't know why" the practice of school prayer was illegal. As astounding as it sounds, when the case arrived on his doorstep, Geller had "not the faintest idea" that the First Amendment had an establishment clause. He did embrace Justice Robert Jackson's dictum that the Bill of Rights was "the fixed star in our constitutional constellation," meaning that the Founding Fathers intended the Bill of Rights to protect minorities, not majorities. As the two law partners discussed the case, Geller told Butler, "This has got to be unconstitutional. You can't force children of other religions, or no religion, to say a prayer."

The national office of the ACLU wanted the experience and resources of the major Jewish defense organizations to help oust the regents' prayer. But Leo Pfeffer, the uncompromising church-state attorney, harbored deep reservations about the New York case. He saw numerous negatives in a potential lawsuit — the weak facts of the case, plaintiffs who were non-Christian, and inexperienced counsel — and thought it would prove disastrous. Believing that the regents' prayer was "as nonsectarian as a prayer can be," he felt that the case would give the courts "another opportunity . . . to become religious and patriotic." In the wake of *Zorach* and *Doremus*, it was not at all clear that the U.S. Supreme Court was prepared to defy popular opinion in favor of pan-Christian practices in the public schools. Jewish organizations decided that their scarce financial resources would be better spent on an education campaign to convince school boards not to adopt the prayer.

When the case proceeded nevertheless, Pfeffer shifted course. He assisted the plaintiffs' attorneys behind the scenes, wrote an amicus brief on behalf of the American Jewish Congress and the National Jewish Community Relations Advisory Council, and coordinated the submission of other amicus briefs. Whereas the American Jewish Committee and Anti-Defamation League relied on education and dialogue with Christian groups to improve the religious climate in the Cold War era, Pfeffer and the American Jewish Congress used the courts to undercut *Zorach* and thereby end formal religious practices in the public schools once and for all.

When Lawrence Roth conferred with Butler, Butler's chief questions concerned the extent of community opposition to school prayer and Roth's ability to solicit public cooperation. Butler told his clients that he wanted fifty plaintiffs, "of all kinds, of all shades, all religious persuasions — and nonreligious persuasions." Roth remembered, however, that Butler at first insisted on excluding agnostics and atheists from the list. Perhaps one atheist in such a suit was all that could be tolerated. Roth believed that "most of the neighbors were upset" as he was — "some because of what they considered to be the school board's high-handedness" — and promised to canvass his community to "get as wide a cross-section of petitioners as possible." To that end, he paid for advertisements in local newspapers, asking "all interested parties" to call him if they would join a "taxpayers suit" against the school. He noted that he had already retained legal counsel for the suit. Given the general popularity of the regents' prayer, one friend thought he was "lucky he wasn't shot."

Roth began recruiting among his neighborhood friends who had children in the Herricks School District. There was an easy camaraderie among the people of Brower's Hill. It was common for neighborhood adults to share the latest gossip, commute to work on the same train, and attend holiday parties in each others' homes, and their children to spend time together playing in backyards, listening to records, going to dances, and walking several blocks to school every day. Roth's next-door neighbor was thirty-five-year-old Steven Engel, a big, balding man who traveled the world for weeks at a time as the international sales manager for a textile company. As a devout Reform Jew, Engel objected to the regents' prayer because it undercut what was sacred. Prayer, in Engel's mind, was intended to be meaningful: "It's really man's communication with what he perceives as his god — his innermost thoughts. It's sacred, and when you rattle these things off and they have no meaning to it at all, I mean, you vitiate the value of religion." He observed that the regents' prayer was optional, but "if your school board chose to use the prayer, your school had to use this one-size-fits-all prayer that doesn't fit the religious faiths of all people."

Engel also found the regents' prayer disturbing because of his own bitter experiences with school prayer. His father, a Russian émigré by way of Denmark and Canada, had always encouraged him to reach his own conclusions: "Never mind what I think. Think for yourself." He had a chance to do exactly that in a Brooklyn elementary public school. He read from the King James Bible several times in front of student assemblies, but one day when the teacher said, "Let us pray," something in the seven- or eight-year-old Engel snapped: "I stamped my foot and said, 'I'm not going to read,'" and stalked off. School officials summoned Engel's father. "Can't you behave yourself?" the irritated father asked his son. "What difference does [the prayer] really make?" Steven firmly defended himself: "They're asking me to pray. That's not the way I pray." Steven was never asked to read from the Bible in school again.

That same evening, the Jewish New Year (Rosh Hashanah) began, and a tremendous argument ensued between Steven Engel and his father. In line with family tradition, Steven's father asked him if he was ready to attend services at the local synagogue. Steven replied testily, "No, I'm not going. I already prayed in school. I don't have to pray there." The bond between the accommodationist father and rebel son was "never quite the same after that."

A generation later, history repeated itself as Steven Engel objected to the school devotions that his own son Michael was saying. Engel paid a visit to Searingtown School and observed Michael bowing his head and clasping his hands. Engel was floored and asked Michael, "What were you doing?" "I was saying my prayers," came the innocent reply. "That's not the way we say prayers," Engel reminded his son. Engel marched into the principal's office to complain in no uncertain terms about state-sponsored religion. In a letter to the school board, Engel asked that the prayer be withdrawn because it had "proved divisive": "Where heretofore there was understanding and respect between denominations, there is now rancor and bitterness."

An uproar enveloped Searingtown School, which had a substantial Jewish enrollment — the largest in the district. Searingtown teachers were already "upset" over their compensation. Rumors abounded that a "Catholic provocateur" was in their midst, a female colleague with John Birch Society sympathies who was scrutinizing them for signs of disloyalty. The presence of an informer was disquieting news indeed because Long Island was already awash with anticommunist investigations, protests, and boycotts. In the neighboring school district of Sewanhaka, "all hell had broken loose" when the school board abruptly canceled a speech on the American presidency by Henry Steele Commager, one of the nation's leading historians. Commager was deemed "too controversial" after he signed a petition to release sixteen convicted communists as part of a Christmas amnesty. Worse still, there was a McCarthyite witch-hunt among the Sewanhaka faculty to ferret out alleged communists. The regents' prayer compounded these anxieties for Searingtown teachers, several of whom were Jews. They felt the prayer was "divisive," but "nobody wanted to be on record" as opposing it. In addition, many parents were disturbed about the prayer for apparently violating their constitutional rights. These parents included Lawrence Roth, Steven Engel, Monroe Lerner, and Daniel Lichtenstein, each of whom had a child in that school.

Ruth Rippon, the Searingtown principal, became "distraught" and "miserable" over the unfolding events. A native of New York City and a graduate of the Jamaica Teachers Training School, Rippon was a buoyant and extroverted Protestant woman whose creative outlets included designing hats, illustrating children's books, and modeling professionally. Although Rippon was a "wonderful leader" who dazzled young children and "worked very well" with parents and the community, her administrative skills would be severely tested in the months ahead.

With the partial exception of Herricks Junior High, the other schools in the district did not suffer this level of unrest. The other elementary schools had student bodies that were overwhelmingly Christian, and their parents supported the regents' prayer. The high school did not suffer the same problems because Principal Thomas Langley exercised unusual leadership in preventing much religious conflict. He ordered Christmas trees removed from the cafeteria and religious symbols of all kinds from the building. Scott Finegan, a young social studies teacher and burly football coach, was assigned the task of policing the school grounds for violations of this policy. When a fun-filled school festival, replete with camp games like volleyball, turned into a contest between Catholics and Jews, Finegan notified the principal. Before Finegan left the office, an announcement over the public address system put an end to the event. Another time, the school's football team divided along religious lines — not the school's colors (blue and silver) — to play a pick-up game on the Herricks field. Once more, school officials quickly stopped a potentially divisive activity. Not only was the high school principal vigilant about religious symbols and conflict, he was evidently uninterested in rigorously enforcing the recital of the regents' prayer.

With his sons attending elementary and junior high schools, Lawrence Roth neither knew nor cared about the religious atmosphere at Herricks High. The fact that the Herricks School District as a whole had instituted the regents' prayer kept weighing on his mind, and he shared his continuing frustration over it with two neighbors on Hillturn Lane, an adjoining street. One was Daniel Lichtenstein, the son of Eastern European Jews who survived the pogroms. The forty-two-year-old Lichtenstein, who attended City College briefly, was charming and gregarious, which he used to full advantage as a sales representative for a ladies' handbag company. In his leisure, he enjoyed playing handball and bridge, swimming at Jones Beach, and listening to classical music. He had, ironically, been the campaign manager for Mary Harte when she first ran for the school board. Daniel and Ruth Lichtenstein had three schoolchildren—Judith (fifteen), David (twelve), and Naomi (ten), all of whom were beatniks, as was Daniel Roth. They, too, attended a leftist summer camp and dressed unconventionally. Ruth Lichtenstein was concerned about the probable adverse reaction a lawsuit would spark, but her husband plowed ahead anyway.

The other neighbor was Monroe Lerner, a thirty-five-year-old Merrill Lynch stockbroker and fellow commuter with Roth on the Long Island train to Manhattan. The son of Russian Jews, Lerner was a native of Jersey City, New Jersey, and had grown up in a household that regularly entertained socialists and communists. Although Lerner was drawn to radicalism, he asked too many questions to be welcomed into a leftist political party. When World War II erupted, Lerner served in an intelligence unit in the Far East, and after the war ended he earned a master's degree in business administration from the City University of New York. In his spare time, he read nonfiction voraciously, listened to classical music, played tennis, and went jogging every day after work. He and his wife, Julia, who was the daughter of an atheist and niece of a rabbi, were humanists who had long belonged to the ACLU and the Society for Ethical Culture, a group founded in the nineteenth century to promote moral conduct rather than particular beliefs. Instead of relying on public education for moral instruction, the Lerners took their oldest daughter Cynthia to Sunday school, first in West Hempstead, then Garden City, for a steady diet of philosophy lessons, which she "hated." The Lerners observed a few religious traditions for social reasons: at Passover, they went to their cousins' home for a Seder feast, and in December, they invited relatives over to exchange gifts beneath a small evergreen tree trimmed with ornaments.

On the way into New York City one morning, Lawrence Roth and Monroe Lerner agreed that they "ought to do something" about the situation. The Lerners felt the exercise was either a "mockery" of prayer for those who believed in prayer or an "imposition" for those who did not. The prayer, they said, makes "an assumption right away . . . that everybody believes in god, whoever god is, and maybe even a different kind of god." The Lerners rejected the school board's provision for excusing students who did not want to say the prayer. As Julia, a former nursery school teacher, knew full well, "That makes the child a pariah. Now everybody is pointing a finger at this child who has to leave the room because the prayer is being said." The Lerners also dismissed the school's claim that the prayer was innocuous: "If it's innocuous, why have it?" Even though Monroe Lerner anticipated major trouble ahead, he was, by his wife's admission, "braver" about proceeding than she was. "But sometimes," Julia Lerner declared, "you have to stick up for what you believe in." The things you believe in "may be cockeyed [to some people], but that doesn't matter."

In recruiting people for the lawsuit, Lawrence Roth evidently approached only men in his neighborhood. The rigid gender roles of the 1950s dictated this strategy. Julia Lerner explained that "none of the wives were very involved" in the litigation. "This was a time in life when you stayed home and took care of children." All four wives did, however, support the school prayer lawsuit.

Despite the gender roles of the time, the fifth and last plaintiff was a woman. How Lenore Lyons, a forty-two-year-old vivacious homemaker, joined the case remains unclear because it appears she did not know any of the plaintiffs. As a regular newspaper reader, she may have seen the advertisement that Lawrence Roth placed to solicit other petitioners. Lyons's religious convictions as a Unitarian may have led her to challenge the regents' prayer. Unitarians have long cherished the First Amendment, including the separation of church and state. Lyons was a faithful member of the Unitarian Society in Plandome, and her youngest son Douglas suggests that her congregation may have asked her to represent it in the case. As an active PTA member with a strong sense of justice, Lyons may have been prodded into action simply by hearing about the regents' prayer.

Alone among the plaintiffs, Lenore Lyons resided in Williston Park, where she lived with her husband, David, an electronics engineer and salesman with an offbeat sense of humor, and their four children — Wendy (thirteen), David (eleven), Jeanne (nine), and Douglas, a three-year-old preschooler. The Lerners, who became friends with Lenore Lyons, described her as "a very bright . . . and lovely, lovely lady." She had been born into a Jewish family. Her father, Judah Zuckerman, had rabbinical training and moved to Kansas City, Kansas, where he sold kosher foods and fathered ten children. David Lyons, the only child of an Irish Catholic immigrant, had eloped with Lenore when her family shunned her for dating outside her faith. The marriage had been "stormy" from the start because of David's alcoholism. When David turned to the bottle, Lenore escaped by taking long nature walks, swimming in the ocean, watching movies, and chairing her church's Religious Education Committee. The *Engel* lawsuit divided the Lyonses still further, and their marriage would dissolve soon after the prayer was struck down.

The plaintiffs' children refused to say the regents' prayer, either from the first day it was recited or soon thereafter. Daniel and Joe Roth came home from school and complained, "Why [are we supposed] to say this stupid prayer every day?" Daniel, then thirteen years old, remembered being "terribly self-conscious" and "terribly awkward" about never saying it. He compared his feelings to going to a dance where "you're convinced you're the only one with two left feet." Of their own volition, Daniel and his friends walked out of the classroom when the prayer was recited, but later abandoned this conspicuous gesture and sat silently in the classroom during the devotion.

The children of the other plaintiffs faced the same ticklish situation. Wendy Lyons remembered that her mother felt "very strongly that her children should do what they felt was right." When Wendy and several classmates remained silent, their teacher got angry. Naomi Lichtenstein "wasn't very religious as a kid" and had quit attending Sunday school, but she stood and clasped her hands when the prayer was recited. She "somehow had the sense that this was not my religion. It was not a prayer that I would do, and it wasn't the way my family handled religion." Sensing resistance, Naomi's teacher implored her, "Come on. Don't give us any trouble," or she would be sent to the assistant principal's office. As far as the Lerners were concerned, their "very sensitive" seven-year-old daughter, Cynthia, would be affected by what they taught her at home, not by a brief prayer mandated at school. Most of the time, Cynthia remained silent, and her teacher demanded an explanation. Steven Engel did not ask his seven-year-old son Michael to step out in the hall during the prayer: "My kids were small. Do you realize what you're asking of a kid to exempt himself from his peers? You're asking too much."

Although the regents' prayer is burned in Michael Engel's memory to this day, he recalls thinking at the time that "when you said something like that continuously day in and day out by rote, it was not really specifically praying; it was not really anything." He had other things on his mind. As a budding scientist, he had a laboratory in his basement and spent hours tinkering with microscopes and test tubes. He was also a rabid New York Yankees fan who, like most boys of that period, followed the World Series keenly. The issue that impressed him most in school was the possibility of a cataclysmic nuclear attack. In an absurd exercise, schools drilled their students to pin their faces against the wall to deflect deadly radiation from an atomic bomb blast. More immediately, Michael's health was not strong, which meant he spent a lot of time in doctors' offices and in hospitals. For Michael Engel and many other pupils, the regents' prayer was a brief, meaningless annoyance, and nothing more.

Complaints by Lawrence Roth and others against the regents' prayer prompted the Herricks School Board to hold an open meeting in mid-September 1958. Parents (all unnamed) who criticized the board for adopting the prayer called it an "infringement of religious freedom" — "out of place in a public school system." Board President William Vitale, a genial and dapper forty-year-old attorney with a Fordham law degree, staunchly defended the prayer on several grounds. In initiating the prayer, the school board had been motivated by a desire to promote morality, which Vitale presumed was an entirely appropriate objective. He noted that prior to this meeting few objections had been raised against the prayer in Herricks. Moreover, other school districts in Nassau County had readily accepted the prayer with "no fury at all." But one parent predicted that the prayer "will cause such widespread dissension; it is bound to hurt the children." "People should be allowed to pray in their own way," another parent declared.

Ignoring such comments, Vitale clinched his argument by observing that the prayer was not compulsory for children: "They don't have to say a word if they don't want to. No one will say or do a thing if a child chooses to be silent during the observances." Vitale charged the prayer's critics with making a "calculated attack" that undermined "our American heritage." Board member Anne Birch agreed with Vitale that the dispute was not over religion but over differences involving politics and educational philosophy. Birch vowed not to yield to the militant minority. According to Julia Lerner, the school board was referring to Brower's Hill, where it assumed that "everyone . . . was a communist." The Roths, Engels, Lichtensteins, and Lerners all lived in that neighborhood.

Antiprayer sentiment only grew. At the October 16 school board meeting, Lawrence Roth, Monroe Lerner, and other "very, very upset" parents filled the auditorium, demanding an end to the regents' prayer. At least ten times the usual number of attendees came to this board meeting. After considering the request to cancel the prayer, the board promptly denied it, noting that the prayer was optional. Children could sit silently or leave the room, the board pointed out, as long as a parent wrote a letter requesting such excusal. According to school records, 39 of 4,294 students (.01 percent) opted to be excused. The board also noted that the prayer was drafted carefully as an ecumenical devotion, so no one had a legitimate reason to object. Tired of verbal jousting, Board President Vitale told the disgruntled parents: "The board has voted on this. If we say it's in, it's in." He dared the angry protesters to "sue us" to stop the prayer. Two hundred protesters took the dare.

But the controversy surrounding the regents' prayer drove off potential plaintiffs. The number of complainants shriveled to fifty and then to eleven, as some of them moved away, changed their views, or endured withering criticism from neighbors and clergy. Lawrence Roth knew one Protestant couple who said that "they were 100 percent with us until they spoke to their minister." The couple told Roth, "We're still with you, but our minister said this is a controversial matter and we can't join you." The Lerners also knew several people who were "all gung-ho to sue," but the fear of joining a lawsuit changed their minds. Many respondents dropped out because of the economic consequences they would face. One employer told a potential plaintiff, "It's foolish to get mixed up in an unpopular cause." Still, Roth declared, "I never felt I was standing alone, like Atlas holding up the world." By the end of October 1958, Roth gave the final list of complainants to his NYCLU attorney, William Butler.

Butler subsequently pared the list to five, all with young children in the Herricks School District and "the moral starch that would be necessary to deal with the criticism and the crank calls." As Butler recognized, "it isn't easy to stick your neck out. It isn't easy to buck the crowd when most of the community feels the other way. But these five — their fundamental principles were more important to them than living with the Joneses." All of the plaintiffs were of Jewish descent, but the group included several different religious convictions. Two of the plaintiffs (Steven Engel and Daniel Lichtenstein) attended a Jewish temple, one (Lenore Lyons) belonged to the Unitarian Society, and another (Monroe Lerner) affiliated with the Society for Ethical Culture. The litigants believed above all, as Lawrence Roth put it, that "religious training is the prerogative of parents and not the duty of the state."

Lawrence Roth's religious views were enigmatic. He classified himself as "a very religious person, but not a churchgoer." "I have prayed myself, many times," Roth insisted, "not in a beseeching manner, but more in seeking guidance." He added, "I was born a Jew, but I believe in a Creative Process." Still, Roth was "not at all sure we can change anything by petitioning to a higher being." Many years later, Roth told a television interviewer that he prayed daily to overcome his alcoholism. When Roth explicated his ambiguous religious views, Butler exclaimed, "You're the atheist!" Roth surmised, "Apparently you have to have an atheist in the crowd, so we started from there." (As death finally approached in the fall of 2005, the ninety-one-year-old Roth grew agitated and experienced a change of heart: "I have been an atheist all my life, but no longer.")

The first step to litigation was a written request to the Herricks School Board to halt the regents' prayer. On December 4, 1958, the five parents signed and mailed a letter to the Herricks administration. The letter said, "We, and each of us, hereby demand that you discontinue, or cause to be discontinued, the practice instituted for the first time at the beginning of the current school year of having a prayer said daily following the salute to the flag in all the schools of the district, and particularly the schools which our children attend." The parents asserted that the prayer was "a violation of the Constitution of the United States and of the State of New York." When no response was forthcoming, each member of the Herricks School Board was served with legal papers two weeks later. The suit indicated that the board's original plan for reciting the prayer had changed. Not only did the prayer follow the flag salute, instead of preceding it, the prayer was led by the teacher or by a student selected by the teacher. All students — presumably elementary school pupils — who remained in the classroom were to participate in a prescribed manner — "hands clasped together in front of the body, fingers extended and pointed upwards in the manner of a supplicant."

The Herricks School Board tried to head off a potential lawsuit. The district clerk sent a letter to William Butler and Stanley Geller — the petitioners' attorneys — pointing out that the board was acting within its authority to institute the regents' prayer. The clerk informed the attorneys that "no further action on this subject is contemplated." Not long afterward, Herricks School Board President William Vitale defended the board's decision as "perfectly right and legal." He added, "It is our opinion that we are not involved in a question of religion. Nor are we concerned with the question of the separation of church and state, but [we are] confronted with an attack calculated to undermine our American heritage."

These statements did nothing to dissuade Lawrence Roth and the others. To achieve maximum publicity, Butler waited for a newspaper strike to end before filing the case in court. The case came to be called *Engel v. Vitale* after the plaintiff who was listed first alphabetically — Steven Engel — and William Vitale, the Herricks School Board president.

The school board's new attorney, Bertram Daiker of the Port Washington law firm of Gunn, Neier, and Daiker, remembered that the board was "flabbergasted" by the suit. The first that Daiker knew about anti–school prayer sentiment in Herricks occurred when Roth's advertisement appeared in the newspaper. After all, Daiker observed, the regents' prayer came with "the imprimatur of the highest authority in the field of education in the state." Daiker's support for the regents' prayer also stemmed from his Lutheran beliefs and his experience as a public school student in Queens. In the 1920s, he had listened to the Bible being read in the school's assembly each week, and no one objected. Daiker, whose legal education came from Fordham and New York University, had extensive experience in representing institutions. He had, for example, helped two dozen Lutheran churches on Long Island found a "Christ-centered" secondary school in Mineola after World War II. A lifelong Boy Scout leader, Daiker had a reputation as a "tenacious" attorney and a "most honest, straightforward, generous man," his longtime law partner remembered. The school district financed Daiker's defense of the regents' prayer with a bond issue for physical improvements.

Almost immediately, Leo Pfeffer of the American Jewish Congress urged the NYCLU to drop the case. Pfeffer was certain that a parallel case in which he was involved —*Abington v. Schempp* — would make the constitutional point far more effectively than *Engel*. In the *Schempp* case, the school code of Pennsylvania required at least ten verses of the King James Bible to be read at the opening of each day. Pfeffer told the *Engel* attorneys, "*Abington School District* is the better case. You take this up and you're going to foul up *Schempp*." Stanley Geller had never heard of Pfeffer, but was "a firm believer in taking any case up that has merit even though it might lose." When William Butler asked his partner about Pfeffer's advice, Geller dismissed the whole idea of abandoning *Engel*: "Oh, that's the kind of talk that you hear from lawyers that want to push their own case or are developing some theory that I don't particularly cotton to."

Nevertheless, Geller read Pfeffer's tome, *Church, State, and Freedom*, from cover to cover, sought out Pfeffer for advice, and in the process acquired considerable expertise himself in church-state affairs. The apogee of Geller's church-state litigation came two decades later, when he convinced the U.S. Supreme Court in *Aguilar v. Felton* (1985) that public schoolteachers could not tutor impoverished children who attended parochial schools. The Court reversed itself twelve years later in *Agostini v. Felton*, a decision that permitted some government services to needy children regardless of the kind of educational institution they attended.

The Herricks School Board naturally became a focal point for the fevered community reaction to the regents' prayer. Within two months of being sued, the board, which carefully recorded all of its correspondence, received 2,361 pieces of mail supporting the prayer—a ratio of 200 to 1. Nearly 20 percent of district families formally endorsed the prayer. The "complimentary" mail included letters, cards, petitions, and resolutions. In a typical letter to the board, Harold Boss concluded, "Only atheists and/or communists . . . would oppose a nondenominational prayer given at the opening of the school session. It is alarming, however, to know that there are even five such people. I would suggest that all steps be taken to prevent these people from spreading their influence in this respect."

A clear religious divide appeared over the *Engel* lawsuit. Those who favored the regents' prayer came from largely Roman Catholic neighborhoods, while those who opposed it lived in a section where a number of Jews lived. Of the 4,009 names on petitions and resolutions endorsing the regents' prayer or the fourth stanza of the "Star-Spangled Banner," which asserts, "In God is our trust," 47.4 percent came from New Hyde Park, 34.7 percent from Williston Park, 15.6 percent from Albertson, and just 1.2 percent from Roslyn Heights—a small geographic section in the district. Only forty-three signatures came from Roslyn Heights, and nineteen of the signers lived on the same two streets as Roth, Engel, Lerner, and Lichtenstein. One of the signers in Williston Park was David Lyons, Lenore's estranged husband. Whether he signed the petition because he was politically conservative or because he wanted to spite his wife cannot be ascertained.

Eighteen civic, fraternal, business, and religious organizations produced resolutions that endorsed the prayer, most of them from Williston Park, which was largely Catholic. The Williston Park resolutions came from the village board of trustees, Rotary Club, Taxpayers Party, Cub Pack 521, Homeowners Association, Ladies Auxiliary of the Veterans of Foreign Wars, St. John's Lutheran Church Men's Club, Saint Aidan's Holy Name Society, Republican Club, St. Andrew's Episcopal Church, and Notre Dame Rosary Society. One school administrator remembered that much of the friction over the regents' prayer was due to the majority's conviction that "the Jewish population had come in and they were dictating what we could or couldn't do." The school board was "gratified with the voluntary outpouring" of support.

Local newspapers strongly favored the regents' prayer. The *Williston Times* and *New Hyde Park Herald*, which reached 56 percent of Herricks families, ran such sensational headlines as "Suffer the Little

Children and Forbid Them Not," "Let Us Pray," and "Why Is This Group So Afraid of God?" The editors deemed the lawsuit a "publicity stunt" by "Marxists," "crackpots," "the devil's advocates," and "unwitting dupes" who were dividing the community. One editorial cartoon showed a child writing the "Eleventh Amendment" twenty times on the blackboard: "I shall not mention God in School." Underneath the cartoon, readers were urged to "bombard" the school board with postcards commending the prayer: "The bigger the response, the better the ammunition the board will have at the preliminary court trial." Another cartoon warned, "A wrong decision now could well affect the minds of youngsters against prayer so that they will grow up believing that God is only in church and one cannot pray in any case where the 'State' is involved." Almost all of the published letters to the editor endorsed the prayer.

The petitioners were not totally without support. The Herricks Parent-Teacher Association conducted its own survey and found that at least twelve organizations opposed the regents' prayer. At open school board meetings, Mrs. Irving Weiland, the PTA president, forcefully told the board, "School is no place for prayer." But the PTA would not get involved in the lawsuit because it would split the parents into two camps, one favoring, the other opposing the prayer. The Roslyn Civic Association polled its membership and reported that sixty-one members opposed the prayer, two supported it, and five abstained from voting. Between September and November 1958, the school board received ten letters criticizing the prayer. Harold Sander quoted Thomas Jefferson: "No man shall be compelled to frequent or support any religious worship . . . whatsoever." Harriet Mann declared that the prayer was unnecessary because parochial schools were available for children whose parents wanted them to have religious education.

When word leaked about Lawrence Roth's attack on the regents' prayer, he and his family were vilified as anti-Christian, even anti-God. His two sons, Daniel and Joe, took the brunt of the public animus. Working-class Catholic boys crossed their chests as a pointed reminder of Jesus' crucifixion at the hands of Jews. In the school hallways, there were arguments, pushing, and name-calling. "You're a Commie!" the toughs shouted. "Go back to Russia!" Some Herricks teachers considered these harassers the "dregs" from the parochial system who could not afford to attend Chaminade, a fine Catholic high school in Mineola operated by the Society of Mary since 1930.

As "one of the class nerds," Daniel was singled out. "Kids would yell at him," his father recalled, " 'Hey, you Jew bastard!' It felt strange to him to be accused of being a Jew." It was not surprising that the Roth boys did not feel Jewish because, as Daniel recollected, "We didn't grow up with any religious training whatsoever. Zero. Absolutely zero." Daniel's worst tormentor was an eighth-grade teacher who held him up as "some kind of a radical, lunatic." "She would make snide remarks about what my father was doing. . . . I was certainly singled out by her for humiliation." A civics teacher who was "a really, really reactionary right-wing political activist" made Daniel's life "unpleasant and uncomfortable" by "constantly ridiculing me" in front of the class. His classmates, Daniel thought, did not care about the teachers' harassment "because they didn't understand it." The Roths never complained to the principal, but on an assignment that addressed the theme of why the Pilgrims came to America, Daniel wrote at the end of his paper in large capital letters so the teacher could not miss seeing it: "BECAUSE THEY WANTED SEPARATION BETWEEN CHURCH AND STATE."

Such harassment was episodic and corresponded to the developments in the case, which moved up each step of the judicial ladder year by year. Even so, the case took its toll on the Roth boys, and they resented their father for putting them in their predicament as outcasts. Alternately angry and sulking, the Roth boys sometimes gave the bullies a taste of their own medicine, resorting to fistfights to defend themselves.

So quiet were the Roths about the abuse they withstood that many in the Herricks School District were unaware of the epic lawsuit. The students generally did not discuss the regents' prayer among themselves. Prolific author David Fisher, a sophomore when the case was decided, recalled: "I'd like to tell you the case was a major event in our lives. It wasn't. I don't think we even knew about it." Wendy Lyons remembers that there was "no big hullabaloo" about the suit until the prayer was struck down years after it had been filed. Michael Engel agrees that "the proverbial shit did not hit the fan until the Supreme Court vote. Prior to that moment, it was not very big news for anyone." The student newspaper never mentioned the case. The high school principal almost never discussed it with the faculty, and many teachers knew little about it and did not mention it in their classes. "Most people never thought much about the case," one teacher recalled, because nobody "supposed that it would make it to the Supreme Court." History was being made, and few either knew about it or cared.

Some Herricks residents did care deeply about the regents' prayer and went to court to retain it. This third party to the suit consisted of sixteen parents — seven Protestants, five Roman Catholics, three Jews, and Evelyn Koster, who had no religious affiliation but sent her children to Sunday school at the Williston Park Reformed Church. At the center of the group was Henry Hollenberg, an Orthodox Jew who worked for the U.S. Navy. Hollenberg felt that the prayer was not at all sectarian. Another member was Thomas Delaney, who described himself as "violently in favor of prayer in schools."

Their attorney, Thomas Ford, a Pearl Harbor survivor and the son of an Irish Catholic police officer, knew several of the intervenors through his service as a Williston Park trustee. Although Ford doubted that the trial judge would permit intervenors to join the case, he nonetheless filed an affidavit explaining why they wanted to retain the regents' prayer: "If the board should be directed to drop this [prayer] . . . it could be the first step in an advance which could culminate in the removal of every vestige of the belief in the existence of God, and America's deep spiritual heritage must be upheld." The court allowed these parents to intervene, provided their counsel stuck to the constitutional issues.

At the suggestion of Francis Cardinal Spellman of New York, the nation's most powerful Roman Catholic prelate, the intervenors also retained an imposing, prominent Manhattan attorney named Porter Chandler. Born on a farm near Buffalo, New York, Chandler received highest honors at Harvard, Oxford, and Columbia Universities, served in both world wars, and became chair of the New York City Board of Higher Education. As the former president of the Guild of Catholic Lawyers for New York, Chandler had the reputation of being the "cardinal's lawyer" and the city's "dean of Supreme Court practitioners." Most notably, Chandler helped win two important establishment cases — *Everson* and *Zorach*. At a fancy New York restaurant, the cardinal introduced Chandler to New Hyde Park School Board President

Frank Picciano who, in turn, introduced him to William Vitale, president of the Herricks School Board. Picciano and Vitale knew each other from the Fordham alumni association, and Picciano had helped Vitale win election to the school board. With this double vote of confidence, Chandler telephoned Ford "out of the blue" and asked if there were any objection to his joining the case. Ford welcomed Chandler's involvement, even though it was clear who was now the senior partner in the intervenors' case. Chandler promised to dedicate himself to the case, but did not promise victory.

As the trial date loomed, an acerbic and patronizing column by H. I. Phillips in the *New York Mirror* mocked the very idea of a lawsuit against the "quickie prayer." Phillips thought it was a "queer world" when a brief prayer could be challenged at the same time juvenile delinquents assaulted teachers and vandalized schools. "Fight Prayer in Schools," Phillips charged, makes a curious headline against "Boy Kills Whole Family" and "Schoolgirl Held as Murder Accomplice." To cope with the alleged insanity of the school prayer lawsuit, he suggested that mothers "take another tranquilizer." The communist world, Phillips guessed, must be amused: "Hey, Soviet Russia! You can ease up on your drive to kill religion among the young in America. You're getting an 'assist' on the home grounds."

CHAPTER 6

"Why Are These People So Afrai⸝ of God?"

The trial judge in the initial *Engel* proceeding was forty-three-year-old Bernard Meyer, an Averill Harriman appointee who was hearing his first important case. The son of a prosperous Jewish haberdasher in Baltimore, Meyer had recited the King James Version of the Lord's Prayer in the city's public schools and recalled that "there wasn't any controversy about it." He graduated with an economics degree from Johns Hopkins University and a law degree from the University of Maryland and then established a tax consulting practice. After marrying, serving in World War II as a lieutenant, and fathering two daughters, Meyer emerged from the hurly-burly world of local politics to become the leader of the Nassau County Democrats and then a justice on the Nassau County Supreme Court, formally called the New York Supreme Court, Tenth Judicial District.

A witty, self-effacing, and compassionate man, Meyer was so worried about the *Engel* case, which attracted national attention, that he thought a more experienced judge should handle it. Veteran Supreme Court justice Courtland Johnson had the greatest confidence in Meyer, casually telling the new jurist during the trial: "Bernie, this is the way you get your feet wet. You wanted to be a judge, now face up to your responsibilities." After Meyer rejected the plaintiffs' request to prohibit the regents' prayer in the Herricks School District, the case of *Engel v. Vitale* reached the spacious county courthouse in Mineola on February 24, 1959. Behind Meyer's bench hung the motto, "In God We Trust."

That very morning, the *Long Island Post* carried a column by George Sokolsky, a Columbia University–educated Hearst newspaper writer who attacked "this crazy fear of prayer." As a boy, Sokolsky had attended public school on New York City's East Side, where the daily assembly opened with Bible reading and hymn singing. His father, an Orthodox _ı from Poland, knew about the devotions, but "did not object as long as no one attempted to convert us to Christianity." Though Sokolsky did indeed convert to Catholicism, he was "sure" that he was "in no manner harmed by this little ceremony."

"Why," Sokolsky asked in his column, "are these people in Herricks so afraid of God?" Sokolsky thought the suit ridiculous and noted that the New York Constitution's preamble thanks "Almighty God" for the people's freedom. If the plaintiffs triumphed, the logical conclusion of the *Engel* suit, Sokolsky averred, would be to abolish or impeach government entities and officials that used the word "God," including Congress and the president. Sokolsky, who identified himself as a fierce anticommunist and "a star-spangled spieler for capitalism," doubted that the school prayer litigants were representative of many Americans. To make sure that his readers knew who the "cranks" were who brought the case, Sokolsky reproduced Lawrence Roth's newspaper advertisement — the one that solicited complainants — and gave Roth's home telephone number. It was, Daniel Roth asserts, "an act of journalistic terrorism."

Sokolsky's syndicated column was picked up by newspapers nationwide and created "something of a public relations problem" for the American Civil Liberties Union (ACLU), which sent a rejoinder to editors around the country. Patrick Murphy Malin and George Rundquist, executive directors of the ACLU and NYCLU, respectively, insisted, "Religion is not, either directly or indirectly, placed under attack by the Herricks lawsuit, and those who say otherwise do so either because of inadequate information or through other motivations." Rather, the directors argued, it was "a specific religious practice, instituted in our public schools by a handful of public officials" that was being "challenged as dangerous — not only to the free public school system but to the cause of religion." In standing by the Bill of Rights, the ACLU sought to safeguard "religion — all religion — to flourish in a Nation of many different faiths, with a minimum of civil strife and without the sacrifice of individual liberty."

In his column, Sokolsky declared that "the time has come for all good Americans" who want God's guidance for their children "to assert themselves valiantly" against "divisive," "even subversive" tiny minorities "who seek to impose their wills upon the great majority of our people." Heeding this call, hundreds of protesters crowded into the courthouse yard, calling the plaintiffs "all kinds of names." The courtroom was so packed with spectators — agitated mothers, representatives from parent-teacher associations, and Roman Catholic mother superiors, nuns, and novitiates — that camp chairs were set up in the corridors.

The courtroom atmosphere was the most "hostile" that *Engel* attorney Stanley Geller ever experienced. Geller, but not Justice Meyer apparently, heard constant muttering to the effect that Butler and Geller were "certainly atheists." Porter Chandler, the intervenors' attorney, refused to say "hello" to the plaintiffs' attorneys. Geller thought Chandler considered them "the scum of the earth." Fortunately, Meyer "couldn't have been nicer," and the plaintiffs' attorneys "never had any complaint" against him. Except for one outburst of applause following a closing statement defending the prayer, the courtroom was otherwise orderly during the three-hour hearing, and the six police officers assigned to the case were idle.

When the court opened at 10 A.M., the plaintiffs' lead attorney, the sober-faced William Butler, who was, as always, dressed in a navy-blue suit, spoke first. Armed with a pile of books but no written brief, Butler unexpectedly demanded a jury trial, which the court denied. As the proceeding continued, Butler defended the petitioners against the damning accusation of atheism: "My adversaries are attempting to place me and my clients as the leaders of godlessness in our society. They point to us as atheists. . . . Nothing could be further from the truth. We come before this Court, representing four individuals with deep religious convictions." He insisted that his clients believed "fervently in the right to prayer and belief in God" and appeared in court "to protect religious liberty by keeping religion out of schools and government."

Butler then argued that the regents' prayer abridged both religion clauses of the First Amendment. The prayer violated his clients' religious beliefs and practices, thereby infringing on their free exercise rights. The nonbeliever, Butler pointed out, objected to the very idea of prayer; the ethical culturist objected to the recital of a set prayer; the Unitarian found the prayer "too dogmatic and too conclusive"; and the two Jews objected to saying a prayer in English, instead of Hebrew, to clasping hands, and to saying it with uncovered heads. The more important point, Butler argued, was that his clients came forward "in the spirit of Madison and Jefferson" to seek refuge in the First Amendment's guarantee of "religious liberty for all Americans." That liberty was being threatened by the state, which "was composing its own prayer and inserting it in compulsory institutions which will act as its churches and led by teachers who act as priests." He argued that the case against the Herricks School District was "even stronger" than the *McCollum* released-time case because "there is a compulsion here" that little children found difficult to resist.

Bertram Daiker, the school board's attorney, complained to Justice Meyer that Butler had not prepared a written brief, while he had broken his back to prepare a 100-page argument. Daiker argued that Butler had turned their roles upside down because procedure required petitioners to furnish briefs to respondents, not vice versa. As Daiker demanded his brief back, he scolded Butler: "You brought the case. Why'd you bring the case if you're not ready?"

Daiker's formal argument was based on the assertion that the state was obliged to develop the students' moral and spiritual values. The best way to carry out this obligation, he maintained, was to recite the regents' prayer. The prayer did not, he claimed, violate the First Amendment because the Founding Fathers intended only "to prevent the establishment of a state church or a nation church." Daiker waved aside Butler's contention that children were being coerced to say the regents' prayer. He noted that the prayer was merely "recommended" for use, and that no school official or student was required to say it. School officials claimed — evidently inaccurately — that only one formal request had been made to excuse a student, and that student was excused.

Daiker reminded the court that a child of Jehovah's Witnesses had asked for similar protection in the *Barnett* flag-salute case. Even though the U.S. Supreme Court understood that religious convictions prevented the child from "worshipping" the U.S. flag, the majority said the solution was to make the Pledge of Allegiance voluntary: "We will not require this child to join in this pledge to the flag where it is contrary to her religious convictions, but we will not strike it out for everyone else." Daiker saw a parallel in the circumstances of both cases and asked that the Court render a similar judgment in *Engel*. In other words, let the few who found the regents' prayer objectionable refrain from repeating it without penalizing the rest of the students by removing it.

Porter Chandler, the intervenors' attorney, who habitually grasped his lapels as he spoke, seconded Daiker's argument on compulsion. The school board was not requiring anything of the children, Chandler asserted, so there was no infringement on anyone's religious freedom. The prayer was "an entirely voluntary act by every child in the school. Since they do not charge that any child has been forced to recite it, they have not suffered any breach of their freedom of religion." The petitioners, he argued, had not suffered from the prayer, for if they had, they would have asked for damages. Rather, "the coercion, the infringement of the free exercise of religious liberty, I submit, is all on the other side." The plaintiffs, he went on, were not content with the option of remaining silent during the prayer; they wanted to prevent everyone else from saying it. Chandler thought it strange that the plaintiffs' attorney did not oppose government-sponsored chaplains in the military, in prison, and in Congress, but contended that "it's all wrong for a child to have any mention of God put before him within the walls of a public school." If the plaintiffs were right, Chandler suggested, the courthouse in Mineola should chisel away the statement, "Justice Is God's Idea, Man's Ideal."

To clarify the establishment clause's meaning, Justice Meyer directed Butler and Geller, the plaintiffs' attorneys, to submit a brief within two weeks. To do that, Geller visited the New York City Public Library to conduct research in a special room for rare books. He relished the assignment "immensely" because he got a quick education in the history of church and state, particularly the influential views of Thomas Jefferson and James Madison. Meyer, who had an "inexhaustible capacity for hard work," took the briefs of both sides and conducted his own research before burrowing into his chambers for six months to consider the vital case from every vantage point. As he deliberated, he had to ignore the many emotional letters he received.

Convinced that the case would wind up in the U.S. Supreme Court as attorneys for both sides predicted, Justice Meyer finally handed down his painstaking decision on August 24, 1959. In what he acknowledged was a close call, Meyer found for the school board and the intervenors in an erudite and exhaustive sixty-seven-page opinion.

After tracing the history of the Constitution and referring to the *Zorach* decision (the most recent establishment clause case), Meyer concluded that accommodation of religion was permissible, although compulsion was not. When Meyer determined that the regents' prayer was nonsectarian and recited voluntarily before classes began, he decided that it did not run afoul of the Constitution.

In Justice Meyer's view, the existence of religious tensions arising from the prayer did not mean its recital was sectarian or unconstitutional. He was not concerned about the juvenile crime rate or "the specter of 'Godless' schools," but only whether school prayer was an "accepted practice" at the time the First and Fourteenth Amendments were adopted. He found that it was, even though there were few public schools at the time. "The recognition of prayer," he wrote, "is an integral part of our national heritage," one whose practice stretched back to the time that the First Amendment was ratified. As further authority, Meyer quoted from an 1839 decision of John Spencer, superintendent of New York's common schools, which permitted school prayer as long as it did not "form a part of school discipline." Spencer declared that parents had the right to decide whether their children should recite the prayer; parents did not have the right to remove the prayer from the schools.

At the same time, Justice Meyer ordered the Herricks School Board to "take affirmative steps to protect the rights of those who, for whatever reason, choose not to participate." Every individual, he wrote, has "a constitutional right personally to be free from religion but that right is a shield, not a sword, and may not be used to compel others to adopt the same attitude." Parents had to be given a copy of the regents' prayer "so that a conscious choice can be made whether a child shall or shall not participate." Moreover, the minority had to be protected from sectarian instruction by school officials and teachers, whether in the form of commentary, posture, or dress. He suggested, for example, that nonparticipating students be allowed to arrive at school after the prayer ended. Long after the trial ended, Meyer told Butler and Daiker that he had at first written twenty pages striking down the prayer, which he tore up because his subsequent research convinced him otherwise.

William Vitale, the Herricks School Board president, was "delighted" with the ruling and reported that the prayer was being recited in all classrooms as before. As for the conditions imposed by Justice Meyer, Vitale insisted, "We have been practicing these conditions in fact. Now we will adopt them formally and comply strictly with all of the requirements imposed by the court. We have repeatedly advised teachers that the prayer is not compulsory. No pupil ever sought to be excused from the room. One pupil who did not wish to participate in the prayer was told he did not have to," a claim contradicted by the administration's own records. Vitale said that parents who followed board meetings should have known of the option to have their children not recite the prayer, but now the district principal would notify all parents directly by mail of their right. By the spring of 1960, Justice Meyer dismissed the suit, having determined that the school district had fully complied with his decision.

A disappointed Lawrence Roth found reason for hope in Meyer's call for the protection of minorities: "It seemed strange to me that a judge would render a decision saying in effect . . . that 'This is legal, but if you do so and so, it's going to be even more legal.'" Roth's attorney, William Butler, also saw a silver lining in the loss because Meyer found that a compulsory recital of the regents' prayer would be unconstitutional. In Butler's mind, "That gives us solid ground to work on" for an appeal because any recital of the prayer had a subtle influence on children in what was "tantamount to compulsion."

This defeat in Nassau County fit into Butler's larger plan. Vowing not to "tolerate even a nick" in the wall of separation, Butler wanted the case to reach the highest court in the land so that school prayer could be eliminated in all school districts, not just in Herricks. When Butler told Thomas Ford, the intervenors' attorney, that "I can't wait to get to the Supreme Court and get out of this state," Ford replied, "Well, you may not be as satisfied in Washington as you are dissatisfied here." Thus began a series of appeals that stretched to the white marble U.S. Supreme Court building.

On October 17, 1960, Meyer's decision was affirmed in Brooklyn by the New York Supreme Court Appellate Division, Second Department, which issued a per curiam (unsigned) decision against Engel and the others. Four of the appellate justices agreed fully with Justice Meyer's decision. The fifth justice, George Bedock, added that the regents' prayer must be sustained for the sole reason that it "does not constitute religious teaching." In his view, recital of the prayer "does nothing more than acknowledge the existence of God and dependence upon him. It gives no training or instruction of any religious nature whatever." Borrowing from the *Doremus* decision, Bedock thought there could be "no constitutional objection to a prayer which is said without rites or ceremony or doctrinal teaching, and which serves at the beginning of each day to give each student who believes in God 'a brief moment with eternity' and a feeling of 'humility before the Supreme Power.'"

Then, on July 7, 1961, the New York Court of Appeals, the state's highest tribunal, met in the capital of Albany and upheld the two lower court decisions permitting the regents' prayer. It looked for all the world that Leo Pfeffer was right, that *Engel* was a bad case for separationists. Writing for the majority, Chief Justice Charles Desmond, a Roman Catholic who wrote a religiously slanted opinion in the *Zorach* case, dismissed outright the claim that declaring belief in God violated the First Amendment. Such a claim was "so contrary to history [as] to be impossible of acceptance." Desmond declared, "Belief in a Supreme Being is as essential and permanent a feature of the American governmental system as is freedom of worship, equality under the law and due process of law. Like them it is an American absolute."

Justice Desmond thought that "Saying this simple prayer may be, according to the broadest possible dictionary definition, an act of 'religion,' but when the Founding Fathers prohibited 'an establishment of religion,' they were referring to official adoption of, or favor to, one or more sects." He observed that references to God were already prevalent in the public school curriculum, in the recital of the Pledge of Allegiance, in the singing of "America," and the study of the New York Constitution. It "defies understanding," Desmond concluded, to permit such references everywhere but in organized prayers in the public school classroom. So certain was Desmond of his decision that when the U.S. Supreme Court eventually overruled him, he urged a national group of Catholic college students to "dispel and disprove the current extremist arguments of American secularists" that the Constitution forbids religious practices in public schools.

But there was hope for the separationists. For the first time, the vote was not unanimous. The two dissenting justices in the New York Court of Appeals declared that the prayer was "a form of State-sponsored religious education." Marvin Dye and Stanley Fuld, who once prosecuted mobster "Lucky" Luciano, believed that the state's "salutary" purpose "overstep[ped] the line marking the division between church and state, and cannot help but lead to a gradual erosion of the mighty bulwark erected by the First Amendment." The inevitable result, the dissenters held, was that the prayer "contains the very elements the prayer is supposed to eliminate," namely "divisiveness," "compulsion" that "an immature child is unable to resist because of his inherent desire to conform," and "a subtle interference by the State with religious freedom." Dye acknowledged that Americans are religious, but such religiosity, he maintained, comes from "the protections afforded by the First Amendment." No matter how well-intentioned the state is, Dye argued, religious instruction is the proper province of the family and its faith community.

The court of appeals allowed the case to advance on the petitioners' claim that "a serious constitutional issue," not just a question of law, was at stake. Once more a court had encouraged the complaining parents just enough to continue. Because the state's highest judicial division provided the first votes for an absolutist interpretation of the establishment clause, Lawrence Roth remarked, "It was at this level that I began to really take hope. I felt that we had gotten some measure of recognition in the courts, and that if we could only get to the [U.S.] Supreme Court, that — I felt then that the Supreme Court would rule for us." Likewise, Steven Engel, a constitutional history buff with an unusually sharp memory, "knew the practice was unconstitutional" and never lost faith that his cause would prevail, despite losing in three courts in a row. For her part, Mary Harte, now the Herricks School Board president, was "confident" that the nation's highest tribunal would uphold the regents' prayer that she had so strongly recommended in her district.

The odds did not favor the petitioners, for 90 percent of the time the nation's highest court rejected cases laid before it. Justice Hugo Black was eager for the Court to hear the school prayer case, but wanted to be sure that his colleagues would strike down the regents' prayer. "I want to know what these guys do before I vote to take it," he confided to his law clerk. Potter Stewart and Charles Whittaker — both Eisenhower appointees from the Midwest — opposed hearing the appeal. Stewart, an Episcopalian, felt the lower court's ruling was entirely correct. An emotional Whittaker, who was active in the Methodist Church, wanted to reject *Engel* outright: "I can't agree to hear this case. I feel strongly — very deeply — about this." Even Chief Justice Earl Warren, whose Court established a high-water mark in guaranteeing justice for all Americans, including minorities of one kind or another, did not think that the *Engel* plaintiffs needed legal protection. Warren could not "get excited" about the case because he believed that the regents' prayer was as harmless as the Pledge of Allegiance. Nevertheless, on December 4, 1961, the Supreme Court placed *Engel v. Vitale* on its docket — Case No. 468 of that judicial term. Black was reassured by the seven to two vote to take up the case.

Oral arguments for *Engel* were scheduled for April 3, 1962, three and a half years after Lawrence Roth had retained the NYCLU. For the first time since the Bill of Rights had been ratified, the U.S. Supreme Court would address the constitutionality of school prayer. The Court was down to eight members because the chief justice had forced the utterly overwhelmed Whittaker to resign after a nervous breakdown, and his designated successor, Byron "Whizzer" White, a Rhodes scholar and football star who had clerked for Supreme Court Chief Justice Fred Vinson, still awaited Senate confirmation. There was speculation that the Court might wait for White's confirmation because of the broad implications of the case. An even number of justices also presented the prospect of a tie vote, an eventuality that would affirm the lower court's ruling. Attorney William Butler urged the plaintiffs to stay home to avoid "a great distraction." At the same time, Butler invited his mother to come down from Boston to see him argue the biggest case of his career.

In briefs filed in advance, Geller prepared an eighteen-page argument, "the smallest, shortest brief" he ever wrote. The brief was short because he found that "there was very little law on the subject — very, very little law" — besides the 1948 *McCollum* precedent. Geller's brief omitted the First Amendment free exercise argument in favor of other complaints against the regents' prayer: the prayer was plainly sectarian and offended the plaintiffs' convictions; it favored belief over nonbelief; and it necessarily produced coercion. At a minimum, the prayer formula and the manner of recital were Christian, and therefore violated the beliefs of atheists and those of some theists. As a result of these substantial problems, Geller's brief maintained, the regents' prayer violated the First Amendment and was unconstitutional. Paul

Freund, Felix Frankfurter's successor at Harvard Law School and Stanley Geller's professor, chided his former student for not premising the case on the free exercise clause.

Relying on a Cold War metaphor, the Herricks School Board suggested in its brief that the parents had confused the "wall of separation between church and state" with an "iron curtain" that excluded religion altogether from public life. This separation, the brief continued, was not intended to be antagonistic to religion. There was no evidence that any pupil had been subjected to "any sectarian or other formal religious teaching. Undisguised [this] attack is against any voluntary public recognition of belief and trust in God in an effort to obliterate from our public schools any recognition — even on a voluntary basis — of the existence of a divine being." And such an attack was, in the board's estimation, intolerable.

Thomas Ford filed a separate brief on behalf of the intervenors, although he did not take part in oral argument. The heart of Ford's brief differentiated between conflicting Cold War values: "Belief in a divine being lies at the basis of our institutions and in the recognition of individual worth and dignity. It is also the point at which our American way of life and values differ most sharply from the totalitarian. No pupil can be educated for his duties as an American citizen if the school is forced to ignore the existence of God and assume a completely negative rather than a neutral attitude toward religion." Ford argued that a handful of people were trying to "force all others to conform to their views" by insisting on "the total and compulsory elimination of God's name from our schools." To these parents, the request to remove the regents' prayer was not unlike actions taken by atheist dictatorships behind the iron curtain.

Other groups filed their own briefs. Twenty-two state attorneys general (only one-third of them from the deep South) maintained that the Founding Fathers "would be profoundly shocked were they to have been told in their day that in this year of our Lord, One Thousand Nine Hundred and Sixty-Two, a voluntary, undenominational acknowledgment of a Supreme Being and a petition for His blessings, recited by American children in their classrooms, is being seriously attacked as a violation of the Constitution of the United States!" Although the attorneys general acknowledged "the right of every man to believe in God or not believe, as he chooses," they noted that the

United States had always been a religious nation and that "nearly all Americans . . . worship God." They concluded, "Our children must continue to have every opportunity to gain an appreciation of this heritage and tradition, not only at home and in the Church but also in public schools, and other governmental functions."

Contesting the regents' prayer were the American Ethical Union and most major Jewish groups, including the American Jewish Committee, American Jewish Congress, Anti-Defamation League of B'nai B'rith, National Jewish Community Relations Advisory Council, and Synagogue Council of America. The briefs, which had been prepared by Leo Pfeffer, argued that prayer is sectarian by its very nature. The way a prayer is worded and the way it is said, Pfeffer wrote, must follow one religious tradition or another. If a prayer takes its wording and practice from several religions, that prayer is the genesis of a new religion. Government, these Jewish organizations insisted, has no business in deciding which religion students should follow.

As the attorneys waited nervously for the proceedings to begin, William Butler kidded Bertram Daiker: "I see that you've brought your own cheering squad today." When Daiker asked, "What do you mean?" Butler replied, "Look around." All Daiker could see was a packed courtroom with a sea of nuns and seminary students in black-and-white robes lining the central aisle. He guessed that they were from Georgetown University. The nuns fingered their rosary beads as they quietly said prayers of petition. As was the custom, the case began after the clerk entered the chamber and said loudly, "Oyez, Oyez, Oyez. . . . God save the United States and this honorable Court."

The pressure was enormous in this kind of constitutional case, especially for Daiker, who had never appeared before the U.S. Supreme Court. To prepare for oral argument, Daiker had his co-counsels drill him in his hotel room for four hours the previous day with every question they could think of; afterward, he collapsed on his bed "completely exhausted." Daiker was tense, even though he fully expected to win, as he had in three lower courts. Part of the tension resulted from the book of protocol that the clerk gave the attorneys to follow. Each counsel was to wear a conservative suit and tie, address the justices by name after glancing at photographs in front of them, and adhere to a signal system that indicated when their presentations were to cease. When Daiker faced the justices for the first time, he felt as if he were "the most lonesome person in the world" stranded on a "deserted island. . . . And you realize full well that if they ask you a question, and you don't know the answer, there's no one in that courtroom to help you. You can't lean over to your neighbor, or your associate, and ask a question. You must come up with an answer."

Even though William Butler had once before participated in a U.S. Supreme Court case (as amicus counsel), he, too, was "nervous" and "intimidated." As attorney for the petitioners, he went first and asserted that the regents' prayer "raises, in our opinion, grave constitutional problems." Butler called attention to a 1951 statement by the New York Board of Regents that referred to the "eventuality of teaching our children . . . that Almighty God is their creator." This transparently religious intent, Butler declared, was "the motive of the prayer." Butler was then thrown into "disarray." He had prepared himself "for a very thorough argument" lasting almost an hour — the maximum time allotted for presenting the case — only to be interrupted at the outset.

The give-and-take between Butler and the Court produced heated exchanges, occasional outbursts of laughter, and a few misstatements of fact. When Butler asserted that the regents' prayer was designed "to inculcate into the children a love of God" in order to "preserve the religious and even Christian heritage of our society," a troubled Justice John Marshall Harlan II asked, "Is that a bad thing?" Butler scrambled to clarify his position, raising his voice and thumping the lectern with his hand for emphasis. Insisting that he did not come "as an antagonist of religion," he maintained that his clients were "deeply religious people," who wanted, as Roger Williams, the founder of Rhode Island, had wanted, to divorce religion from public life. "My clients," Butler declared, "say that prayer is good. But what we say here is, it's the beginning of the end of religious freedom when religious activity such as this is incorporated into the public school system of the United States."

All of the justices, except Earl Warren, raised question after question, particularly about the nature of the plaintiffs' grievance. When Potter Stewart learned that two of the petitioners were Jewish, he seemed not to comprehend their complaint: "What is there in this prayer that people of the Jewish faith find objectionable?" He noted that the regents' prayer "doesn't talk about a Christian God. It doesn't talk about a Methodist or an Episcopalian or Presbyterian God." Stewart felt it necessary to verify that Jews "believe in God, do they not — Jehovah?" Butler assured the justice that is so and explained gently that the issue was constitutional, not religious. Moreover, Butler pointed out, the regents' prayer violated the manner in which some Jews (though none of the litigants) pray — only in the synagogue, wearing yarmulkes, facing east. Stewart then questioned whether the Pledge of Allegiance with its phrase "One Nation under God" already brought religion into the classroom, prompting Butler's interpretation that the pledge affirmed a merely political belief. William Brennan inquired whether there was a meaningful distinction between teaching religion and teaching *about* religion. Butler contended that such a distinction could be made and that religion could be taught as an academic subject. Felix Frankfurter demanded to know Butler's legal bottom line: "Is it your position that our public schools, by virtue of our Constitution, are frankly secular institutions?" Butler fairly blurted out, "Absolutely, yes."

The justices were keenly interested in whether other types of religious activity might be permissible. Harlan, an inactive Episcopalian whose namesake grandfather had served on the Court for thirty-four years, wondered aloud about the constitutionality of a ten-minute period of Bible reading. Butler asked which Bible Harlan had in mind. When Harlan replied that he was thinking of the King James Version, Butler pronounced that scripture unconstitutional. Frankfurter then inquired as to Butler's view of a five-minute period for "silent meditation." Butler could find no constitutional objection to that idea. William O. Douglas, who was fascinated by Far Eastern religion and thought that Christianity "turned men into vandals," inquired about reading from the Book of Mormon or the Qur'an. Butler maintained that reading devotions from any religious tradition would "definitely" be unconstitutional. When Douglas asked why, Butler explained that "any kind of religious activity, any attempt by the State to impose any religious view or to engage in any kind of religious activity" was prohibited by the First Amendment. Butler thought that if the objective was merely to teach about a religion, that would be a different matter altogether.

Butler had little difficulty repudiating the arguments made in his opponents' briefs. The case he had to dismiss adroitly was *Zorach*, in which the U.S. Supreme Court had permitted released time for religious instruction. Butler reminded the Court that *Zorach* represented the state's accommodation to a religious practice held away from school property. In *Engel*, Butler maintained, the Herricks School Board was directly involved in a religious practice that took place in public school classrooms. As for the school board's claim that the regents' prayer was legal because the complaining parents were in the minority, Butler reminded the justices that "the very purpose of the Constitution is to protect the minority against the majority, to protect the weak against the strong in matters of keeping separate forever the functions of the civil and the religious."

In his prepared remarks, Bertram Daiker defended the regents' prayer by looking at the establishment clause. The heart of the matter, in Daiker's mind, was that the prayer was not religious instruction, but religious expression, which is guaranteed by the First Amendment. Daiker admitted that if the prayer were compulsory then it was unconstitutional, but, he insisted, it was strictly voluntary. School administrators would readily grant any parent's request to excuse his or her child from the classroom during the opening prayer; but, Daiker claimed, no child or parent had yet made that request. In fact, however, more than three dozen students had asked to be excused from saying the regents' prayer and several of them had been disciplined for their refusal to recite it.

Daiker declared that in instituting the prayer the Herricks School Board was doing no more than recognizing the existence of a supreme deity, something that was mentioned in the Declaration of Independence and in every state constitution except one. He concluded, "We are not trying here in the Herricks School District to teach religion . . . any more than . . . the prayer used in this Court." Both prayers, Daiker maintained, were part of the civil religion, employing language that was used almost universally among believers. The lawsuit was trivial, in Daiker's mind, because it took only thirty seconds to recite the prayer, and because there was no evidence of harm to children who did not like it. Besides, he argued, the New York Board of Regents was legitimately using this prayer to help prevent juvenile delinquency.

Chief Justice Warren then made a lengthy query that caused Daiker's mind to wander. The school board attorney decided to bank on honesty and admit his loss of concentration. Such a frank admission took everyone by surprise. When Warren conceded that his question "got pretty involved," his fellow justices and the audience enjoyed a good laugh. Strangely, it was Warren whose face turned beet red, and he slapped his thigh in utter amazement that an attorney would admit to losing his train of thought. A federal marshal had to gavel for order.

The justices then peppered Daiker with more questions. Earl Warren inquired about the obvious character of the prayer: "Is it not a religious practice to say a prayer?" Daiker replied that an opening prayer in a variety of settings was merely an important custom. The regents' prayer, he maintained, was "no more [a religious practice] than the saying of any prayer on any public occasion is a religious practice. . . . Whenever people gather together in a group and utter a prayer, a recognition of the Almighty, as has been consistently done since the founding of the country hundreds of years ago, we don't find constitutional objections. How then can we say that prayer is all right on any public occasion in a state-paid-for building, with state employees, except in the school?" The crucial question for Daiker was whether the regents' prayer unconstitutionally established religion, by which he meant a national or state church. He was certain it did not.

With Daiker ostensibly defending prayer in all public venues, Warren and Frankfurter zeroed in on the vulnerable age of schoolchildren. It was one thing, these justices said, for politicians, lawyers, and the general adult public to hear a religious affirmation like that uttered by the Court's crier; it was something else when youngsters heard their teachers recite a prayer or read from a holy book. Daiker warned the Court that the petitioners had larger game in mind than the regents' prayer. They wanted nothing less than to remove any mention of God from public schools altogether. It was a charge calculated to inflame the issue.

After Daiker finished, Porter Chandler represented the intervenor parents with eloquence. He began his remarks with a little levity, observing that there could be "no question of mootness here" because when the case started his clients had thirty-seven children in the public schools, a number that had now reached forty-one. To make sure he did not cover the same ground as Daiker, Chandler addressed the flip side of the First Amendment. He explained his clients' motivation: "They are here in the name of the free exercise of religion, if you want to put it that way. They are here because they feel very strongly that it is a deprivation of their children's right to share in our national heritage, and that it is a compulsory rewriting of our history in the fashion of George Orwell's *1984* to do what these petitioners are now seeking to do, namely to eliminate all reference to God from the whole fabric of our public life and our public educational system." Chandler observed that the U.S. Supreme Court had once upheld the rights of Jehovah's Witnesses, who asked only to be excused from the flag salute in classes, but did not ban the salute altogether. He closed his remarks with a poke at Butler, calling on the plaintiffs' attorney to recite Jefferson's phrase in the Declaration of Independence that Americans are "endowed by their Creator with certain unalienable Rights."

After oral arguments concluded and the justices departed, Butler asked his mother, a devout Roman Catholic, what she thought of his performance. She replied, "Well, I think you made a good argument, and I even think you're a good lawyer and you might even win this case, but I hope nobody in Boston hears about it."

In its conference deliberations, the U.S. Supreme Court quickly reached a decision on the case. Earl Warren said that the respondents "practically conceded that this is religious instruction, and is so intended." For him, "the fact that we speak of God with reverence does not mean that we can take the prayer into the school — it is the camel's head under the tent." All of the sitting justices agreed, except Potter Stewart, who was "still in doubt." Felix Frankfurter had no such doubts, labeling the regents' prayer as "a disguised religious practice in public school." The decision hinged, he thought, on whether a prayer "is saved merely because children may include themselves out." He thought not, noting that religious exercises produce an "inherent compulsion on children to take part and to force parents to acquiesce." Even John Marshall Harlan would reverse the lower courts, albeit "reluctantly." Given the string of church-state precedents, he felt the Court had no choice but to strike down the regents' prayer. But, he said, "If this were *de novo*, I would say that it was no violation."

When Hugo Black and Chief Justice Warren conferred afterward to decide who would write the majority opinion, Black requested the assignment — a reasonable request, given his twenty-five years on the High Bench and his seminal church-state jurisprudence. As a results-oriented jurist interested in justice above all, Warren entrusted this important opinion to Black, who along with William O. Douglas, was the Court's leading civil libertarian. After the chief justice departed, a smiling Black told his clerk, George Saunders, the good news.

As Black roughed out his opinion, he directed his clerk to scour the Court library for books on religion and history. Saunders recalled, "The Judge had religious references [at] his fingertips. He read them and told me to go to the library to get more. . . . If I thought a book were worthwhile, I'd give it to him and he'd take it home. If I didn't think so, we'd talk [about] whether he should read it. But he ended up reading everything I took out." Among other works, Black reread the Book of Common Prayer and John Bunyan's Christian allegory, *The Pilgrim's Progress*, which he kept readily available at his desk. His reading of history was that "when one religion gets predominance, they [*sic*] immediately try to suppress others." Black confided in his wife about the excesses of true believers: "People had been tortured, their ears lopped off, and sometimes their tongues cut or their eyes gouged out, all in the name of religion."

The Roman Catholic Church was especially given to such oppression, Black believed, a view that was reinforced by his reading of Paul Blanshard's best-selling polemic, *American Freedom and Catholic Power*. Blanshard, once a minister and then special counsel for Protestants and Others United for Separation of Church and State, came to think that Christianity was "full of fraud." He was convinced that the Catholic Church's policies on birth control, divorce, and parochial education seriously harmed women, the world's poor, and U.S. democracy. Blanshard may have shared his anti-Catholic views in person with Hugo Black because both men attended All Souls Unitarian Church in Washington, D.C.

Even before the decision was announced, the Supreme Court justices expressed concern over how far the principle of church and state should be extended. William O. Douglas found Black's drafts unconvincing and scribbled a brief note to Black: "I still do not see how most of the opinion is relevant to the problem." Douglas simply did not discern any penalty for the Herricks students who did not pray. Even more troubling, Douglas thought, how could the Court clearly differentiate what the government could or could not do with respect to religious activities? How, he wondered, could the Court order teachers not to say a prayer although the Court's own marshal opened its sessions with prayer? How could the Court authorize, as it did in *Everson*, a plan to pay parents to transport their children to parochial schools, and prohibit the practice of paying public schoolteachers who led prayers? The entire matter of church and state relations seemed to be a conundrum to Douglas.

As the Court deliberated over classroom prayer, major events unfolded elsewhere. The Cold War and social inequality at home remained American preoccupations. The United States instituted a trade embargo against communist Cuba, and a Cuban military tribunal convicted 1,179 CIA-trained Cuban exiles for their involvement in the ill-fated Bay of Pigs invasion designed to overthrow dictator Fidel Castro. The civil war in Vietnam appeared more frequently on the front pages of the *New York Times*. East German guards shot anyone caught scaling the newly built Berlin Wall. U.S. mobster Lucky Luciano died in Naples, Italy, and Nazi war criminal Adolf Eichmann was hanged in Israel. Aboard *Friendship 7*, John Glenn orbited the earth three times in five hours, the first American to do so; he returned to a hero's welcome in New York City. In Albany, Georgia, a shrewd local sheriff stalled Martin Luther King, Jr.'s civil rights campaign. Disturbed by inequities at home, the Students for a Democratic Society completed the Port Huron Statement, a manifesto calling for major political and economic reforms. In the short term, none of these developments would hit the U.S. public harder than the decision the Court was about to make.

On the warm summer morning of June 25, 1962, the U.S. Supreme Court dropped a bombshell when it invalidated the regents' prayer in the Herricks School District and voided laws in eleven states requiring religious exercises in public schools. In a six-to-one decision that was the logical extension of *Everson* and *McCollum*, Justice Hugo Black ruled that the regents' prayer was "wholly inconsistent with the establishment clause." Leaning forward in his chair, the seventy-six-year-old Black read the majority's fifteen-page opinion with considerable emotion, in a deep voice that contained the "faintest tremble," one observer reported. Two justices did not vote. Two days after oral argument, Felix Frankfurter, then eighty years old, was hospitalized by a crippling stroke that left him paralyzed and unable to speak; Byron White, Charles Whittaker's replacement, was new to the Court.

The regents' prayer, Black decided, was unconstitutional because a government body had placed its "official stamp of approval" on what was obviously a religious activity. He held that the entire idea of a state-mandated or state-sponsored prayer was contrary to the spirit and command of the First Amendment's ban on the establishment of religion. He dismissed outright the school board's claim that the prayer was permissible because it was purportedly a brief, bland, and voluntary petition. Black maintained that abridgements of the establishment clause, unlike those involving the free exercise clause, do not require "any showing of direct governmental compulsion," only the enactment of laws that "establish an official religion." The very fact that the government paid for the schools where the prayer was said and the salaries of the teachers who led it created indirect pressure for everyone to conform, including nonbelievers. Black concluded, "It is no part of the business of government to compose official prayers for any group of the American people to recite as a part of a religious program carried on by government." Religion, he averred, is "too personal, too sacred, too holy, to permit its 'unhallowed perversion' by a civil magistrate." Echoing the thoughts of Jefferson and Madison, Black maintained that "a union of government and religion tends to destroy government and to degrade religion." By homogenizing prayer, the regents' prayer amounted to a bland entreaty addressed "to whom it may concern."

To reach this conclusion, Black delivered a heartfelt history lesson about church-state relations in the United States. Whereas Bernard Meyer, the trial judge, had used history to sustain the regents' prayer, Black used (and sometimes misused) history to outlaw it. Black asserted that the Founders devised the establishment clause "upon an awareness of the historical fact that governmentally established religions and religious persecutions go hand in hand." After all, he continued, "this very practice of establishing governmentally composed prayers for religious services was one of the reasons which caused many of our early colonists to leave England and seek religious freedom in America." The First Amendment, Black explained, stood as "a guarantee that neither the power nor the prestige of the federal government would be used to control, support, or influence the kinds of prayer the American people can say. . . ." In an extemporaneous remark, Black added, "The genius of the First Amendment" was that "the prayer of each man from his soul must be his and his alone." Remarkably, Black did not cite a single substantive case in support of his argument. This omission would provide valuable ammunition to those who criticized *Engel*.

Black foresaw that his decision would create a backlash, so he waived aside the charge that the Supreme Court had expressed "hostility" toward religion: "Nothing, of course, could be more wrong." Responding to Daiker's claim that banning prayer would be hostile to both prayer and religion, Black asserted that the Court was not against God or praying to God: It was "neither sacrilegious nor antireligious to say that . . . government . . . should stay out of the business of writing or sanctioning official prayers and leave that purely religious function to the people themselves." In an important footnote (number 21), Black tried to make clear that his opinion did not at all foreclose brief references to religion in government mottoes or ceremonies: "There is of course nothing in the decision reached here that is inconsistent with the fact that schoolchildren and others are officially encouraged to express love for our country by reciting historical documents such as the Declaration of Independence, which contain references to the Deity, or by singing officially espoused anthems which include the composer's profession of faith in a Supreme Being, or with the fact that there are many manifestations in our public life of belief in God."

In a concurring opinion that did cite legal precedents, Justice William O. Douglas tossed a hand grenade against religious establishment, and in so doing stirred the greatest fears of *Engel*'s critics. *Everson* had been a terrible mistake, Douglas decided, because any government aid to religion would muddy the constitutional waters, bring renewed demands to dismantle the wall of separation, and produce squabbling between competing religious sects. To Douglas, even one penny of government money for religious activity was illegal, including military/congressional chaplains, tax exemptions for churches, and the slogan "In God We Trust" on the nation's currency. "For me," Douglas wrote in *Engel*, "the principle is the same no matter how briefly the prayer is said." Any audience for prayer — whether in a school, court, or legislature — is a "captive audience" and therefore illegal. Douglas dipped into psychology to protect the nonconformist student who might be "induced to participate for fear of being called an 'oddball.'" "[T]he atheist or agnostic — the nonbeliever — is entitled to go his own way," Douglas thought.

The chief justice sided with the majority, in part because of the bloody Philadelphia Bible riots of the 1840s. Earl Warren was a profoundly religious man who attended the Baptist Church, kept a Bible on his nightstand, and thumbed through the Talmud in search of moral truths. In a frank interview published posthumously, Warren remarked, "A person who has no religion of any kind is almost a lost soul." For Warren, religious instruction was a personal matter for families to decide, not the duty of the state. Although Douglas wondered how the Court could logically strike down the regents' prayer and begin its own proceedings with prayer, Warren viewed the two customs as entirely different. In the case of Court sessions, the justices were merely invoking God's benevolence; in the case of school classrooms, state officials were compelling a prayer. In a rare moment of political tone-deafness, Warren did not anticipate the fallout from the case.

The sole dissenting voice came from Eisenhower's appointee, Potter Stewart, the son of an Ohio Supreme Court chief justice. Stewart, who gave greater weight to free exercise guarantees than the danger of religious establishment, thought that the regents' prayer was a compromise between those who wanted to pray and those who did not. In the absence of direct coercion, he believed the voluntary prayer was permissible. Stewart thought it ironic that the establishment clause, which was designed to prevent Congress from interfering with religion in the states, was now being used to do just that.

Stewart was mystified how "an official religion" was established by allowing those who want to say a prayer to say it, particularly one that was so brief and nonsectarian in nature. He observed that similar divine supplications emanated from a number of institutions: the president is sworn in under an oath to God; Congress and the U.S. Supreme Court open their sessions with prayer; and the "Star-Spangled Banner," which mentions God, is officially recognized as the nation's anthem. None of these examples established religion, Stewart maintained. They simply recognize the "deeply entrenched and highly cherished spiritual traditions of our Nation." School prayer, to his mind, was yet another example. As for Black's extended discussion of English history, Stewart thought it irrelevant to the question of prayer in U.S. public schools. To clinch his argument, Stewart became the first U.S. Supreme Court justice to question Jefferson's "wall of separation" metaphor, noting that it is "nowhere to be found in the Constitution." Many Americans quickly embraced Stewart's minority view.

The Warren Court had little choice but to side with the petitioners in *Engel*. Given the ever-growing religious pluralism in U.S. society, the Court simply accommodated constitutional law to reality. Although the Court could no longer permit one religious group to hold a privileged position, it was not hostile to religion in general.

Attorney William Butler, who expected a one-vote victory, believed that *Engel* would have the same far-reaching effects on public education, if not on civil religion itself, as the *Brown* desegregation decision had for Jim Crow. "Every school board in the country," he predicted, "is going to have to reappraise its position on the use of its buildings for religious practices, and on the use of its curriculum, too." It was very clear, Butler continued, that "the Supreme Court has laid down new rules for the doctrine of separation of church and state — that public facilities can never be used for religious instruction." Nor could tax monies be used for religious education. Having won a landmark victory in court, Butler celebrated by going mountain climbing with his family on the West Coast.

To stop all religious activities in public schools, the NYCLU called for a coast-to-coast drive by the ACLU's thirty-three affiliates: "We are confident that as other . . . religious practices are brought to the court's attention," including Christmas and Hanukkah observances, Bible reading, Lord's Prayer recitations, and baccalaureate services, "they likewise will be declared unconstitutional." The New Jersey affiliate received a dozen requests to go after such practices.

Although attorney Bertram Daiker was "completely shocked" by the decision and had "never expected" to lose, the Herricks School Board at once made its peace with the ruling. William Vitale, the former school board president, thought all along that the Supreme Court would overturn the regents' prayer. Vitale disagreed with Black's decision, but "as a good citizen, more so as an attorney, I must respect that decision." Mary Harte, who had called for the regents' prayer in the beginning, said the board "would have to abide by their decision." She hoped, however, that James Allen, the New York education commissioner, would permit some morning exercise in the public schools. When Allen suggested that a moment of silence was a legal exercise, the Herricks School Board readily adopted that practice following the Pledge of Allegiance.

Thomas Ford, who represented the intervenors, was also disturbed by the decision. He called Porter Chandler, the lead counsel, and told him that *Engel* "went much further than I thought it would. This is very bad. This is the end of prayer in school and maybe the end of prayer." Chandler thought Ford was "overreacting." When the press caught up with him, Ford showed mixed emotions: "Well, life just goes on. We've had tragedies and triumphs and joys and sorrows and life just goes on." But how, he wondered, could the U.S. Supreme Court be reversed? "The enormous task of overruling a Supreme Court decision, of legally opposing that mandate is really impossible. We had to have a civil war to outlaw slavery. What are we going to do to abolish abortion or get prayer back in the schools? Our Founding Fathers never intended to place in them such power. That power has gone unchecked." Given the six-to-one ruling, Ford said it was "futile" to request a rehearing by the Supreme Court. He did suggest to Mary Harte that the national motto, "In God We Trust," be placed in each classroom and that an "appropriate stanza" from the national anthem or "America" substitute for the regents' prayer.

Dan Reehill, a Roman Catholic and one of the sixteen parents Ford represented, blamed his church for sitting on the sidelines as the case proceeded, only to criticize the adverse result: "Where were they when we needed them?" The firefighter lieutenant vowed to work for a constitutional amendment overturning *Engel*.

In the Herricks School District, some faculty were very surprised by the *Engel* decision. Drama coach John Snyder recalled hearing the news during a late afternoon rehearsal. "We were all shocked that it happened." Snyder and his colleagues had heard of the case, but "we never thought that anything would come of it." The conversation then turned to the petitioners, and the teachers worried about possible retaliation against them. One teacher said, "I hope nobody torches the house" of any of the plaintiffs. Another teacher added, "I hope they don't burn a cross." These fears proved remarkably prescient. Although the teachers feared for the safety of the petitioners, they were also concerned that any violence would tarnish Herricks' lofty reputation.

Engel reinforced the disposition of newspapers to keep supporting or opposing the Warren Court. In general, liberal newspapers applauded *Engel*, and conservative ones condemned it and fed the negative public reaction to the school prayer ruling. An examination of the forty-two largest metropolitan areas that commented on *Engel* revealed that a majority opposed the decision. A particularly stinging rebuke came from the *Los Angeles Times*, which accused the Court of having fallen under the sway of "a small group of guardhouse sophists." The result, the *Times* argued, was to make a "burlesque show of the world's first complete declaration of religion toleration." Likewise, the *New York Mirror* lambasted the Court and the opinion's author: "It is difficult to understand how any six men in the United States could agree on this decision, written by Justice Hugo Black, who started his political career in the Ku Klux Klan but who, on the bench, became the leader of the radical left. Here is a decision without a quoted precedent, with no roots in law, with no historic basis." The *Mirror* reprinted the regents' prayer several times in the hope that its readers would memorize it.

Editorials against *Engel* also appeared in the *Baltimore Sun, Boston Globe, Chicago Tribune, Cincinnati Enquirer, Dallas Morning News, Indianapolis Star, Kansas City Star, Los Angeles Times, New York Journal-American, New York Daily News, Philadelphia Bulletin, Rocky Mountain News* (Denver), *San Francisco News–Call Bulletin, Seattle Times,* and *Washington Star.* The *New York Herald Tribune* recognized that "so many otherwise responsible newspapers are getting completely swept off their feet by the tide of emotionalism."

Other papers were more restrained in their reactions. *Newsday* wrote, "The ruling was a bad one, but the headlong rush to amend the Constitution is equally bad. . . . We must accept the decision while seeking other means to preserve the principle of a Supreme Being for our children." "Monday's decision," the *Atlanta Constitution* editorialized, "has not dealt a blow to religion. . . . On the contrary, it has fortified constitutional guarantees that our Government must leave each individual free to worship in his own way." Supportive editorials also appeared in the *Chicago Sun-Times, Cleveland Plain Dealer, Des Moines Register, Detroit Free Press, Hartford Courant, Louisville Courier-Journal, Milwaukee Journal, Minneapolis Star, New Orleans Times-Picayune, New York Herald Tribune, New York Post, New York Times, Pittsburgh Post-Gazette, San Francisco Chronicle, St. Louis Post-Dispatch,* and *Washington Post.*

Legal scholars were divided in their analyses of *Engel*'s meaning. Some scholars criticized Black's decision as poorly written and accused the Court of taking a far broader approach than the facts warranted. Harvard law dean Erwin Griswold, a Frankfurter student, thought it was "unfortunate" that the case ever reached the U.S. Supreme Court. Griswold could not understand how the Court could have misinterpreted the First Amendment phrase "Congress shall make no law," because Congress had made no law in this instance. Further, he found it "difficult to see how what was done in New York, with respect to the school prayer there, can appropriately be regarded as an establishment of religion." The regents' prayer, to his way of thinking, was simply the "free exercise of religion." Griswold, who would become solicitor general in the Johnson and Nixon administrations, contended that the United States "has been, and is, a Christian country, in origin, history, tradition, and culture." He conceded that U.S. religious minorities — he mentioned Muslims — were welcome to worship freely and hold office, but such tolerance did not mean the majority had to abandon its religious heritage.

John Satterfield of Mississippi, president of the American Bar Association and a leader in the Methodist Church, also disagreed with *Engel* and would have dissented from the majority opinion had he been on the Court. Satterfield pulled a coin out of his pocket, pointed to the inscription, "In God We Trust," and declared, "If the use of that prayer is unconstitutional, then the words on this coin are also unconstitutional."

Still other law professors believed that although *Engel*'s full implications were unclear at first, the decision would prove wise. "To read into this decision the implications that have been read into it is to expound a parade of imaginary horrors," remarked University of Chicago professor Philip Kurland, a former Frankfurter law clerk and an authority on church-state relations. Although he had reservations about the ruling's soundness, Kurland believed that the ruling was "important but narrow in breadth." He foresaw a day when *Engel* would be recognized even by its contemporary detractors as "one of the bulwarks of America's freedom from the ills that continue to plague those countries where 'toleration' rather than 'freedom' and 'separation' are the guides to government action." In the short run, however, the petitioners endured a living hell to defend their First Amendment rights.

CHAPTER 7

"Almighty God Has Been Given Walking Papers"

When Lawrence Roth received word of the *Engel* decision at work, he was stunned and gratified. Heaving a sigh of relief, he remarked, "Thank God for the Civil Liberties Union." That night, there was a victory party at his home for all the petitioners and their children. The mild-mannered Roth was weary, but he explained to a reporter why they persevered for more than three long years: "What started out as a feeling within us grew eventually to a test and a demonstration, let's say, of what I consider to be really the essence of the American way of doing things — the right of the citizen to petition his government for a redress of what he considers to be a wrongdoing. I can't emphasize how strong I feel about that, because I feel that if we lose that, we have lost everything." Roth expressed a grim satisfaction that the petitioners had weathered great abuse to protect U.S. liberty: "None of us are sorry that we became involved in the case. We all feel that we have had a small part in clarifying and strengthening a vital constitutional safeguard. For this, we were more than willing to endure whatever came our way."

The other petitioners were jubilant and let off steam until midnight. Frances Roth blurted out, "We're so excited, we can't think straight." She added, "I'm very proud of our country, where a group of people can take a stand on an issue, take it through the courts and be backed by the highest court in the land." She called the regents' prayer "a silly kind of prayer, but that wasn't the point." Insisting again that the plaintiffs were not intent upon removing "In God We Trust" from the currency or even removing religion from academic study, Roth maintained, "It's the actual act of praying I object to, no matter how innocuous the prayer was." There was, she observed, considerable pressure to learn the regents' prayer, with one teacher requiring

.getful child to write it out dozens of times. Daniel Lichtenstein hailed the ruling as "a great victory for democracy and a reaffirmation of the basic principle of separation of church and state." In a victory photo staged on the Roths' front steps, Ruth Lichtenstein could not help asking: "Does it look to you like we're against God? But we were called un-American because people thought we were against God."

The relief, even euphoria, the plaintiffs experienced immediately after the ruling gave way to nonstop harassment by the local community. "When we won the case," Steven Engel remembered, "all hell broke loose." Critics of *Engel* took the decision as a personal rebuke and saw in it the death knell of "Christian America." According to a Gallup poll, 85 percent of Americans disapproved of the ruling.

The plaintiffs received a deluge of "chilling" hate mail, snubs from erstwhile friends, and telephone threats of job dismissal, arson, and kidnapping. Monroe Lerner recalled that neighbors "stopped talking to us," but harassing telephone calls came well into the night. "We had to take our phone off the hook," he recalled. "Terrible things were said to us." The Lerners' mailbox was jammed with anonymous letters composed of words cut out of newspapers, a sign of "how intense the feelings were." To the Lerners' shock, a Roman Catholic woman in their neighborhood stopped speaking to them. They had known the woman to be bright and respectful of religious differences and were taken aback at the unexpected show of intolerance. Their daughter Cynthia could no longer play with a Christian girlfriend two houses away. Some of Monroe Lerner's clients punished him by taking their stock market investments to other brokers.

The Lyons family also paid for its involvement in the case. They received numerous crank calls, some with vile sexual innuendo — "all in the name of God." An old woman would telephone, asking, "Is Mrs. Lyons there? Well, tell the Commie to go back to Russia." The calls came so frequently that David Lyons made a game with his friends. They would take turns answering the phone, waiting for the invective to get well along and then reply, "Joe's Pizza Parlor." Even so, Lenore Lyons had no regrets: "It's fatiguing answering the phone. It's uncomfortable. But I'm thrilled with the decision." The early elation faded, however, and later on, when Lyons found out the name of one young caller, she marched to his house to demand an apology from his mother. In school the Lyons children endured continual taunts and threats because they remained silent during the prayer. After the decision was announced, a Catholic mother broke off her son's friendship with Douglas Lyons and tried — unsuccessfully — to isolate the Lyons family in the neighborhood.

No one suffered more than the Roths, because their name, address, and telephone number had been published in the newspaper. Ministers called Lawrence Roth a devil, and picketers marched in front of his house with signs reading, "ROTH — GODLESS ATHEIST." Within days of the decision, the Roths received at least seven hundred "poison-pen letters which belonged in Himmler's book." The sons guessed whether letters backed or opposed them based on how the envelope appeared. Many of the "crackpot" letters contained anti-Semitic phrases, such as the following: "This looks like Jews trying to grab America as Jews grab everything they want in any nation. America is a Christian nation." Another letter connected Jews to communism: "If you don't like our God, then go behind the Iron Curtain where you belong, Kike, Hebe, Filth!" Lawrence Roth admitted, "Toward the end, it got so bad that my wife or I made it a point of getting the mail before the children could see it."

The Roths received angry telephone calls literally around the clock — 8,000 in the first week alone. The apparently orchestrated campaign invariably included many anonymous threats: "We're going to blow up your car. . . . Don't leave your house; something is going to happen to it. . . . We'll get you." One caller identified himself as from the Brooklyn Protective Association and threatened the litigants, "We took a vote and decided to kill you." At 3 A.M. one morning, the Roths received a bomb threat from the Union Street Benevolent Society, forcing them to scour their house for a deadly device. The calls were so incessant that on many nights Lawrence Roth had to get up to remove the receiver from the hook.

The abuse deeply affected young Joe Roth. "They'd tell us to go home to Russia, to die of cancer. It was rough," Roth remembers, especially because he was shunned by his classmates: "I was a really alienated kid, and it didn't help. I refused to pray because my father asked me [not] to, but at the same time I resented it all along." More accurately, he resented his father for launching the case that caused his predicament. Joe showed a large rebellious streak, cutting class and stealing automobiles, apparently for joyriding. Tired of being an outsider with low self-esteem, the insular youth finally found his niche in extracurricular school activities. Avoiding politics altogether, Joe dove into sports with single-minded passion, partly to follow a different path from that of his bookish older brother and partly because he was on his "own emotionally in my own house." He belonged to several leadership and service clubs and worked on the student newspaper and yearbook, but he was happiest when he played basketball and soccer. He finally felt like he belonged when he was named captain of the soccer team. Still, Roth's soccer coach noticed that his fullback "wasn't the happiest fellow. He didn't go around joking and smiling. He was kind of serious."

Appropriately enough, Joe Roth's favorite movie in those days was *The Loneliness of the Long Distance Runner*, a story about an idealistic teenager who feels betrayed by his parents and indeed all adults. When the boy gets caught robbing a bakery and ends up in reform school, the cunning headmaster trains him to be a champion cross-country runner. In the race of his life — a race intended to bring glory to the headmaster — the boy stops one step from victory and loses. Determined to be true to himself, he rejects the corrupt system that misused him. "That's me," Joe Roth says. "I am that guy."

Lawrence Roth was "unprepared" for the vituperation he and his family faced: "There's just no way I could have imagined that what seemed to me to be such a clear-cut . . . issue, one that our Founding Fathers fought, and one that went on in England for umpteen generations, the right for the separation of church and state . . . it just never occurred to me — ever — that it would be misinterpreted to be an attack on religion in general." Roth admitted to having "qualms" about "exposing my children to danger." The "torrent of abuse" that was the "penalty" for "being an instigator" caused him to ask himself a soul-searching question: "What . . . have . . . I . . . done?" Roth's wife, Frances, tried humor to cope with the constant tension, telling her husband, "You had to be the big shot, didn't you?"

In the midst of this maelstrom, the Roth boys desperately needed parental support, but their father was unable to provide it. He took them instead to the Center for Emotional Re-Education (CER), a now-defunct group that specialized in group-therapy sessions. "The cult," as Joe Roth describes CER, was led by "a hippie with a law degree" and was supposed to help people "find themselves." Lawrence

Roth encouraged his sons to join, which they did. It nearly destroyed Joe, and the breach between father and son never quite healed.

Steven Engel recalled that critics of all kinds "came out of the woodwork" to question the decision. He was shocked when members of the Jewish community attacked him personally. He believed that ultraorthodox Jews saw the U.S. Supreme Court's decision as threatening their claim to government aid to Hebrew schools, the perspective shared by Roman Catholic Church officials. Even local Reform rabbis "spoke up against us": "Hey, do you know what you're saying?" some rabbis demanded to know. Most probably, these rabbis were concerned about reawakening anti-Semitic feelings in the larger society. The lowest point for Engel came at work when an anonymous caller told him, "We have your children." Beside himself with worry, Engel jumped into a taxicab and headed to the school to see whether his son had been kidnapped. It was a false alarm. To fight such outrages, Engel helped found the Nassau chapter of the New York Civil Liberties Union, in which he was joined by Monroe Lerner, Daniel Lichtenstein, and Lawrence Roth.

Not all of the threats were idle. Nine members of the right-wing National Party, newly formed to expose "communist fronts," marched up and down in front of Roth's home. On cue, the screaming protesters waved signs that read, "FBI PLEASE INVESTIGATE MR. ROTH" and "IMPEACH THE PRO-RED SUPREME COURT." They also carried leaflets attacking public schools, racial integration, public housing, and George Lincoln Rockwell's rival American Nazi Party. The Roths were not at home then, but the noisy demonstration terrified the Engels who lived next door. For Engel's parents, the incident revived painful memories of the brutal Russian pogroms that they had barely survived.

Incensed, Steven Engel charged outside to defend his family. He jabbed one protester, a "natural-born coward," in the chest with a baseball bat and warned him: "If you don't get them off my property, I'm going to beat your bloody head in." Finally, neighbors took matters into their own hands, wielding shovels and pitchforks to defend the plaintiffs. At that point, four police officers interceded and moved the picketers along. Such episodes meant that Engel's son Michael "never really left the house again" without his parents until he went to college in Binghamton, New York.

The vitriol poisoned at least one New York political primary that summer. James McGinniss, an independent Democrat, made a blatantly anti-Semitic pitch to Catholic voters in the Queens County Eleventh Assembly District. It was Jews, his campaign hinted, who removed the regents' prayer, which Catholic voters overwhelmingly supported. "These are the names you should know," the McGinniss leaflet read: "Stephen [*sic*] Engel, Daniel Lichtenstein, Monroe Lerner, Lenore Lyons, and Lawrence Roth. These people brought the legal action which resulted in the banning of the 'prayer' in our public schools." McGinniss urged Democrats to elect him "if you want a public official who will remember the 'Presence of God' and who will sponsor and work for laws which will permit us to live and raise our children as God-fearing citizens." McGinniss's coldly calculated bigotry failed, as he finished last in a three-way race, behind winner Hyman Greenberg, who lost in the general election.

Although William Butler commiserated with the Roths over the constant abuse they received, the stress of being in the vortex of the hurricane became too much for them. The Roths temporarily escaped the tumult by vacationing in New England. Before she departed, Frances Roth remarked, "I have a feeling of sadness, because these are so-called godly people. If their God teaches them to wish my kids get polio and my house be bombed, then I think He hasn't done a very good job with them."

The revilement never deterred the petitioners, in part because they also received "friendly letters and telegrams of congratulations" thanking them for their sacrifices. Lawrence Roth pushed negative thoughts aside, convinced that "there are just certain things a man's got to do." He "expected some people to be offended, but our feelings on the matter haven't changed a bit. We felt then and feel now that the state has no right to impose religion on citizens. Our country was founded by a group from England who resented imposition of religion by a state, and therefore, they formed their own state." He insisted that he was not opposed to prayer per se or to religion in general. Julia Lerner declared, "We never even considered dropping the suit. We didn't go into it lightly. We had strong feelings about this. We as people were not important. The issue was monumental, and we just lent ourselves to it."

On Monday, May 6, 1963, the Roths were subjected to yet another hate crime. After Lawrence Roth appeared on a CBS television program reviewing the case, vandals laid out gasoline-soaked rags in the form of a 5 x 10' cross on the Roths' driveway, dangerously close to an automobile gas tank. At 10 p.m., the flames shot up high in the air before the Roths noticed the blaze from their living room, where they were entertaining a visitor. Lawrence Roth and his guest rushed outside and doused the fire with a garden hose and a chemical extinguisher before the fire department arrived. "We might all have gone up in smoke," Roth remarked as he recalled the terrifying incident. As Daniel Roth returned from his girlfriend's house, he was numbed by the sight of fire engines, police cars, and a street filled with gawking neighbors. Just as the Roths began to catch their breaths, a series of anonymous telephone calls came; each time, the caller hung up without speaking. The police were put on alert because the Roths feared the cross-burning marked the resumption of the harassment campaign against them.

Frances Roth signed a complaint against the perpetrators, who were caught within days. Arthur Anderson, Bernard Koppen, John Skura, and brothers Joseph and James Losgar — all teenagers from Williston Park who attended Herricks High School — were charged with "outraging public decency," a misdemeanor, and their picture appeared in local newspapers. Police detectives described the incident as a "prank" that the young men hatched at a soda parlor to exact vengeance for the *Engel* decision. When Herricks teacher Scott Finegan learned that one of the arsonists was a student of his, he pulled the senior aside and said disgustedly, "Artie, that was the worst possible thing you could've done. And I can't stand your being sneaky and lying about it, so don't — you can talk to me in class — but don't talk to me afterwards." In the end, the delinquents were not prosecuted. Steven Engel remembered that the Roman Catholic Church "intervened" on behalf of the vandals: "Please," the church official reportedly said, "they're altar boys; they're nice kids."

The avalanche of abuse convinced the plaintiffs to shun the public limelight, lest the harassment resume, even decades later. Other litigants who challenged religious practices in the public schools — Vashti McCollum and Madalyn Murray (O'Hair), for example — wrote memoirs of their baptism of fire, but none of the five *Engel* plaintiffs, their spouses, or their children has done so.

The turmoil notwithstanding, the plaintiffs' older children were active and accomplished in school. Judith Lichtenstein was a "Mathlete," cheerleader, and dancer; a member of the Chemistry Club and the Quill and Scroll literary society; vice president of the sophomore class and the Honor Society; and editor in chief of the *Tartan* yearbook. She was voted "nonconformist" of the senior class. Her brother David was a Mathlete and vice president of the Latin Club, Symposium, and the Service Squad; president of the Honors Service Squad; and chief justice of the Student Court, an apropos activity for a member of a family that was suing the school board. David Lyons was involved in band, lacrosse, and intramural sports. Daniel Roth played tennis; wrote for the student newspaper and literary magazine; and joined the Student Court, International Relations Club, Varsity Club, and Honor Service Squad. His appropriate yearbook motto came from Ralph Waldo Emerson: "Each man is justified in his individuality."

Reaction on Long Island to the "unholy mess" created by the U.S. Supreme Court was highly negative. At Trinity Episcopal Church in Northport, the Rev. Graham Walworth erected an outdoor display that chastised the Court for helping the Soviet Union: "Congratulations [Premier Nikita] Khrushchev! School Prayer Held Illegal. God *Help* America!" In an editorial that appeared in the *New Hyde Park Courier*, Joe Meredino accused the "learned gentlemen" of the Supreme Court of not understanding the plain meaning of "establish" and "religion." The Court, Meredino concluded, was "not interested in constitutional rights but in stopping children from acknowledging God . . . any God that their own religion taught them to believe in. Getting to the children of a nation is an old trick used by others [read "communists"] who wished to 'change the world.'" The net effect of the ruling, Meredino declared, was "to drive religion out of our lives," which "we must stop somewhere." Most letter writers on Long Island agreed with Meredino. Richard DiLoreto of Jamaica expressed outrage over *Engel*: "Almighty God has been given his walking papers. He is persona non grata in America's public schools. . . . The Supreme Judge has Himself been judged and found unconstitutional by six of His peers."

Many local officials called for *Engel* to be reversed because, as one town supervisor put it, the people were "deeply upset and disturbed." Milton Gibbons, the seven-term mayor of Tuckahoe, urged the impeachment of the U.S. Supreme Court justices who sided with the plaintiffs. He personally went door to door to collect 2,000 signatures for a petition demanding a constitutional amendment. North Hempstead town supervisor Clinton Martin, whose township included the Herricks School District, asked Congressmember Steven Derounian of Manhasset to prepare legislation that would remedy the "constitutional defects" of the regents' prayer. Derounian, a naturalized citizen from Bulgaria who investigated the quiz-show scandals of the 1950s, chided the Supreme Court for "nit-picking at its worst" and called for a legislative remedy so that "the meaning of the Constitution not be further distorted." To that end, Derounian proposed a constitutional amendment reauthorizing the regents' prayer. Derounian, who was later appointed to the New York Supreme Court, was convinced that Congress would approve his amendment by an "overwhelming majority."

A variety of local organizations mobilized to oppose *Engel*. The 1,300-member General Federation of Women's Clubs, a middle-class reform organization, voted almost unanimously to support a constitutional amendment permitting voluntary, nonsectarian devotions in the public schools. The American Legion distributed 100,000 copies of a prayer and suggested that students recite it as the school day began. Although the organization claimed that it supported *Engel* in theory, it believed that the Constitution permitted students to recite a voluntary prayer. The Manhasset Republican Club had an "immediate and unfavorable" reaction from most of its 500 members. Albert Groh, the club's leader, characterized *Engel* as "a shocking affront to God-fearing, dedicated Americans. It is a triumph for godless communism. . . . This is an example of why sound thinking people must organize and make themselves heard." The Ozone Park Catholic War Veterans were "deeply shocked" by the ruling because every president had prayed for "Divine Guidance." In a letter to the U.S. Supreme Court, the veterans declared, "action of this type plays directly into the hands of the Communists, the arch-enemies of all religions."

What happened on the local level after *Engel* was magnified nationwide. Constitutional experts maintain that *Engel* was "a wildly unpopular decision," engendering more public hostility than almost any previous opinion in the Court's history, certainly since it had sanctioned slavery a century earlier. Indeed, Rodney Smith, a scholar of religious establishment jurisprudence, says the "public furor" after *Engel* was decided was "without equal in any prior case before the Supreme Court." The decision was greeted first by alarm, then anger, because *Engel* challenged Protestant hegemony and seemed to portend a full-scale attack on the civil religion of U.S. society. The *Engel* decision jolted Americans because their sense of national identity was inseparable from their religious feelings.

The nation's political class led the way in denouncing *Engel*, almost with a single voice. The two Republican ex-presidents were shocked by the decision. Herbert Hoover, a Quaker from Iowa, described the ruling as "a disintegration of one of the most sacred of American heritages." He urged Congress to act immediately to "submit an amendment to the Constitution which establishes the right to religious devotion in all governmental agencies." Dwight Eisenhower, who attended Presbyterian services, was appalled by the ruling, too. "I always thought that this nation was essentially a religious one," he said publicly. "I realize, of course, that the Declaration of Independence antedates the Constitution, but the fact remains that the Declaration was our certificate of national birth. It specifically asserts that we as individuals possess certain rights as an endowment from our Creator — a religious concept." But Eisenhower had appointed Earl Warren and William Brennan to the Court, and they had concurred in the *Engel* decision.

At the annual Conference of State Governors, then meeting in Hershey, Pennsylvania, all governors except Nelson Rockefeller of New York condemned the decision and called for a constitutional amendment overturning it. Rockefeller, a Baptist, suggested initially that, after adjustments were made, the regents' prayer could be recited, perhaps in a different form or under different conditions. He told a news conference that the spiritual foundation of the United States came from the Judeo-Christian heritage of the "brotherhood of man" under the "fatherhood of God." The inculcation of these "fundamental beliefs" was "a very important thing." The next day, however, Rockefeller sounded more pessimistic about organized school prayer because his counsel believed that a long-shot constitutional amendment would be required. George Wallace, the flamboyant governor of Alabama, had no second thoughts about the evils of *Engel:* "It is the bitter fruit of the liberal dogma that worships human intelligence and scorns the concept of divinity. . . . It is part of the deliberate design to subordinate the American people, their faith, their customs, and their religious traditions to a godless state."

In Congress, every politician who spoke the day after the Supreme Court announced *Engel* blasted the decision. Their outrage was fueled by a mixture of righteous indignation and political self-interest. The leading voice against *Engel* was Frank Becker, the Republican congressmember for Nassau County, which included the Herricks School District. He was stunned by *Engel*: "This is not the first tragic decision of the Court, but I would say it is the most tragic decision in the history of the United States, and June 25, 1962, will go down as a black day in our history." Because the U.S. Supreme Court was "writing law" in *Engel*, as Becker saw it, rather than interpreting law, he called for a constitutional amendment to permit "the offering, reading from, or listening to prayers or biblical scriptures, if participation therein is on a voluntary basis, in any governmental or public school, institution, or place." As a Roman Catholic and an American Legionnaire, Becker took the lead to do just that until his retirement in 1965. Without his zeal and adept parliamentary maneuvering, the effort to add a school prayer amendment might have fizzled quickly.

Other congressional politicians — mostly southern Democrats who were Protestant — echoed Becker's outrage. In part, white southerners saw *Engel* as yet another blow to their worldview. Already furious over the Warren Court's school desegregation decision in *Brown v. Board of Education* (1954), southern Democrats saw a heaven-sent opportunity to make political capital out of endorsing God and simultaneously destroy an institution they hated. In the most published remark, Alabama Congressmember George Andrews lambasted the Court for forcibly integrating public schools and then expelling Almighty God: "They put the Negroes in the schools; now they put God out of the schools." In fact, there was not a single black student attending a white school in Alabama at that time, but Andrews' inflammatory rhetoric was immensely popular among his white constituents.

Twisting *Engel* almost beyond recognition, southern politicians fumed that this decision was a misbegotten victory for atheism and proposed dozens of constitutional amendments to reverse it. They firmly believed that history was on their side, maintaining that the Fourteenth Amendment had not been adopted legally, thus preventing the U.S.

Supreme Court from applying the First Amendment and its establishment clause to the states. By charging ahead anyway, the Court had allegedly usurped state power in the domain of religion.

James Eastland of Mississippi, who chaired the Senate Judiciary Committee, maintained that the prayer decision "brings home to every Christian family in the nation how far down the road the U.S. Supreme Court has gone toward judicial tyranny." Eastland advanced a long-since discredited theory that the decision affected only schools in New York and was not the law of the land. "Frankly," he continued, "I don't believe that the schools of America are going to stop their morning devotions and I don't believe the President is going to call out the troops or the attorney general call out the marshals to enforce the Supreme Court's decree." In a narrow sense, Eastland was right. No president ever sent troops to enforce *Engel*, whereas two presidents — Dwight Eisenhower and John Kennedy — used armed force to desegregate public schools.

A parade of southern politicians joined Eastland in denouncing *Engel*. Senator A. Willis Robertson of Virginia, the son of a Baptist preacher and father of television evangelist Marion "Pat" Robertson, accused the justices of siding with "atheists and agnostics": "We will not stand for this any longer. You have gone as far in misinterpreting the Constitution and our form of government as we will stand for; and if you go further, you will do so at your peril." Senator Sam Ervin, Jr., a folksy, Harvard-trained lawyer and an ordained Presbyterian elder from North Carolina who memorized the Bible as a child, concluded, "The Supreme Court has held that God is unconstitutional." Senator Strom Thurmond of South Carolina, then a pillar of the Jim Crow South, inserted negative comments about *Engel* in the *Congressional Record* for ten weeks. Congressmember Eugene Siler, a Kentucky Republican, proposed amending the Constitution "so as to recognize our nation as a Christian nation and thereby legalize the prayers mentioned."

As the ramifications of *Engel* became apparent, still more southern politicians skewered the U.S. Supreme Court. "An outrageous edict!" thundered Senator Herman Talmadge from Georgia. The Court, he charged, had "set up atheism as a new religion" and "put God and the devil on an equal plane." Congressmember John Bell Williams of Mississippi, who lost an arm in World War II, discerned "a deliberately and carefully planned conspiracy to substitute materialism for spiritual values and thus to communize America." An indignant South Carolina congressmember, Mendel Rivers, could hardly restrain himself: "What is wrong with this prayer? Only a court composed of agnostics could find its defects." Rivers, a high-ranking member of the Armed Services Committee, knew of nothing in his lifetime that "could give more aid and comfort to Moscow than this bold, malicious, atheistic, and sacrilegious twist by this unpredictable group of uncontrolled despots." A Georgia gubernatorial candidate promised that if he was elected, he would "not only go to jail, but give up my life" to protect school prayer.

Some pundits perceived more than a touch of hypocrisy in these congressional complaints against *Engel*. *New York Times* columnist Anthony Lewis accused southern politicians of doing "their best to suggest that the prayer ruling only showed how equally wrong the Court had been to outlaw segregation." *Newsweek* columnist Kenneth Crawford charged southern Democrats with being "not a little demagogic" in reviling the Court. The Bible-belt Democrats, Crawford asserted, had castigated the Court for handing down "an atheistic anti-prayer, anti-church decision that will have the effect of turning American youth away from the nation's religious heritage." Such shrill accusations misrepresented Black's opinion, which confined itself to public school prayers composed and recited by government officials. Although Crawford suggested that Black's concern about religious persecution of nonconformists was "far-fetched" in the twentieth-century United States, he blamed most of the brouhaha over *Engel* on lawyers-turned-politicians who knew better.

Some politicians, particularly northern and western Democrats, tried to calm the public furor. Former president Harry Truman, a Southern Baptist, said simply, "The Supreme Court, of course, is the interpreter of the Constitution," implying that he backed the ruling. In a press conference, President John F. Kennedy, the first Roman Catholic to hold the nation's highest office, cautiously urged Americans to accept *Engel* despite their personal reactions to it. Answering a planted question, Kennedy said it was "important" to "support the Supreme Court decisions, even when we may not agree with them. In addition, we have in this case a very easy remedy, and that is to pray ourselves. And I would think that it would be a welcome reminder to every American family that . . . we can make the true meaning of prayer much more important in the lives of all our children. That power is very much open to us." He urged Americans to pray "a good deal more at home and attend our churches with a good deal more fidelity." This commonsense interpretation of the *Engel* decision was exactly what the Court had in mind.

Having been singed by religious bigotry in his quest for the presidency, Kennedy was not about to break his promise of religious neutrality in this major test. To improve his chances for reelection in 1964, Kennedy could ill afford to revive the anti-Catholicism that had tarred him with being a puppet of the pope. It was unsurprising, then, that Kennedy put the Constitution and his presidency before his church and endorsed a decision that seemed to drive religion out of politics. Kennedy also shored up support for an administration measure that would provide $1.5 billion in federal government grants, as well as loans, to church-related colleges. A Democratic strategist commented, "Logically, the Supreme Court ruling shouldn't have any bearing [on the bill], but it just gives some people the heebie-jeebies." Moreover, Kennedy genuinely liked Earl Warren for compiling a progressive record on the Court, and the president had no desire to reproach his friend. Warren, for his part, was relieved that Kennedy unequivocally and publicly supported the Court, such a marked contrast from Eisenhower's deafening silence after the *Brown* desegregation decision.

The young president's appeal for calm did not dampen the political outcry for reversing *Engel*. Over the next half-century, conservative senators and representatives proposed several methods to restore school prayer, principally via constitutional amendment, jurisdictional limitation, substantive legislation, and sense-of-Congress resolutions. It is likely that no previous Court decision spawned such congressional hostility. Nearly one thousand constitutional amendments have been proposed to overturn the regents' prayer ruling. Some measures were aimed at terminating the federal judiciary's jurisdiction over school prayer. Other proposals would have left the final determination of school prayer cases with the states' appellate courts and the U.S. courts of appeals. If *Engel* were not reversed, conservatives demanded that U.S. Supreme Court justices stand for reelection every ten years or face impeachment charges. Another tactic was to cut off federal funding for any state in which public schools did not permit voluntary prayer.

None of these proposals succeeded. Changing the Constitution to permit school prayer was a long shot at best. It was Senate Minority Leader Everett Dirksen of Illinois, a staunch Republican and staunch Presbyterian, who gauged the temper of the time: "The proposition of separation of church and state is so ingrained into our people that I doubt that such an amendment would be adopted." No "amen amendment" ever passed, though it was not for want of trying. The Founding Fathers deliberately made constitutional amendments a particularly difficult, though not impossible, political task. As the U.S. Supreme Court repeatedly excluded government-sponsored religion from public schools, public anger mounted, but the amendment process meant that the anger could not be translated into structural change.

The U.S. Supreme Court, which served as an escape valve, if not a scapegoat, on the issue of school prayer, received 5,000 letters about the *Engel* case, more than on any previous case in its history. Most of them were highly critical of the ruling. Previous controversial decisions such as the anti–New Deal "sick chicken" case had largely faded because they were not followed by other polarizing rulings. But the Warren Court had embarked on a judicial revolution, stirring the constitutional pot again and again. Major decisions concerning racial desegregation, pornography, communism, and legislative reapportionment preceded *Engel*, and major decisions concerning Bible reading, the rights of the accused, and antiwar protesters would soon follow. The Court had, for example, recently restored postal privileges to three gay magazines. Some Americans were furious at the new jurisprudence. William Bernreider, a realtor in Houston, Texas, exploded: "The Court blesses these rags peddling their photographs of nude male models, but makes a prayer to God a violation of the Constitution!"

An outcry arose from archconservatives that Chief Justice Earl Warren had to be removed. An obscure organization known as the Committee to Restore God and Prayer in Our Schools picketed the White House and waved signs that read, "The Flag Is Next" and "Remove Warren, Restore God." The Liberty Lobby, a neo-Nazi group, spread vicious rumors that Warren had murdered his father and covered it up. The most significant of these groups was the John Birch Society, founded by candymaker Robert Welch, Jr., a Baptist-turned-Unitarian. The Birchers paid for hundreds of billboards alongside the nation's highways that demanded Warren's job. The anti-Warren billboards that had sprouted following *Brown* were modified after *Engel* to add the phrases, "Save Prayer" and "Save America." The jingoistic John Birch Society members believed that Warren; Dwight Eisenhower; his brother and adviser, Milton Eisenhower, who was president of Johns Hopkins University; Central Intelligence Agency director Allen Dulles; and former secretary of state John Foster Dulles were all part of the international communist conspiracy to subvert the United States.

Chief Justice Warren was unperturbed by the call for his ouster. He said matter-of-factly, "I can understand why they were against me because I was against everything they were for." He shrugged off the billboards as the price of free speech. In his memoirs, Warren recalled that one newspaper headline screamed, "Court Outlaws God," but he chose not to respond to the rising furor because he assumed that "the hysteria concerning the decision will subside." In the meantime, he wrote to an old friend in California that there was considerable historical ignorance about the nation's past and its founding documents: "It is strange how many people, including a number of the clergy, have forgotten the essentials of American history and particularly the reason for the Bill of Rights. It bears out the statement of one writer to the effect that the only thing we learn from history is that we do not learn." Warren kept a sense of humor as a cloud of criticism enveloped him. On his apartment wall, he hung a framed cartoon from the *New Yorker* magazine in which artist James Whistler's mother embroidered a pillow cover with the words "Impeach Earl Warren."

The public outcry was so great that U.S. Supreme Court justices felt the need to respond to their critics — a highly unusual occurrence. As a prime target for the widespread hostility to *Engel*, Hugo Black received an unending series of telephone calls and at least one thousand letters. He got a "real education" from reading them — the hostile and the "nice" ones alike. He noticed that "the biggest percentage of approving letters came from Baptists, Jews, and Quakers." Such support convinced him that "it would practically require a miracle" to ratify a constitutional amendment that would overturn the First Amendment, as angry congressmembers sought.

Black had refused to respond to critics of his *Everson* and *McCollum* decisions, but he answered critical letters of *Engel* one by one. He asked Protestant correspondents this question: "How would you like it if the Catholics were to force you to say 'Hail Mary' every morning in the schools?" It was a question that recalled a deep-seated strain of anti-Catholicism in U.S. history. Black also wrote to a woman who condemned him to hell without a hearing, sarcastically urging her to have the local librarian help her find a book called the Bible — he presumed she did not have that book at home — and read the passage that urges the devout to "Pray in your own closet." As the barrage continued, Black wrote a letter to his niece, Hazel Davis, criticizing those who demanded that, to be effective, "prayer must be recited parrot-like in public places" and predicted that intelligent people would not "think this constitutional principle wrong on mature second thought." The implication of Black's remark was that those who criticized *Engel* were being driven by their emotions, not by logic or history.

In a San Francisco speech to the American Bar Association, Justice Tom Clark went public with his defense of *Engel* — an almost unprecedented step. Criticizing adverse press coverage and critical lawyers as misinformed, he declared that the Constitution provides "that both state and federal governments shall take no part respecting the establishment of religion or prohibiting the free exercise thereof. 'No' means 'No.' That was all the Court decided." Later that year, Clark wrote an article in *This Week* magazine, which accompanied Sunday newspapers across the country. In it, he criticized the "recent loud chorus" for school prayer, noting that too many parents now looked "to the state to provide spiritual training." Prayers, he argued firmly, belong at home for constitutional, religious, and social reasons.

Much of the alarm about — if not outright hostility to — the *Engel* ruling came from the Roman Catholic Church. Although the diocesan newsletters of Cleveland, Ohio; Indianapolis, Indiana; Kansas City–St. Joseph, Missouri; and Portland, Maine, agreed, at least in part, with the decision, the Catholic hierarchy overwhelmingly condemned the ruling. One bishop attacked Black's opinion for promoting atheism and suggested the need for public schools "to start bootlegging religion into the classrooms." The leading Catholic voice against the decision was Francis Cardinal Spellman of New York, who had attended public schools and "learned a reverence for God and religion" at the hands of his Protestant teachers. During World War II, Spellman became the living embodiment of the American Catholic as patriot, and he largely succeeded in bringing Catholicism into prominence for the first time in U.S. history. This image as well as his lofty position added weight to Spellman's comment that he was "shocked and frightened" by *Engel*, which "strikes at the very heart of the godly tradition in which America's children have for so long been raised." In an address to a humanitarian organization, Spellman connected the opposition to school prayer and parochial school aid as "a two-pronged attack on the American way of life." For Spellman, the purpose of this attack was "to take God out of the public schools and to force the child out of the private school."

Many Protestant organizations and leaders, though not all, supported *Engel*. After some equivocation, the National Council of Churches in Christ, which included 31 mainstream denominations, 146,000 churches, and 40 million Americans, voiced approval of *Engel* for protecting religious liberty, but insisted that public schools recognize the importance of religion in U.S. society. It cautioned the U.S. Supreme Court not to set up a "virtual Chinese Wall between religion and government." The nation's two most important Protestant journals — *Christian Century* and *Christianity Today* — the one liberal, the other conservative — endorsed *Engel* in separate editorials for protecting "the integrity of the religious conscience." Franklin Clark Fry, president of the Lutheran Church of America and a founder of the World Council of Churches and National Council of Churches, thought the decision was hardly worth noticing because the regents' prayer was a meaningless devotion. Called "Mr. Protestant" for his tireless ecumenical work, Fry commented, "When the positive content of faith has been bleached out of prayer, I am not too concerned about retaining what is left."

The Episcopalian Church moderately endorsed the decision as "a gain rather than a loss for true religion," but two prominent Episcopalians condemned it. James Pike, an attorney and the liberal bishop of San Francisco, accused the Court of having "deconsecrated the nation" in steering clear of a state church. The Rt. Rev. Percy Goddard, a suffragan bishop in Texas, compared the decision to the public prayer room in the United Nations: "They removed the cross so they wouldn't offend the Jews. They removed the Star of David so they wouldn't offend the Mohammedans. They wound up with a tree stump — a stump of nothing."

The *Engel* decision split Baptists between absolutists who had long opposed any abridgement of the wall separating church and state and a new faction that dismissed the idea as a legal fiction aimed at conservative Christians. *Engel* was endorsed by the Baptist Joint Committee on Public Affairs, which represented 17 million Baptists. Herschel Hobbs, president of the Southern Baptist Convention (SBC), confessed that what he first saw as "tragedy" was "one of the greatest blessings that could come to those of us who believe in the absolute separation of church and state." At the same time, Louie Newton, a former SBC president, remarked: "We just weren't ready for six men to tell us that our fathers and mothers were all wrong about this business of acknowledging God as the supreme ruler of the universe." Evangelist Billy Graham, the nation's most celebrated Southern Baptist minister, scorned *Engel* as "another step toward the secularization of the United States. . . . The framers of our Constitution meant we were to have freedom of religion, not freedom from religion." Graham thundered: "God pity our country when we can no longer appeal to God for help." Because the Protestant faith community as a whole was divided over *Engel*, any concerted action to overturn it was improbable.

Except for Moses Feuerstein, president of the Union of Orthodox Jewish Congregations of America, who feared that religion would be excluded from public life, the Jewish community overwhelmingly approved of the decision. Most Jewish organizations rallied behind *Engel*, many rabbis delivered sermons supporting the decision, and the Union of American Hebrew Congregations prepared a kit of materials that denied the United States was a Christian country. *American Jewish World*, a leading periodical, praised the First Amendment for permitting "the unfettered development of religion, on the one hand, and the enrichment of democracy, on the other." The American Jewish Committee, American Jewish Congress, Anti-Defamation League of B'nai B'rith, and the Synagogue Council of America, which is the coordinating body of Reform, Conservative, and Orthodox congregations, similarly hailed the decision "as a great milestone in the struggle for religious freedom" — the Jewish equivalent of the *Brown* school desegregation ruling. These groups particularly seized on President Kennedy's endorsement of *Engel*.

As counsel for the American Jewish Congress, Leo Pfeffer had been deeply concerned that the Supreme Court might uphold the regents' prayer. The outcome in *Engel* pleased him no end, and he praised the decision as consistent with the U.S. value "that religion is a private matter. The nature of our democracy is to create a society which proposes that man's relation to God is nobody's business but his own." He wondered why there was a demand for school devotions in the first place. "Is God only in the public schools?" he asked. "Why can't children be taught to pray in the home? There are certain responsibilities of parenthood which should not be forwarded to the public schools." The peripatetic Pfeffer reminded audiences across the country that "the Catholics and not the Jews" pushed for the secularization of the public schools beginning with the lawsuits of the mid-nineteenth century. Several weeks after *Engel* was announced, Pfeffer observed with considerable relief that the U.S. public had recovered its equilibrium on church-state matters and increasingly embraced the decision after widespread hostility to it. A calming influence, he thought, had come from leading national newspapers, prominent Protestant leaders, and many influential organizations that publicly supported *Engel.*

What worried Jews more than anything else about *Engel* were signs that anti-Semitism was resurfacing. The *Catholic Standard and Times* of Philadelphia warned Jews that their "anti-God" campaign would "awaken the dragon of racial and religious hatreds which sleeps restlessly in our midst." The Jesuits' highly regarded magazine *America* published a condescending editorial, "To Our Jewish Friends," which mirrored Roman Catholic wrath everywhere. The magazine called the decision "asinine," "unrealistic," "doctrinaire," and "stupid," one that "spits in the face of our history, our tradition, and our heritage as a religious people." In the magazine editor's view, this outrageous decision could be laid directly at the feet of a "small but overly vocal segment" within Jewry, especially the American Jewish Congress as well as atheists and the ACLU, the Ethical Culture Society, and Unitarians. *America* accused these groups of seeking not only to eliminate prayer in public schools but to eliminate funding to parochial schools altogether. Such a prospect was intolerable. The "time has come," the editorial went on, "for these fellow citizens of ours to decide among themselves precisely what they conceive to be the final objective of the Jewish community in the United States — in a word, [they must decide] what bargain they are willing to strike as one of the minorities in a pluralistic society." The Catholic weekly did not mention that the Catholic president, John Kennedy, endorsed the ruling.

Most Jews were appalled by the article. The Synagogue Council of America and the National Jewish Community Relations Advisory Council scored *America*'s editorial as "repugnant" for its suggestion that "any group must barter its right to free speech in exchange for its security." American Jewish Congress president Joachim Prinz, who was forced to make the sign of the cross as a schoolchild in Germany, said it was a sorry day for religious liberty when efforts to safeguard the First Amendment "should evoke thinly veiled threats of anti-Semitism from so respectable a journal of opinion as *America*." Sidney Regner, executive director of the Central Conference of American Rabbis, and Albert Vorspan, director of social action for the Union of American Hebrew Congregations, blasted *America*'s "threatening and patronizing" editorial: "In the guise of a kindly warning, *America* is encouraging the very evil it claims to be trying to avert. It is not the United States Supreme Court, nor those who support the law of the land, who are arousing religious tension in America. If there is a 'harvest of fear' in America, it is caused by those who have planted seeds in a highly charged emotional attack upon those who support the Supreme Court decision." Vorspan and Regner wondered aloud what Catholic reaction would be if a Jewish magazine published an editorial entitled, "To Our Catholic Friends," warning Roman Catholics to stop campaigning for government money to parochial schools lest a wave of anti-Catholic bigotry surface.

To dampen the blazing controversy, *Commonweal*, a liberal lay Catholic periodical, rebuked its sister journal. *Commonweal* thought that the prayer decision was "crude, legalistic, and naïve," but asserted that *America* had chosen a "very odd" method of combating any signs of rising anti-Semitism. "If there is . . . any real danger of anti-Semitism among Catholics," *Commonweal* told its readership, "then it is the Catholics who ought to be warned. . . . It does little good — as Catholics ought to know — to be told, much less warned, by others whether to press one's claims or not. . . . If the result of the prayer decision is to break down community relations, the fault of this breakdown will lie with those Americans who single out particular groups to blame for the decision."

During the summer and fall of 1962, the widespread dissatisfaction over *Engel* spilled over into the educational arena. A national survey conducted by the *Nation's Schools* journal revealed that 50 percent of school administrators returning the questionnaire wanted the *Engel* decision reversed; 48 percent of them supported it. An Idaho administrator remarked, "I feel that the Court has placed itself in the position of making laws rather than interpreting them." Sterling McMurrin, U.S. commissioner of education and a former philosophy professor and Mormon Church official, tried to put a positive spin on the decision: "I believe it is no loss to religion but may be a gain in clarifying the matter. Prayer that is essentially a ceremonial classroom function has not much religious value." Edgar Fuller, executive secretary of the Council of Chief State School Officers, a nonpartisan, nonprofit national lobbying group, likewise viewed the decision favorably: "My judgment is that the Supreme Court is right. . . . *Engel* [will] make the schools a little more strictly secular for the peace of mind of the minorities."

Some Long Island school districts followed and others defied the U.S. Supreme Court decision. At the time of the *Engel* ruling, a survey of sixty-one districts showed that forty-six of them had provided time for prayer or meditation. Of these forty-six, eighteen superintendents said *Engel* left them no choice but to comply with the decision, twenty others said they would wait for their school boards to deliberate on the ruling, and eight vowed to resist. Four of the resisting districts — Bridgehampton, Freeport, Mattituck, and Port Jefferson Station-Terryville — insisted that *Engel* did not foreclose their continued use of the Lord's Prayer. As an alternative, school officials in Baldwin, East Meadow, Herricks, Malverne, and New Hyde Park instituted periods for silent meditation in lieu of the regents' prayer.

Herricks teachers were required by the school board to provide a moment of silence in place of the regents' prayer, and for the most part, the religiously neutral substitute was implemented smoothly. In the beginning, the question inevitably arose about the purpose of the exercise. One student asked, "Do we have to think religious?" Scott Finegan, the social studies teacher who rejected the Catholicism of his youth, replied, "You can think dirty thoughts if you want to. Just keep quiet, that's all. Let everybody else do what they want to do." Once in awhile, a student would refuse to stand for the moment of silence. The rest of the students tried to pressure their defiant classmate. "Oh, just get up," they demanded. "No, I'm not going to," came the reply. More often, defiant students remained seated and were ignored by teacher and classmates alike.

Elsewhere on Long Island, school officials had difficulty coming to terms with *Engel.* One defiant superintendent remarked, "A school without a prayer is not a school." New Hyde Park School Board Trustee Emil Bobek agreed: "To eliminate prayer completely from our schools is to substitute atheism by default." Levittown School Board President Robert Hoshino, an admirer of Joe McCarthy, excoriated the ruling for playing "right into Khrushchev's hands." He vowed that his district would "not vote out the Regents' prayer" because most historical documents "give recognition of God." Hoshino interpreted *Engel* as outlawing only state-mandated prayer and argued that local school districts could legally order that same prayer. The board contemplated calling together religious leaders in the community to draft a nonsectarian prayer that would be put to a vote by area taxpayers.

In Hicksville, School Board President Robert Eaton drafted his own thirty-word "nonsectarian" prayer for board approval. Asserting that 90 percent of district residents backed school prayer, Eaton issued a defiant promise: "If [Education] Commissioner [James] Allen won't stand up and fight, we will." Allen replied that such statements did not provide a good example for schoolchildren. At the next school board meeting, the proceedings erupted into a shouting match over the meaning of *Engel* and the legality of school prayer, and Eaton was forced to scream for order. The board finally rejected Eaton's prayer in favor of the fourth stanza of the "Star-Spangled Banner." Hicksville resident Howard Van Allen circulated petitions to challenge the board's action, but he obtained only 450 of the 6,000 necessary to force a referendum.

In the wake of such open defiance, particularly on Long Island, New York officials had to respond. Attorney General Louis Lefkowitz, a close associate of Governor Nelson Rockefeller, interpreted *Engel* as banning prescribed prayers, not necessarily prayer in general. Charles Brind, counsel to the New York Board of Education, went further, declaring that it was illegal for students to recite a prayer, even a "voluntary" prayer. He did concede that silent meditation was probably permissible and that the state would not object to it. Frederick Morse, the regents' secretary, declared that the board was "law-abiding," but wondered whether school Christmas pageants were permissible; whether the board had a legal obligation to enforce compliance with *Engel,* since it had never required the regents' prayer; and whether it had to stop New York City students from reciting the fourth stanza of "America," which ends with the words, "Protect us by Thy might, Great God, our King."

Despite being surprised by *Engel*, New York education commissioner James Allen took the lead in supporting it. He admitted, "The ruling comes as a disappointment because I felt [the regents' prayer] was not a violation of the U.S. or state constitutions, nor a violation of the principle of separation of church and state." But Allen respected the principle of constitutionalism and ordered all public schools to comply with the decision. He expected complete compliance by the fall, when emotions likely would have abated and schools reopened. At the same time, Allen had no plans to monitor the schools to verify compliance. He would act against a district only in the event legal action was threatened. School prayer subsequently proved to be a minor distraction to Allen, whose tenure was increasingly preoccupied with racial desegregation. For handling the education challenges of a large state with aplomb, Allen was named U.S. commissioner of education in 1969.

As New York State education officials urged quick compliance with *Engel*, leaders in half of the other states breathed open defiance to it, at least initially. Rual Stephens, deputy superintendent of schools in Atlanta, Georgia, vowed, "We will not pay any attention to the Supreme Court ruling." At the same time that Stephens defied the Court on school prayer, he was "gingerly" implementing the Court's eight-year-old ruling on school desegregation. In Alabama, W. A. Lecroy, the fire-breathing state superintendent of education, insisted that public schools should retain religious practices "regardless of what the Supreme Court says." South Carolina education superintendent Jesse Anderson regretted that "the issue would even come up" and predicted that schools in his state would continue reciting prayers. State officials in Mississippi, North Carolina, and South Carolina passed off to the teachers the responsibility for following *Engel*. Some states beyond Dixie also retained religious practices in the public schools. In New Jersey, the state attorney general ruled that grace before meals was illegal in public school classrooms, but the state supreme court upheld the reading of five Old Testament verses each day and permitted the recital of the Lord's Prayer. Owen Kiernan,

Massachusetts education commissioner, noted that *Engel* did not mention Bible reading, so that practice would continue in the Bay State.

As formal religious exercises were outlawed, or at least questioned, some Christian parents considered alternatives to the public school system. One possibility was to withdraw their children from the public schools and put them into parochial schools, a practice that was common even for Protestants in the late nineteenth century. Another possibility was "shared time" or "dual enrollment," an idea advanced by Harry Stearns, superintendent of schools in Englewood, New Jersey. Stearns proposed that children attending church-affiliated schools be permitted to take some courses in public high schools. Children could attend their own schools for religion and history and attend public schools for gifted education and instruction in "neutral" subjects such as mathematics, foreign languages, natural sciences, music, home economics, vocational education, and physical education. The idea was meant to apply to children of all major faiths, though it was almost exclusively a program for the Roman Catholic Church. In this way, Catholic schools could cut costs and Catholic parents could get some use out of the public schools they supported with their taxes. Protestant leaders hoped that shared time would head off Catholic demands for direct government aid to parochial schools, a notion they deemed unconstitutional.

Heretofore, Protestant parents had shown little interest in shared time because public schools provided a modicum of acceptable religious instruction to their children. Such instruction reinforced the religious training their children received at home and in Sunday schools. The *Engel* decision apparently forced some parents to face the fact that their children received little in the way of solid religious education, even if they faithfully attended Sunday school. One estimate was that Protestant children received only twenty-five hours of religious instruction from all sources in a year. Because Protestant churches already had classrooms that went unused six days a week, church officials considered recruiting a professional staff who could teach a curriculum with a high "value" content, including English, history, and such explicitly religious courses as Bible study. By the late 1960s, thirty-five states had at least one school system with shared time programs in education.

For all of the initial fears expressed about *Engel*, the larger import of the case was to uphold constitutionalism, as construed by the Supreme Court, and to recognize that the United States was being transformed from a largely Protestant country to an increasingly pluralistic nation. As Independence Day approached, *Newsweek* magazine wrote presciently, "The upsurge of fury will subside, but the electrifying impact of the decision — striking at the very core of cherished customs — is likely to rumble through much of American church, political, and personal life for some time. But disruptive as the ruling may seem now, eventually what so many view as a violation of sacred traditions may be seen as a judgment which reaffirmed and strengthened these same traditions, expressed in Philadelphia just 186 years ago this week. When the tumult and the shouting have died, the New York prayer decision may well be hailed as a landmark in the never-ending search to strike a proper balance between church and state." The shouting would take decades to subside, as *Newsweek* predicted, in no small measure because of the lawsuit brought by the founder of modern atheism in the United States.

CHAPTER 8

"The Most Hated Woman in America"

The tumult touched off by *Engel* in the summer of 1962 continued the following year, when the U.S. Supreme Court forbade public schools from reciting the Lord's Prayer and reading from the Bible. In two cases, *School District of Abington Township v. Schempp* and *Murray v. Curlett,* the question before the Court was whether school officials in Pennsylvania and Baltimore, Maryland, could require students to participate in daily devotions, including listening to Bible verses and reciting the Lord's Prayer. These cases had broad implications because thirty-nine states either required or permitted Bible reading in public school classrooms.

In Pennsylvania, Bible reading had existed in the public schools before the Civil War. In 1913, the state legislature voted to require the practice to help young people develop lives of "good moral training," "honorable thought," and "good citizenship." As the Cold War divided the world into two camps — one democratic and God-fearing, the other communistic and atheistic — many U.S. politicians believed that Bible reading was indispensable to the nation's survival. With that thought in mind in 1949, the state required Pennsylvania public schoolteachers to read ten Bible verses without comment every school day or face dismissal. In Baltimore's public schools, the Bible had been required "as a reading book" since 1839, a rule that was superseded in 1905 by a requirement for daily devotions consisting of a chapter from the King James or Douay Versions of the Bible and/or recital of the Lord's Prayer.

The *Schempp* case arose in 1956 when sixteen-year-old Ellory Schempp, a popular honors student and track athlete at Abington High School in suburban Philadelphia, objected to the required scripture reading. Every day at 8:20 A.M., a few students led their classmates in a familiar ritual. Using the public address system, they opened with a "fact for the day" to get the rest of the students thinking, followed by ten Bible verses, the Lord's Prayer, the salute to the flag, and school announcements. Although state law did not require the Lord's Prayer to be recited in public schools, the Abington School District mandated it anyway. In the lower grades, which were attended by Ellory's younger sister, Donna, and brother, Roger, entire classes recited the Lord's Prayer with bowed heads and closed eyes. In the junior high and high schools, teachers asked a student in each classroom to read scripture. The school provided a King James Bible, but the student chosen to read sacred text could use a different version, including the Revised Standard (Protestant), Douay (Catholic), or Old Testament (Jewish) scriptures.

In Ellory's homeroom, some boys thought it would be amusing to read Old Testament passages that had sexual overtones. Ellory himself chose the Song of Solomon, which contains a series of erotic poems about two lovers. In one passage he read, a bride and groom frankly admire their physical features and hint at the consummation of their love. After their adolescent humor fell flat, the students found the whole procedure tiresome. Treated like robots, the students were told what to do and when to do it. For Ellory, it added up to "mumble, stand, mumble some more, then sit down." It became so meaningless, that he compared the exercise to "peeing — you just do it; it has no meaning."

Before long, Ellory became deeply offended by such indoctrination as patently unconstitutional. He had been taught to think for himself, surrounded as he was by supportive liberal adults — his parents, his church leaders, and his teachers. Ellory's father, Edward Schempp, a self-taught electronics engineer, could not believe in the Old Testament's bloodthirsty God of vengeance, and he completely rejected the idea that the sins of the fathers would be visited on their sons, even to the fourth generation. Raised in the Unitarian tradition of free thought, Ellory likewise rejected core Christian teachings about Jesus of Nazareth — that Jesus was conceived by the Holy Spirit and was part of a triune godhead — which had been asserted in biblical passages read in homeroom. Ellory examined the First Amendment in his social studies class, and it dawned on him that the devotions in his own school violated the law.

Ellory's mentor, English teacher Allan Glatthorn, assigned weekly essays on timely issues and urged his students to meet outside class to continue the discussions. Ellory and a dozen friends met at each other's homes on Thursday nights, talking about "everything from politics to civil rights to sex." "It was a wonderful forum for testing ideas," Ellory recalled. One night, school prayer and Bible reading came up. Although Ellory's circle agreed that these devotions were probably unconstitutional, "a lot of them thought it was trivial — who cares?" A few friends, including a Roman Catholic and a Greek Orthodox, made a compact to protest the devotions, but "they all chickened out when they thought of the principal calling their parents. So it came down to me," Ellory remembered, which was "a little scary." As a teenager, he did not grasp the enormity of the matter: "In my naiveté, I thought I could point out the error and someone would make things right. I don't think I understood the extent of how jolting this would be to the American public."

On Monday, November 26, 1956, Ellory borrowed a copy of the Qur'an from a friend and began reading it silently while Bible verses were read over the public address system. He continued reading at his desk when the rest of his classmates stood to recite the Lord's Prayer. Ellory later told reporters that he picked the Qur'an because "I wanted to indicate that Christ and the Bible were not the only holy scriptures of the world." Ellory stood to say the Pledge of Allegiance, but this did not pacify his flabbergasted homeroom teacher, who rushed over to tell him: "You know you have to obey the rules about Bible reading." Ellory replied, "I've been thinking about that, and I have decided that in good conscience I can no longer participate." Ellory admitted that he was "terribly, terribly nervous, nervous as a cat."

Ellory's homeroom teacher was taken aback by his recalcitrance and ordered him to the principal's office. The lonely walk down the school corridor began a journey that led to the U.S. Supreme Court. The principal, W. Eugene Stull, was furious over Ellory's protest and tried to isolate him in a face-to-face conference. Stull asserted that Ellory was the only Unitarian he knew who would protest Bible reading and the only student of the 1,100 Abington high schoolers who did not "show respect" for mandatory devotions. Ellory defended himself by citing the First Amendment, only to find himself shuffled off to the guidance counselor's office for months.

To stop the devotions, Ellory laboriously typed a letter to the American Civil Liberties Union (ACLU), with his parents' full blessing.

They were, after all, ACLU members. "Gentlemen," Ellory wrote rather pretentiously, "I thank you for any help you might offer in freeing American youth in Pennsylvania from this gross violation of their religious rights as guaranteed in the first and foremost Amendment in our United States Constitution." To entice the ACLU to pay attention to his letter, Ellory enclosed a $10 check. The ACLU did not need an inducement because it had been looking for a plaintiff for years, going so far as to ask Joseph Lewis, president of the Freethinkers of America, if he could find a petitioner to stop Bible reading.

ACLU attorney Bernard Wolfman, a University of Pennsylvania law professor, interviewed the Schempp family to determine the feasibility of filing a lawsuit. Ellory's parents told Wolfman, "Talk to the kids," then abruptly left the room. After pointing out that the community might well be hostile to a legal challenge against Bible reading, Wolfman asked the children to whom they prayed. Twelve-year-old Donna replied, "You are Jewish, aren't you? Well, Unitarians are like Jews and they are individualistic." When Edward Schempp returned to the room, Wolfman asked whether the elder Schempp wanted to proceed. The father replied, "If the children agree, we will support them." Wolfman was impressed by this "attractive, well-balanced" family which was "very keen mentally." He recommended that the ACLU take the case. "How could I not, after this?" he asked rhetorically.

As it turned out, the ACLU Philadelphia affiliate had doubts about the case. The board of directors split down the middle over whether it could pay for such a lawsuit. Board chair Charles Byse, the Harvard law professor who inspired the television show *The Paper Chase*, cast the deciding vote in favor. Although he was Roman Catholic and regarded Bible reading as a source of morality, Byse was convinced that the Abington School District had abridged the establishment clause. The ACLU spent the next year soliciting other plaintiffs of various religious convictions and mapping out its legal strategy. The ACLU particularly hoped for a "*real* Christian family." When no one else in Abington signed up other than the Schempps, the ACLU proceeded with the suit anyway, cautioning that legal action could take five years.

At the trial, the Schempps told the federal district court that a literal reading of the Bible ran contrary to their religious beliefs. Expert testimony on the Bible followed. Rabbi Solomon Grayzel, a distinguished scholar who had translated the Torah into English, outlined the harm that could come from presenting religious works in a public school environment. In Judaism, scriptures are sources to be studied and not merely recited, as they were in the Abington School District. The rabbi maintained that Bible reading without study would degenerate into an empty ritual. Moreover, he observed, there are marked differences between Jewish and Christian scriptures besides the obvious one that the New Testament is found only in the Christian Bible. Grayzel noted that the concept that Jesus is the son of God was "practically blasphemous" to Jews. Grayzel also examined the crucifixion account in which Jews ask for condemnation: "His [Jesus'] blood be on us, and our children," a phrase, Grayzel commented, that had been "the cause of more anti-Jewish riots throughout the ages than anything else in history."

Abington school officials argued that Bible reading was not a religious practice: "It requires only that those who wish to do so may listen to daily readings without discussion or comment from a great work that possesses many values. . . . [It] does not involve proselytizing, persuasion, or religious indoctrination. It involves no avowal of faith, acceptance of doctrine, or statement of belief." The school board attorneys went so far as to contend that even if Bible reading were religious, the practice need not be outlawed because the Constitution does not require government to be "hostile to religion." To outlaw Bible reading, the school board attorneys alleged, would blaze a trail that would eliminate from public life customs that "are now and have long been cherished and accepted by a vast majority of the people."

The Schempps anticipated that their lawsuit would result in harassment, if not worse. "We figured we would be the objects of a certain amount of hate," Edward Schempp said. In the mail, the Schempp family received hundreds of New Testaments and letters that opposed them by a two-to-one margin. One postcard read, "You must be either Catholics, Jews, or Communists. Why don't you go back to Russia?" Vandals pelted the Schempp home with rotten fruit and smeared dog feces on the doorknobs. At school, the younger Schempp children were hounded and beaten, which caused fourteen-year-old Roger to develop a stuttering problem that compounded his learning difficulties. As the afternoon school bus passed by the Schempp home, the youngsters pointed to the "Commie camp" or the "devil's house." The harassment occurred despite efforts by the Schempps to portray themselves as religious. A posed photograph of them reading the Bible at home appeared in the local newspaper.

The mistreatment of Ellory was especially serious because his future was on the line. Principal Stull found out where Ellory had applied to college and urged institutions of higher learning to reject him as a "troublemaker," if not a communist. When Tufts University in Boston, Massachusetts, nonetheless accepted Ellory for its new class, Stull escalated his campaign by calling on Tufts to rescind Ellory's admission. Tufts very much wanted the gifted science student and declined to reject him. In the end, Ellory continued his outstanding academic performance, graduating from Tufts with Phi Beta Kappa honors and then earning a doctorate in nuclear physics at Brown University. He subsequently helped to develop magnetic resonance imaging (MRI) diagnostic technology, worked at the Lawrence Berkeley National Laboratory, and managed a firm specializing in high technology superconductors.

In 1959, a federal district court ruled that Bible reading and the Lord's Prayer in Abington High School were unconstitutional because such practices illegally established religion. The court held that the Bible is "primarily a book of worship," which the school used for "the promotion of religious education." As the school district appealed the decision, the Pennsylvania state legislature rushed to save the law by excusing students from participation in religious rituals, provided their parents sent written notes to school. Edward Schempp charged that the amendment of state law did not change the establishment of religion, but decided against asking school officials to excuse his children. He thought that if his children were excused and stood outside the classroom door they would miss important school announcements and be stigmatized as "oddballs," called "un-American," and tied to "atheistic communism."

In February 1962, the same federal court ruled against Pennsylvania's excusal provision because Christianity was still promoted at taxpayer expense. Chief Judge John Biggs, Jr. wrote: "The fact that some pupils, or theoretically all pupils, might be excused from attendance at the exercise does not mitigate the obligatory nature of the ceremony. . . . Since the statute required the reading of the 'Holy Bible,' a Christian document, the practice . . . prefers the Christian religion." The latest setback prompted the Abington School District to appeal the decision to the U.S. Supreme Court, at which point the case was consolidated with a similar case that had arisen from Baltimore, Maryland.

In 1960, Madalyn Murray, a forty-one-year-old social worker, sued to stop Baltimore public schoolteachers from reading the Bible aloud and leading their students in reciting the Lord's Prayer. Murray's lawsuit against such "brainwashing" was the first since the rule had been implemented a half-century earlier. She explained that as an atheist she doubted "the historicity of Jesus Christ" and denied the "efficacy of prayer." More importantly, in her view, "state-sponsored religious practice for children" violated the First Amendment because the school subjected their "freedom of conscience to the rule of the majority." Murray's recollection is that her fourteen-year-old son, William III, made the momentous decision to resist saying the prayer and called her a "hypocrite" for not having the courage of her convictions to support him. According to Murray, William said, "I don't know if there is a God or if there isn't, but I do believe one thing: it's fruitless to pray to him if there is one, and damn stupid to pray if there isn't, and no one should be forced into doing either one." William's recollection is that his domineering mother coerced him to support her complaint.

Exactly why Madalyn Murray, who was raised Presbyterian and had her sons baptized, became antireligious remains ambiguous. Whatever her motivation, she attacked religion as a dangerous superstition that created a repressive society. Only irrational people, she wrote in a letter to *Life* magazine, would follow a "nauseating" Bible that was "replete with the ravings of madmen" and a God who was "sadistic" and "brutal." An atheist, by contrast, "loves his fellow man instead of God" and "believes that a hospital should be built instead of a church." As for the Lord's Prayer, which was mandated in her son's school, Murray said that people who uttered it were mere "worms, groveling for meager existence in a traumatic, paranoid world." Religion, she concluded, did not belong in public education because children should be prepared to address problems on earth, not get ready for heaven — "a delusional dream of the unsophisticated minds of the ill-educated clergy."

Madalyn Murray found herself increasingly alienated from a "decadent" U.S. society in which a capitalist economy abandoned the poor.

As she drifted from job to job, Murray gravitated to socialism and tried to defect to the "strong and beautiful nation" of Russia, which had launched *Sputnik*, the first artificial satellite. When Moscow rejected her application — a turn of events she blamed on a sinister CIA — she returned to Baltimore and enrolled her son William in the ninth grade at Woodbourne Junior High School. As they walked down the long hallway to the school office, they passed by classrooms with students reciting the Lord's Prayer. Enraged, Murray barreled into the administrative office and tore into the young school counselor. "Why are those fucking children praying?" she shouted. "It's un-American and unconstitutional." The flustered counselor completed an enrollment form and marked it with a large "T" for "troublemaker." When Murray persisted in her outburst, he finally challenged her: "If you don't like it, why don't you sue us?"

A light went on in Madalyn Murray's mind, and she vowed to become an atheist Joan of Arc, committed to the destruction of God and the Church. She once described herself as an "offensive, unlovable, bull-headed, defiant, aggressive slob" who loved "a good fight." All of those qualities would come into play in the fight of her life. The key part of Murray's battle plan to end school prayer was for her son William to record every classroom activity with religious overtones. William reluctantly played along with his mother's plan, but had no interest in her crusade, preferring to watch television, hang out with his friends, and chase girls. Insisting that William be her spy, Murray delivered a Marxist harangue tinged with anti-Semitism: "Listen, kid, the United States of America is nothing more than a fascist slave labor camp run by a handful of Jew bankers in New York City. They trick you into believing you're free with those phony rigged elections. . . . The only way true freedom can be achieved is through the new socialist man." William came to consider *Murray v. Curlett* — a case against organized religion in public education — as his mother's plan to get even with God and to persuade the Soviet Union, an officially atheist country, to grant her citizenship.

Furious over the school's ongoing religious activities, Murray kept William home for almost three weeks on "strike." She sent registered letters to school officials explaining why her son was truant, but received no reply. Tired of being ignored, she wrote a plaintive letter to the *Baltimore Sun*, defending atheists as persecuted people, like Jews, and objecting to the "collective madness" of prayer in the public square. Although her letter went unpublished, it did attract the newspaper's attention and led to a front-page photograph and feature article about her son, including the entire text of his school paper on the Soviet Union. The shocking headline read, "Boy, 14, Balks at Bible Reading." The David versus Goliath story implied that William's motivation in challenging school devotions stemmed from communism. Murray declared that she felt so strongly about the matter that she would fight it by going on a hunger strike in jail and litigating all the way to the U.S. Supreme Court.

The news created a national sensation, and Madalyn Murray milked the developing story for all it was worth. In contrast to every other school prayer plaintiff before or since, Murray assiduously cultivated the media, providing reporters with free beer, scripts of her next actions, and an endless stream of quotable comments. According to her son, Murray was a "perfect media maven" who loved being a celebrity — even one stigmatized as "the most hated woman in America." She reveled in the contributions that arrived in the mail from atheists, communists, Orthodox Jews, and antigovernment conservatives. A particularly generous donation came from Carl Brown, a wealthy wheat farmer who gave her $5,000 and 160 acres of land to found an atheist/nudist university near Centralia, Kansas. With two young sons to support, as well as her mother, alcoholic father, and chronically unemployed brother, Murray desperately needed every donation.

When the case came to the attention of the Maryland chapter of the ACLU, it advised Madalyn Murray to return William to the school immediately so a workable church-state case could be developed. But the relationship between Murray and her private attorney, Fred Weisgal, who chaired the local ACLU legal committee, was tempestuous and short-lived. According to Murray's recollection, Weisgal opposed the case almost from the beginning. He told her, "You are wrong, wrong, wrong, Madalyn. I know in my heart you are wrong. You should not be doing this. I went to public schools. I'm a Jew. *I* had to say that prayer to Jesus Christ. *I* had to go through what your son is going through. Look at me. Did it change me? Does a Jew accept Jesus Christ because he hears about him in public schools constantly?" When Murray defended her course of action, Weisgal said flatly, "You, Madalyn, are some sort of nut. You see injustice everywhere you look. . . . What do you hope to gain?" Such sentiments offended Murray, who was in any case upset about Weisgal's strategy of letting other school prayer cases come ahead of hers, potentially making hers moot.

The national office of the ACLU refused to take the case, repelled by Murray's admission that her financial backers were rabid anti-Semites and preoccupied by the *Schempp* case in Pennsylvania and the *Chamberlin v. Dade County Board of Public Instruction* case in Florida, which were similar to Murray's case but not tainted by atheism. Murray retorted, "The ACLU can go to hell, and take their opinions with them."

That left Murray's fate in the hands of Leonard Kerpelman, a thirty-two-year-old Baltimore attorney who sought out high-profile, if sometimes wacky, cases, including one involving bullfighting. He had pestered the Murrays to let him represent them, even though it opened him to the charge of being an ambulance chaser. (Twenty years later, Kerpelman would be disbarred for unprofessional conduct.) Murray was not impressed with Kerpelman, whose scruffy appearance and physical deformities were off-putting, but she had nowhere else to turn.

They were an odd couple to be sure: Madalyn Murray was an unapologetic atheist and anti-Semite who called her attorney a "grossly inept little Jew, Sammy the Shyster"; Leonard Kerpelman was an Orthodox Jew who later gained notoriety for jumping into public fountains fully clothed. For all his weaknesses, Kerpelman offered to work without a fee, and, as a graduate of the Baltimore public schools, he could fully empathize with William because both of them had endured mandated devotions. Still, Kerpelman seemed to be nearly hopeless in oral argument, so Murray, who had graduated from the YMCA's South Texas College of Law but never passed the bar exam, did much of the legal work herself.

Once Woodbourne school officials recognized what Murray was up to, they tried to forestall a lawsuit in two ways. The administration proposed a deal: if the Murrays dropped the school prayer lawsuit, the school would allow William to graduate; if they kept on, he would be ineligible for graduation because he had not completed all of his homework while on strike. The Murrays declined the offer. At the same time, school officials kept William out of homeroom so that he would not hear the devotions and therefore have no case. Male teachers escorted William to the administrative office, where he filled out paperwork, took aptitude tests, and received counseling.

After two weeks of this cat-and-mouse game, William entered the school building through a back door and sneaked into his homeroom. The tall, muscular youngster was impossible to miss, but his teacher believed that the office had cleared him to return. As the prayer began, William's heart was pounding as he blurted out: "This is ridiculous." He then grabbed his coat and books and stormed out. "Communist pig," a classmate hissed at William as he departed. When William told his mother what had happened, she laughed with glee: "That's great, Bill. Let's see what they do about this!" Thus was set into motion the challenge to another prayer, this one not written by school officials as in the *Engel* case, but an officially sanctioned prayer nonetheless.

William Murray endured all manner of harassment. He was assaulted daily on the playground. His classmates — some of whom were children of Polish and Hungarian Catholics who had broken through the iron curtain — taunted him as a "Commie lover! Why don't you move to Russia?" William thought to himself, "We tried, but they wouldn't take us!" William's classmates punched, kicked, and spat upon him as he made his way down the school corridors. Boys used rosaries as weapons, swinging the attached metal crosses to lacerate William's skin. At one point, hoodlums cornered William and shoved him in front of a city bus. Teachers shunned William, allegedly on Principal Dorothy Duval's orders. When Madalyn Murray complained to Duval about this abuse at "Stalag Woodbourne," the principal purportedly replied, "Why should I be concerned with your son's special rights, when you and he both flagrantly disregard the rights of our Christian children in the school?" Another time, Murray barged into the vice principal's office and threatened to kill "that son of a bitch" unless the violence against William stopped. The principal's answer was to isolate William from his classmates, designating where he could enter the school and forbidding him to use the library or cafeteria.

Madalyn Murray herself endured month after month of heavy abuse. Taunters spat in her face so much that spittle dripped on her dress. She was called a "dirty atheist," an "anti-Christ," a "slut," and a "masculine lesbian bitch," and was threatened with murder unless she left town. A letter smeared with feces accused her of bestiality and threatened to "kill you, kill you, kill, kill, kill, kill, kill." Postal workers tampered with her mail, forwarded the contents to the Communist Party, or delivered empty envelopes. Crank telephone calls came incessantly, day and night. Some callers tried to convert the Murrays; others cursed them, breathed heavily into the telephone, slammed receivers in their ears, or jammed their telephone line so that no one else could call. False telephone orders ruined their credit. The Murray flower garden was trampled upon, the car tires slashed, the electricity short-circuited, and their home pelted with buckshot and stones. Murray was arrested for having barking dogs, and the family cat's neck was wrung. When Murray complained about the abuse, the police arrived belatedly and, she claimed, treated her like a " 'Nigger' in a white block."

As the controversy escalated, Maryland attorney general C. Ferdinand Sybert issued an opinion stating that all students had to attend school, even if they objected to the Lord's Prayer. In his view, children "had the right and the duty to bow their heads in humility before the Supreme Being." Anyone who was absent from school, except for reasons of ill health, could be prosecuted for truancy. Sybert, who graduated from Catholic preparatory schools and Loyola College of Maryland, conceded that any student who did not say the prayer might well be embarrassed, but such was "the inevitable consequence of dissent." He recommended that students who objected to devotions be permitted to remain silent, or, if their parents submitted a written request, be excused from the exercise. The Baltimore School Board, led by President John Curlett, took the attorney general's advice and directed all of the district schools to make sure that excused students were not held up to "ridicule or scorn." In the first week after the new excusal rule was adopted, only 3 students, including Murray's sons, asked to be excused, out of a district student population of 170,000.

After the Maryland Court of Appeals ruled against her case in April 1962, Madalyn Murray became an ever-more-visible target. The Federal Bureau of Investigation (FBI) opened a file on her after she wrote a letter to the *Washington Post* protesting the government's censorship of the *Daily Worker*, a communist newspaper. The day after appealing her school prayer case to the U.S. Supreme Court, Murray was fired from her job as a caseworker for the Baltimore Department of Public Welfare. Her supervisor claimed that Murray had "brought disgrace" to the city by her actions. William contends that his mother was fired for not passing the state bar exam within a year of beginning employment, which had been stipulated at the time of hiring. To stay afloat financially, Murray worked for the Communist Party, managing its left-wing bookstore and recruiting new party members.

As their world came apart, the Murrays learned of the related case being fought against Bible reading in nearby Pennsylvania. Hoping for moral support, the Murrays drove up to Abington to meet the Schempps. The meeting was a disaster. In Madalyn Murray's eyes, the Schempps were hypocrites and cowards because, she claimed, they were really atheists who attended the Unitarian Church as a "cover" for their unconventional convictions. Edward Schempp admitted to speaking to and writing for a free-thought group, but was apparently worried about jeopardizing his livelihood if his atheism became publicly known. Murray deeply resented Schempp's decision to keep his children in homeroom so that they would not be lumped with "atheists" and "traitors" during the Cold War.

Still, the Murrays charged ahead to the nation's highest court. On the day of oral argument, attorney Leonard Kerpelman hesitated to enter the U.S. Supreme Court building. "I can't go in. I'm afraid," he blurted out. His fears may have been because he realized that his case was based on Murray's superficial research and his own unsophisticated arguments. Murray finally steadied Kerpelman enough to proceed into the hallowed room, only to be horrified when the clerk cried, "Oyez, Oyez, Oyez! . . . God save the United States and this Honorable Court!" How, she wondered, could such a court "impartially judge an Atheist's rights with this all too obvious commitment of fortunes to the deity?"

His voice quavering, Kerpelman contended that tradition did not make an unconstitutional act constitutional. Relying on the *Engel* decision, he told the Court that the Constitution had erected a "wall of separation" between church and state. Justice Potter Stewart interrupted to ask Kerpelman exactly where this wording appeared. Kerpelman was stumped and remained silent for an embarrassing moment. Finally, Kerpelman regained his composure, with Justice Hugo Black's help, and commented that that phrase was indeed not in the Constitution but that the First Amendment had been so interpreted.

Whereas Kerpelman stumbled, Henry Sawyer III, the Schempps' ACLU attorney and a former Philadelphia city council member, performed superbly. With Leo Pfeffer's assistance, Sawyer insisted that the state law amounted to religious establishment, preferring one religion to another. He disputed the claim that the King James Bible was a guide to morality rather than a sectarian scripture. "It is the final arrogance," he argued, "to quote constantly about our religious traditions and to equate those traditions with this Bible." Such an argument, Sawyer asserted, "suggests that the public schools of Pennsylvania are a Protestant institution to which others are cordially invited." He noted the obvious, that many Americans, including Jews, Catholics, and his clients, did not subscribe to the King James Bible. Some passages are plainly anti-Semitic, Sawyer maintained, and the introduction describes the pope as "that man of sin." He urged the Court to extend the *Engel* decision to the Pennsylvania practice.

Philip Ward, the Abington School Board attorney, conceded the "religious character" of Bible reading and the Lord's Prayer, but claimed these devotions promoted "moral values" that helped counter "the materialistic trends of our times." Ward asked the Court, "Must the government rip out that document, that tradition, simply because it involves a religious book?" Besides, he argued, the schoolchildren in Abington were not forced to recite the devotions but only had to listen to them, or could be excused.

Such arguments proved unpersuasive. When Ward asserted that it was a "debatable" contention that the Lord's Prayer was sectarian and might well be compared to the Jewish prayer the Kaddish, Justice Black retorted, "Then why not use that one?" Justice Byron White wanted to know why children needed to be excused from devotions if they were not religious. "If it is *only* moral, and not religious, they should be compelled to attend." Several justices asked why, if the schools simply wanted to promote a good atmosphere, they did not use scriptures from other traditions, including Islam and Buddhism? When Ward characterized the dispute as one between theists who supported school prayer and atheists who opposed it, Chief Justice Earl Warren contradicted him, noting that Jews and other "fine groups" of theists had filed amicus briefs to strike down school-led devotions.

Ordinarily, Justice Hugo Black would have written the *Schempp* decision because he had written *Engel*. But Warren's instincts led him to assign the opinion to Justice Tom Clark, a Presbyterian church elder from Texas who might placate conservative critics because of his sensitivity to public opinion. Clark had written articles in the lay press that trumpeted the value of prayer and religious piety, and Madalyn Murray was certain that he would vote against her. As Truman's attorney general during the early stages of the Cold War, Clark unapologetically developed the administration's loyalty program for federal employees, drafted a list of allegedly subversive organizations, and prosecuted top Communist Party leaders. But other experiences led Clark to identify with religious and ethnic minorities. At the University of Texas, he had at first been blackballed by fraternities because his roommate was Jewish. During World War II, he was the civilian relocation coordinator whose job it was to handle the legal aspects of interning Japanese Americans. Though he supported the policy at the time, he later rued his actions as one of the worst mistakes he ever made. Clark was far more progressive with respect to African Americans, taking unprecedented action against restrictive housing covenants and other Jim Crow practices.

On June 17, 1963, Justice Clark agreed with the plaintiffs in *Abington v. Schempp* and *Murray v. Curlett*. Writing for an eight-to-one majority that included justices who were Protestant, Catholic, and Jewish, Clark upheld and expanded the *Engel* decision. A prime objective was to quiet the public furor left over from that earlier ruling. Although *Murray* was docketed first, Clark listed *Schempp* as the lead case and treated the cases unequally in his opinion, evidently to avoid the appearance of endorsing Madalyn Murray's atheism. In ringing language designed to reassure the faith community, Clark paid homage to the importance of religion in U.S. society by observing, "many people have devoutly believed that 'More things are wrought by prayer than this world dreams of.'"

In simple, direct prose, Clark dismissed the argument that school prayer is permissible because the Founding Fathers did not object to it. He noted that U.S. education had changed remarkably since the First Amendment was ratified. For a long time, education was confined to private schools, and only gradually passed into the hands of public officials. "It would, therefore, hardly be significant," Clark concluded, "if the fact was that the nearly universal devotional exercises in these schools of the young Republic did not provoke criticism;

even today religious ceremonies in church-supported private schools are constitutionally unobjectionable." The central idea of the establishment and free exercise clauses, Clark wrote, was that the Constitution prohibits the union of "governmental and religious functions."

Justice Clark declined to mention Jefferson's rigid "wall" metaphor, fashioning instead a twofold test of legislation to guide lower federal courts on church-state suits. Maintaining that government may not sponsor religious activities, Clark insisted that "wholesome 'neutrality' " requires that a statute or regulation have (a) "a secular legislative purpose" and (b) "a primary effect that neither advances nor inhibits religion." The classroom exercises in Abington and Baltimore failed this test on both counts.

Clark rejected several arguments the state made in favor of religious exercises. "It is no defense," he wrote, to say that Bible reading and school prayer were "minor encroachments" on the First Amendment: "The breach of neutrality that is today a trickling stream may all too soon become a raging torrent and, in the words of Madison, 'it is proper to take alarm at the first experiment on our liberties.' " Recalling the storm of criticism over *Engel*, Clark dismissed the claim that his ruling established a "religion of secularism," something *Zorach* had already prohibited. He declared that "one's education is not complete" without instruction in the objective history of religion, especially comparative religion and the Bible as literature or philosophy. *Schempp* was Clark's most controversial opinion in his fourteen years on the Court.

Potter Stewart almost made *Schempp* unanimous, but in the end, he dissented, as he had in *Engel*. Stewart criticized his brethren for adopting Jefferson's "sterile metaphor," which, he claimed, was likely to produce "a fallacious oversimplification" of the establishment clause. Stewart maintained that it was neither necessary nor desirable to have a "single constitutional standard" concerning religion and government. "Religion and government must interact in countless ways," he thought, and most of them are harmless enough. He favored sending the case back to the lower court because there was insufficient information to render a sound decision. Stewart wanted the plaintiffs to demonstrate that coercion had occurred before the Court agreed with them. For him, coercion was not the inevitable result of government involvement in a religious activity.

In light of the *Engel* decision that had just preceded it, the *Schempp* ruling was scarcely a surprise, and it did not engender quite the same outpouring of hostility, even though *Schempp* directly affected far more schools and students than *Engel* did. Although civil liberties attorney Leo Pfeffer hailed the momentous decision as marking the end of Christian hegemony and the beginning of religious equality in the United States, he thought that *Schempp* was "certainly universally expected and came almost as an anticlimax." The U.S. Supreme Court received fewer than one hundred letters about *Schempp*.

A year had passed since *Engel*, and most Protestant leaders and groups concluded that the U.S. Supreme Court was correct in outlawing organized religious activities in public schools. Indeed, to minimize hostile reaction, some religious groups spoke out before *Schempp* was announced. The General Assembly of the United Presbyterian Church issued an unqualified endorsement of church-state separation a month prior to the decision. C. Emanuel Carlson, executive director of the Baptist Joint Committee on Public Affairs, spoke for millions of Baptists when he declared that the Bible should not be used for devotional purposes in the public schools. Even the National Council of Churches declared that "neither true religion nor good education is dependent upon the devotional use of the Bible" in public schools.

Howard Kennedy, dean of the Episcopal Cathedral of St. James in Chicago, explained why he had rejected *Engel* but accepted *Schempp:* "Unlike last year when I reacted emotionally, illogically, and nonintellectually, this decision doesn't disturb me." He commended the ruling, arguing that it "dissipates the myth that ours is a Christian country." The decision "should clear the air and put the challenge squarely up to the churches and Christian parents."

Schempp was still bitterly attacked in statehouses, the halls of Congress, the news media, and some churches. Many Americans believed that the Court was more interested in protecting a few kooks than in protecting the majority's assumed right to read the holy scriptures aloud in public schools. *Schempp* seemed to be one more sign that the country was splitting at the seams. Evangelist Billy Graham was "shocked" by the *Schempp* decision, and said the Court was "wrong": "At a time when moral decadence is evident on every hand, when race tension is mounting, when the threat of communism is growing, when terrifying new weapons of destruction are being created, we need more religion, not less." He described *Schempp* as a penalty for the 70 percent of Americans who supported Bible reading and prayers in public schools. "Why," he asked, "should the majority be so severely penalized by the protests of a handful?"

Catholic reaction was not uniformly hostile toward *Schempp* because the decision was expected. Archbishop Joseph McGucken of San Francisco commented, "We should . . . work harder at letting our children know of God and religion in our homes and churches." Only three of the five U.S. cardinals then meeting in Rome to choose Pope John XXIII's successor lashed out against *Schempp*. Francis Cardinal McIntyre of Los Angeles remarked that the decision "can only mean that our American heritage of philosophy, of religion and of freedom [is] being abandoned in imitation of Soviet philosophy, of Soviet materialism, and of Soviet-regimented liberty." The Jesuit magazine *America*, which bitterly opposed *Engel*, issued no incendiary editorials and opposed a constitutional amendment to allow prayer and scripture reading in public schools. *America*'s editor took small comfort that the Court had relied this time on the notion of "neutrality," not Jefferson's "wall" metaphor, and quoted *Zorach*'s declaration that Americans are "a religious people whose institutions presuppose a Supreme Being."

In Congress, the rhetoric after *Schempp* was more temperate than it had been following *Engel*, but school prayer amendments languishing in committee received new life. The House Judiciary Committee received 1 million signatures and more mail backing a school prayer amendment than on any other topic, primarily from Protestant and Catholic women. The most important support came from the National Association of Evangelicals, which drew much of its membership from Pentecostal and Holiness churches. Other supporters included fundamentalist Carl McIntire, president of the International Council of Christian Churches; Gerald L. K. Smith, the silver-tongued minister of hate who led the Citizens Congressional Committee; and evangelist Billy James Hargis, whose Christian Crusade advertised itself as a "weapon against Communism and its godless allies." Francis Burch, the city solicitor who represented Baltimore in the *Murray* case, and George Brain, the superintendent of Baltimore schools, launched a group called the Constitutional Prayer Foundation. Its illustrious membership included former president Dwight Eisenhower, newspaper magnate William Randolph Hearst, Jr., Francis Cardinal Spellman, hotelier Conrad Hilton, and the governors of several states, but other than impressive stationery, little came of this glittering roster of names. Perhaps the largest such campaign was Project America, whose supporters came from the American Legion, Catholic War Veterans, International Christian Youth in the United States, and state groups, such as the Massachusetts Citizens for Public Prayer.

After months of drum-beating for school prayer, House Judiciary Committee Chair Emanuel Celler, a New York Democrat and Reform Jew, grudgingly consented to open hearings on 150 proposals to amend the Constitution, but he dug in his heels as deeply as he could. When the committee met on April 22, 1964, the large room was packed to capacity, with a long line of spectators waiting for admittance. Reporters crowded the press tables inside the room, and television lights glared outside to illuminate interviews with key players. New York Congress-member Frank Becker, whose amendment dominated the proceedings, commented on the high stakes involved: "The welfare and entire future of our beloved America depends upon how we handle the most dynamic tradition in our national life — dependence upon Almighty God." At the first hearings ever held on school prayer, Becker reminded the committee that the U.S. Supreme Court had once ruled that the United States was a Christian nation. The hearings quickly devolved into partisanship, prejudice, and flaring tempers, as congressmembers grilled each other in the name of God and the Constitution.

Prominent politicians endorsed the Becker Amendment, including Republican presidential candidate Barry Goldwater of Arizona, House minority leader and future president Gerald Ford, and John Sparkman of Alabama, a former Democratic vice presidential nominee. The nation's governors supported the amendment at their annual meeting. Eager for another showdown with the federal government one week after trying to keep the University of Alabama lily-white, Alabama Governor George Wallace urged disobedience to *Schempp*, a "ruling against God." The pugnacious former boxing champion noted that the nation was founded by men who believed in the Bible, adding, "I don't care what they say in Washington, we are going to keep right on praying and reading the Bible in the public schools of Alabama." The state law requiring daily Bible reading in the public schools was not struck down until a federal court reiterated the *Schempp* decision in 1971.

Even though a Gallup poll showed that 77 percent of Americans supported the Becker Amendment, it never got beyond the House Judiciary Committee. The amendment failed in the wake of a grassroots effort by civil libertarians, Jews, and many Protestants, especially Dean Kelley, a Presbyterian minister who worked for the National Council of Churches. Together, these groups organized meetings, sponsored speakers, and launched a letter-writing campaign to protect the First Amendment. Numerous interest groups, along with prominent theologians and 223 constitutional law professors, spoke against the amendment in congressional hearings. One judiciary committee member sighed, "We have just been hit by 223 bricks." Rabbi Joachim Prinz, a refugee from the Nazis and president of the American Jewish Congress, testified at the hearings that sterile religious training failed to prevent the German people from slaughtering millions of innocents. The committee also received 13,000 letters on the matter, with 5,000 of them against the amendment. A rising crescendo of editorial opinion from across the nation warned against tampering with the First Amendment. The sustained effort swung congressional sentiment from support to opposition, and the first of several attempts to win approval of a school prayer amendment failed.

Compliance with *Schempp*, as with *Engel*, depended on local willingness to enforce the law because the U.S. Supreme Court has no police force of its own. Such willingness revealed considerable regional variation. In Pennsylvania, Superintendent of Public Instruction Charles Boehm thought *Schempp* barred only religious services and rituals. He declared that children would still begin their school days with "silent meditation," followed by inspirational music, art, and literature. "God and religion will remain in our schools," proclaimed Boehm. In New York City, the Board of Education discontinued a century-old practice of Bible reading at all school assemblies. At the same time, the board relaxed the requirement of singing the fourth stanza of "America" at the opening of the school day, permitting instead the singing of any patriotic song. Both actions had been recommended by Calvin Gross, superintendent of schools, to conform to the *Schempp* decision.

Many school district officials concluded that public schools must ban all forms of religious activity. In 1960, just before *Engel* was decided, a survey of the continental United States reported that 41

percent of the public school districts allowed Bible readir
percent permitted teachers to recite prayers. By the mid-19
figures had decreased, as Table 8.1 indicates. The drop ir
practices in the public schools encouraged Leo Pfeffer, wh
that *Engel* and *Schempp* "may well be the last major battle . . . in
area of religion in the public schools." Subsequent litigation proved
Pfeffer correct, as the Supreme Court simply closed loopholes in the
decisive rulings.

Although numerous communities stopped the offending religious
practices in the public schools, others defied the U.S. Supreme Court
decisions. Many states voided their laws on school prayer but quietly
looked the other way as local schools continued with prayers on their
own. Some officials believed erroneously that school prayers and Bible
reading were constitutional as long as students were not directly compelled to participate. Two-thirds of southern schools and one-half of
midwestern schools continued as they had before. Six states —
Alabama, Arkansas, Delaware, Florida, Georgia, and Idaho — still had
laws requiring devotions in the public schools. Delaware's attorney
general ruled that *Schempp* applied only to Pennsylvania and Maryland,
so devotions could continue in his state. Bible reading also continued
in nine other states — Indiana, Kansas, Mississippi, North Carolina,
Oklahoma, South Carolina, Tennessee, Texas, and Virginia — though
as a matter of tradition, not statutory requirement. In Tennessee, only
42 percent of the 121 school districts made any change in their policies, and only 1 district eliminated devotions entirely. In Oklahoma
City, 61 percent of the public schools had mandatory classroom prayers
and 92 percent allowed Bible reading in direct defiance of the Court.

Such defiance forced the federal judiciary's hand. District courts
soon ordered compliance with *Engel* and *Schempp* by striking down
prayers of one kind or another in Florida, Illinois, and New York. In

Table 8.1 Religious Practices in U.S. Public Schools (by Percent of
School Districts)

	1960	*1966*
Baccalaureate services	86.8	84.0
Bible distribution	42.7	37.4
Bible reading	41.8	12.9
Devotions	33.2	8.0

ccordance with New York Department of Education guidelines issued after *Engel*, Elihu Oshinsky, the principal at Whitestone Elementary School in Queens, immediately stopped kindergarten pupils from reciting a brief prayer before they received their morning milk and cookies. A group of Protestant, Roman Catholic, Jewish, Greek Orthodox, and Armenian Apostolic parents formed a group called Prayer Rights for American Youth (PRAY), and sued the school to give their children "an opportunity to express their love and affection to Almighty God each day through a prayer in their respective classrooms." In *Stein v. Oshinsky*, a federal court rejected the suit and struck down the practice, deciding, "The plaintiffs must content themselves with having their children say these prayers before 9 A.M. and after 3 P.M." — a ruling the U.S. Supreme Court refused to review.

The *Oshinsky* ruling outraged Senate Minority Leader Everett Dirksen, who credited prayer with saving his eyesight. Although he had once remarked that school prayer amendments were doomed to failure, the gravel-voiced Illinois Republican proposed his own "amen amendment" in 1966. Evidently acting out of sincere conviction, Dirksen declared, "I'm not going to let nine men say to 190 million people, including children, when and where they can utter their prayers. . . . I can see no evil in children who want to say that God is good and to thank Him for their blessings." Dirksen's proposal precluded school authorities from "prescribing" any particular prayer, which the U.S. Supreme Court had barred. Birch Bayh, an Indiana Democrat who headed the Senate Judiciary Subcommittee on Constitutional Amendments, arranged to kill Dirksen's amendment by proposing that the Senate vote first on a meaningless resolution in support of God and prayer before voting on the amendment. After much soul-searching, Sam Ervin of North Carolina, who had denounced *Engel*, turned against Dirksen's amendment for weakening the First Amendment, and persuaded others to join him. As Bayh expected, the Senate approved the resolution as a face-saving measure, and voted against the amendment on technical grounds.

Hopes for a school prayer amendment did not evaporate with Dirksen's death. His son-in-law, Republican Senator Howard Baker of Tennessee, introduced a briefer version of the prayer amendment, but that failed, too. In 1971, Ohio Republican Congressmember Chalmers Wylie, a much-decorated World War II veteran, offered an almost identical amendment to Baker's, but that also failed. With each failure, a school prayer amendment became ever less likely.

As more religion cases came before the U.S. Supreme Court, the justices made another stab at defining the First Amendment's religion clauses in *Lemon v. Kurtzman* (1971). Spencer Coxe, executive director of the Greater Philadelphia branch of the ACLU, asked for volunteers to test a 1968 state law that provided $5 million annually for teacher salaries, textbooks, and instructional materials in nonpublic elementary and secondary schools, mostly Roman Catholic. Alton Lemon, an African American who had grown up hearing school prayers in Atlanta, Georgia, and who was once president of the Society for Ethical Culture, stepped forward, even though he feared retribution from his boss, who was Roman Catholic.

Finding that such payments violated the establishment clause, Chief Justice Warren Burger, a Presbyterian and a Nixon appointee, tried to strike a more sure-handed formula to distinguish between what was permissible in the church-state arena. This three-pronged *Lemon* test, which built on the *Schempp* decision, declared that a valid law concerning state action and religious entities must (1) have a secular purpose, (2) have a primary effect that neither aids nor hampers religion, and (3) not foster "an excessive government entanglement with religion." Although the *Lemon* test was criticized as vague and confusing, it has been mentioned in almost every subsequent state aid dispute.

As the U.S. Supreme Court fine-tuned its interpretation of the establishment clause, Madalyn Murray, the self-proclaimed leader of U.S. atheism, did her best to bring more church-state cases before it. She sued, for example, to end tax exemptions for churches, to forbid astronauts from reading the Bible in space, and to expunge the motto "In God We Trust" from all U.S. currency. She estimated that if churches had to pay taxes "like everyone else" they would disappear within forty years. Although all of these suits were denied, she managed to build an atheist empire in Austin, Texas, which included a center, a library, a magazine, and frequent television appearances. She once confessed, "I don't really care that much about atheism. . . . But I've gotten into this thing, and I've been driven out of the community. Atheism is all I have to fight my way back in with. I want respect for my right to have any opinion I want — and to live. I could be a damned fascist and do the same thing I'm doing now." Such a high profile convinced many Americans that it was Madalyn Murray, not Steven Engel (much less Lawrence Roth), who won the case against organized school prayer.

Eventually, Madalyn Murray alienated her followers, who detested her egomania, autocratic rule, obscene language, and lavish lifestyle at their expense. Even William Murray broke with his mother, embracing evangelical Christianity and picketing her public appearances. Murray's bizarre death matched her bizarre life. Her former office manager, a convicted felon, kidnapped her, along with her son Jon Garth and granddaughter, Robin, just as they were headed to exile in New Zealand; extorted a fortune from them; and murdered and dismembered them in 1995. When the grisly murders were finally solved, William Murray claimed his mother's mutilated remains and put them in an unmarked grave. In doing so, he followed her oft-stated burial wishes — cremation of the body and no intercessory prayers for an afterlife. The "most hated woman in America" was finally at peace.

lobbyists to work with Republican congressional leaders Dick Armey of Texas, Jeremiah Denton of Alabama, and John East of North Carolina; and established public-interest law firms that battled separationists in federal courts. Among the most effective of these firms were the Alliance Defense Fund, American Center for Law and Justice, Christian Legal Society, National Legal Foundation, and Rutherford Institute.

The public school was conservative Christians' *bête noire*. Not only were organized spoken prayers, Bible reading, and Christmas worship services now outlawed, school curricula promoted evolution in biology, logical positivism in mathematics, and values clarification in social studies. The culprit, as these Christians saw it, was secular humanism, an insidious philosophy that denied the existence of God and therefore destroyed the moral compass of human existence. Ralph Reed, then executive director of the Christian Coalition, lamented: "Sadly, there is a war going on against religious freedom in America."

In *The Battle for the Public Schools*, Tim LaHaye charged that "America's public education is purposely designed to eradicate Jesus from the scene and replace Him with the likes of John Dewey, Sigmund Freud, Wilhelm Wundt, Friedrich Nietzsche, Karl Marx, [and] Charles Darwin." A cartoon in LaHaye's book depicted a tree labeled "Secular Humanism" that produced branches of "Crime," "Divorce," "Abortion," "Homosexuality," "Rape," "Venereal Disease," "Liberal Politicians," and "Public Schools." LaHaye opposed all such manifestations of the allegedly immoral life.

When Congress considered but then rejected various school prayer measures, conservative Christians expected the president to return U.S. society to its moral foundations. In the 1976 presidential election, they voted in large numbers for former Georgia governor Jimmy Carter, a lifelong Southern Baptist who taught Sunday school regularly. But his presidency sharply alienated the religious right because he opposed organized school prayer and favored equal rights for women, including access to abortion. When inflation soared and foreign events spun out of control, Republicans and their clerical allies coaxed conservative Protestants to oust a slew of moderate and liberal Democratic politicians, including Carter himself.

To attract that important constituency in the 1980 presidential campaign, former California governor Ronald Reagan pronounced himself a "born-again Christian" and called for lower taxes and small government. With public opinion polls showing 80 percent of Americans favoring school prayer, Reagan explicitly embraced morning devotions. He also confessed to having "a great many questions" about evolution, and called for the biblical creation story to be taught in the public schools alongside Darwin's theory. Jerry Falwell and other religious conservatives ultimately played a role in Reagan's capturing the White House in 1980 and would be even more involved in his reelection.

As a political payback, Ronald Reagan took unprecedented steps to promote school prayer. Reagan nominated or elevated four moderates and conservatives to the High Court — Sandra Day O'Connor, William Rehnquist, Antonin Scalia, and Anthony Kennedy — in the hope that they would roll back the Warren Court's decisions on school prayer and other matters. In May 1982, Reagan became the first president to introduce a school prayer amendment: "Nothing in the Constitution shall be construed to prohibit individual or group prayer in public schools or other public institutions. No person shall be required by the United States or by any state to participate in prayer." Reagan insisted that the First Amendment "was not written to protect the people and their laws from religious values; it was written to protect those values from Government tyranny."

Reagan's presidency seemed to signify a new day for conservative Christians intent on reversing *Engel*. Cheered by their success at the polls, conservatives pressed local officials to secure the return of organized prayer to public schools. "People want something done," said the Rev. Edgar Koons of Sacramento, California. "The great majority favors God and the pendulum has begun to swing in that direction." Peter Irons, a leading constitutional scholar, estimated that teachers in more than half of the nation's 15,912 school districts led their students in prayer in the early 1980s.

Examples abounded of local defiance of the U.S. Supreme Court and its rulings against government-sponsored school prayer. Ignoring the Tennessee attorney general, high school football coaches encouraged their players to assemble in the middle of the football field to recite the Lord's Prayer. When the Louisiana legislature passed a law permitting school boards to institute daily prayers, Jefferson parish invited student or faculty volunteers to lead devotions among pupils whose parents signed consent forms. In Lubbock, Texas, the school board permitted teachers to recite prayers and read from the

Bible, the Gideons to distribute New Testaments to elementary school pupils, and the Fellowship of Christian Athletes to evangelize at school assemblies. In Columbus, Ohio, the school board adopted a carefully worded policy that promoted the teaching of all theories of creation, including a biblical version. Billie Jean Keirns, a teacher in Bell, Oklahoma, filled her classroom with religious drawings and plaques, interpreted the Bible in class, and told eleven-year-old Turene Griffin that she would go to hell unless she was baptized.

Another way to insert religion into public school classrooms was to post the Ten Commandments on the walls. The "Hang Ten" movement argued that the Decalogue was not just religious; it was the very foundation of U.S. law. In Kentucky, State Representative Claudia Riner persuaded the legislature to require the display of a 16 x 20 inch plaque of the Ten Commandments in every classroom. Riner tried to avoid constitutional problems by having evangelical and fundamentalist churches pay for the plaques. In addition, each plaque would carry the following disclaimer: "The secular application of the Ten Commandments is clearly seen in its adoption as the fundamental legal code of Western Civilization and the Common Law of the United States." There was no explicit mention or endorsement of the biblical code by teachers or school officials. The plan largely succeeded, thanks to her husband, Tom Riner, a Baptist minister who headed the Kentucky Heritage Foundation. The foundation raised $200,000, which paid for 21,000 copies of the Ten Commandments, enough to have them posted in two-thirds of the state's classrooms.

With the aid of the Kentucky chapter of the ACLU, the Hang Ten statute was challenged by a group of Kentuckians of various religious beliefs, including a Roman Catholic, a rabbi, a Unitarian, and a nonbeliever. In November 1980, the U.S. Supreme Court invalidated the statute as a poorly disguised attempt to evade the First Amendment. In *Stone v. Graham*, a per curiam opinion, the Court applied the *Lemon* test to determine that the display had a "plainly religious" purpose. The Court noted that the commandments included religious exhortations, along with principles accepted in secular law. The faithful were admonished, for example, to have only one God (religious) and not to murder (secular). It made no difference to the Court that the Ten Commandments were passively displayed, rather than formally read, or that they had been purchased with private funds, because the state promoted religion simply by displaying the posters. The Court did permit the study of the Ten Commandments, as it had done ever since the *Schempp* case, as long as the Decalogue was "integrated into the school curriculum" as part of a more general study of history, ethics, or comparative religion. The State of Kentucky had not intended such an objective study.

Although the *Louisville Courier* endorsed *Stone*, no voice for or against it was lifted by leaders in education, business, labor unions, and the professions. The void in public opinion was filled by the religious right, for whom the decision represented both a legal defeat and a fund-raising opportunity. Jerry Falwell, the head of Moral Majority, accused the Court of "attempted censorship" of the Ten Commandments and repudiating "our American heritage." On the local level, Kentucky school districts came under heavy pressure from Baptist ministers to retain the Decalogue plaques. As many as forty school districts resisted the decision, either by replacing the Ten Commandments plaques with posters containing presidential quotations about the Bible or by distributing sweatshirts with Moses on the front and the Ten Commandments on the back.

In the wake of this defeat, the Reagan administration pressed Congress to approve the president's school prayer amendment. In the debate that followed, Illinois Republican Congressmember Henry Hyde drew a laugh when he compared school prayer to chicken soup: "It might not help, but it sure won't hurt." Although Senate Majority Leader Howard Baker predicted that a prayer amendment had "the best chance in decades," it nonetheless failed in 1984. A member of Reagan's own party — Lowell Weicker of Connecticut — led the opposition to what he called a "mess of speculative, political pottage." Even Barry Goldwater, the patriarch of the modern Republican party, voted against Reagan's proposed prayer amendment. Goldwater had voted for the Becker Amendment twenty years earlier, but subsequently embraced his libertarian instincts to oppose the mixing of government and religion. Other critics opined that a prayer amendment might someday result in a theocracy like the fundamentalist Islamic State of Iran.

Despite the views of cynics that the Reagan administration simply used school prayer for political advantage, Reagan always deeply regretted the defeat of his prayer amendment. The subject came up unexpectedly when Daniel Roth, then working for Simon and Schuster, helped the former president make an audiotape of his autobiography. During a production break, Reagan confessed that the greatest single regret of his public life was his inability to get the *Engel* school prayer decision overturned. "Oh, really, Mr. President?" Roth replied, trying not to reveal his identity. "He had no idea that he was sitting there with the devil incarnate and that I was significantly responsible for that decision." Roth just kept his "mouth shut," because he "didn't see any benefit in opening it."

With Congress unwilling to approve a prayer amendment, legislatures in half the states pursued other avenues to permit devotions in school. A favorite tactic was a moment of silence because *Engel* had forbidden only organized spoken prayer. The idea had been suggested by Justice William Brennan in his lengthy *Schempp* concurrence as one of several ways that the state could accommodate religion to achieve secular goals, such as "fostering harmony and tolerance among the pupils, enhancing the authority of the teacher, and inspiring better discipline." During the designated quiet moment, students could think what they wanted, including praying to their deity, as long as they were quiet and respectful, exactly the conditions that believers considered ripe for divine petitions.

The Alabama legislature led the way. In 1978, the legislature authorized a moment of silence for meditation at the beginning of the school day; three years later, it authorized a moment of silence for "meditation or voluntary prayer." This 1981 statute soon stirred up a hornet's nest in Mobile, Alabama, and would produce the first serious test of the *Engel* decision.

In September 1981, five-year-old Chioke Jaffree was upset by his kindergarten class at the E. R. Dickson Elementary School in Mobile. The initial cause for complaint concerned spoken prayer, not silent meditation. At lunchtime, Charlene Boyd, a young black teacher who was a born-again Christian, led Chioke and the other children in singing a prayer: "God is great, God is good, Let us thank him for our food, Bow our heads we all are fed, Give us, Lord, our daily bread. Amen!" When the outspoken Chioke asked his teacher to stop, Boyd replied that although he did not have to participate, the prayer would continue. Chioke complained to his father, Ishmael Jaffree, an African American attorney with the Legal Services Corporation, a federally funded agency that assisted poor people. Jaffree soon discovered that his older children — Jamael Aakki and Makeba — were also subjected to school prayers orchestrated by teachers.

Such devotions did not sit well with the Jaffree family, who vowed to end them. Ishmael, once a child evangelist in Cleveland, Ohio, had repudiated religion after meeting atheists in college and studying comparative religion. As an agnostic, he concluded that religion was an opiate, a crutch for the weak to cope with the unknown. His "very religious" wife, Mozelle, subscribed to the tenets of the Baha'i faith, a sect of Middle East origins that espouses religious and racial tolerance. In this religiously mixed household, the parents agreed that their children should "be exposed to different philosophies" so they could choose their own religious faith or have no faith at all. The Jaffrees stood united in their belief that public schools should play no role in inculcating religion in their children. Their mission would not be easy because Mobile was a Bible-belt community of 200,000 inhabitants and 56 religious denominations, including 192 Baptist churches.

Embarking on an anti–school prayer crusade, Ishmael Jaffree told Chioke to inform his teacher that organized devotions were prohibited by the U.S. Supreme Court. When Charlene Boyd ignored the remark, Jaffree confronted her, only to learn that the teacher seemed more concerned that Chioke was puncturing his classmates' belief in Santa Claus. Boyd remembered that Jaffree "hated to discuss this with me because I was black, but I was doing something that was against the law. He said I could go to jail for what I was doing." When Jaffree asked why Boyd led Chioke's class in prayer, Boyd replied matter-of-factly, "That's who I thank." After the schoolteachers, principals, and superintendent ignored Jaffree's personal pleas, telephone calls, and letters for most of the year, Jaffree was at his "wit's end." He "didn't want to bring this lawsuit," because he realized that Mobile was "a very conservative area and people have grown up with the Bible from Day One."

Nevertheless, Jaffree sued his children's teachers for $115,000 in punitive damages for proselytizing his children for eight hours a day in "fundamentalist, Christian philosophy." When other parents learned about Jaffree's suit, they remarked, "My God, what's wrong with that man?" Jaffree explained that he was not opposed in principle to children praying, as long as they initiated the prayers themselves. He was certain that children "accept what they hear" from teachers:

"They would accept a belief in the tooth fairy, just because it is told to them by adults."

Once the suit was filed, the State of Alabama virtually declared war on the Jaffrees. Dan Alexander, the school board president, told the board that it could not admit wrongdoing, so the prayers would have to be defended as far as necessary. Governor Forrest "Fob" James, Jr., like his demagogic predecessor, George Wallace, characterized the *Engel* decision as a "dangerous usurpation of power" and insisted that no court had jurisdiction over "the Most High God." Determined to make religion, rather than race, the fulcrum of Alabama politics, James denounced Ishmael Jaffree for attacking teachers who were doing nothing except teaching pupils how to pray, which seemed no offense at all deep in the heart of Dixie.

In June 1982, Governor James convened a special session of the state legislature, which approved a prescribed prayer to be led by teachers and recited by "willing students." The devotion, which was written by the governor's son and namesake, a twenty-five-year-old Mobile attorney, declared: "Almighty God, You alone are our God. We acknowledge You as the Creator and Supreme Judge of the world. May Your justice, Your truth, and Your peace abound this day in the hearts of our countrymen, in the counsels of our government, in the sanctity of our homes, and in the classrooms of our schools. In the name of our Lord, Amen." There was no provision to excuse students who objected. In light of the *Engel* decision, Alabama's state-prepared prayer — the first since the New York regents' prayer — was obviously unconstitutional, but the governor nonetheless asked Alabama school-teachers to defy a federal court order and recite the prayer. "Fine me," James taunted the judiciary. "I dare them to do that."

Jaffree's lawsuit made him a pariah, especially in the black community, which expected him to be a "good Christian." He remarked wearily, "the black community doesn't understand," insisting that he was never "anti-church, anti-Christ, [or] anti-prayer." Unconvinced by such assurances, local radio talk shows urged him to go back to Africa. A flood of hate mail arrived — some of which wrongly believed that he was a Black Muslim — and his car was pelted with eggs. Hostile telephone calls, including death threats, were made at all hours of the night. Worst of all, Jaffree's children were attacked, shunned, talked about, and laughed at. Aakki and Makeba called the lawsuit "stupid" and told their father that they wished he had never filed it. A dispirited Jaffree knew from studying previous school prayer lawsuits that even in victory the plaintiffs paid a steep price. "My children," he said, "will be forever stamped as the children of the father who tried to take religion out of the public classrooms."

Jaffree lost his case in federal district court, in an opinion that the U.S. Supreme Court derided as "remarkable." Judge W. Brevard Hand, a Nixon appointee who was once described as "the last surviving Confederate," ruled that *Engel* and *Schempp* were wrong. In upholding the Alabama statutes, Hand asserted that the First Amendment establishment clause did not apply to the states. Hand's audacious claim amounted to a frontal attack on the Supreme Court, which, he charged, "erred in its reading of history" and acted despotically in controlling the states. Hand thus ignored a half-century of precedents and the entire judicial concept of incorporation — the idea that the First Amendment applied to the states through the Fourteenth Amendment. Rightly anticipating that his decision would be reversed on appeal, Hand warned that if that happened, he would "hunker down" and "purge" school textbooks that denigrated Christianity in favor of "the secular humanistic ethic."

When the case reached the U.S. Supreme Court, it was politically charged. The Reagan administration strongly supported a moment of silence as a means of reinterpreting the First Amendment's establishment clause and permitting voluntary school prayer. The White House proposed nothing less than lowering, if not obliterating, Jefferson's wall of separation between church and state. In its amicus brief, the administration claimed that the state had an obligation to accommodate religious activity because the Constitution "guarantees religious freedom." In a weekly radio address, President Reagan declared that "the good Lord who has given our country so much should never have been expelled from our nation's classrooms." *Engel* had done no such thing, but the president's misunderstanding of that decision was not unusual and reinforced the misunderstanding of others.

As the *Jaffree* case wended its way up the judicial ladder in the early 1980s, the U.S. Supreme Court decided a series of cases that suggested it might well overturn *Engel*. The Court affirmed direct payment of public funds to religious schools, permitted state income tax deductions for education expenses in religious schools, upheld government-paid legislative chaplains, and required states to make public facilities, including schools, available to religious groups, if nonreligious groups were permitted to use them.

Perhaps the most memorable of these cases was the Supreme Court's decision in *Lynch v. Donnelly* (1984) to allow municipalities to erect nativity scenes of Jesus' birth as part of their December displays. Chief Justice Warren Burger ignored his own *Lemon* test to hold that the crèche's eclectic mixture of sectarian and secular figures rendered it a merely "passive symbol." To justify his decision, Burger claimed that the Constitution "affirmatively mandates accommodation, not merely tolerance, of all religions, and forbids hostility toward any," a view that stood three decades of establishment-clause jurisprudence on its head. *Engel* seemed to be hanging by a judicial thread.

In the end, these church-state cases did not foretell a defeat for *Engel*. In June 1985, the U.S. Supreme Court overturned the 1981 Alabama statute in *Wallace v. Jaffree*. Justice John Paul Stevens, a Protestant and a judicial maverick who had clerked for Wiley Rutledge and been appointed by Gerald Ford, wrote for the six-to-three majority. His strongly worded opinion, which did not overturn a moment of silence per se, was filled with familiar separationist arguments and precedents. In matters of religion, Stevens believed that state governments had to be neutral and their statutes had to have a nonreligious intent. He indicated that he would have upheld a straightforward moment-of-silence statute, which the Alabama legislature had approved in 1978, but that statute was not before the Court. The 1981 statute, he ruled, was clearly intended to promote religion as "a favored practice" during the moment of silence.

The bill's sponsor, State Senator Donald Holmes, admitted as much in the legislative record and again in district court: "Since coming to the Alabama Senate I have worked hard on this legislation to accomplish the return of voluntary prayer to our public schools and return to the basic moral fiber." The state already had enacted a law that permitted meditation, so the 1981 statute adding "voluntary prayer" obviously intended to promote religious activity — a violation of the "secular purpose" test devised in *Lemon*. The state moved explicitly to promote religion the following year when it wrote its own prayer.

The dissenting justices fashioned striking arguments to keep Alabama's moment of silence. Chief Justice Warren Burger and Byron

White, a Kennedy appointee who read the Bible but did not attend church, declared that Alabama's statute was an example of "benevolent neutrality" permitted by the U.S. Supreme Court's accommodationist precedents. The most spectacular dissent came from William Rehnquist, a Lutheran who had clerked for Robert Jackson, campaigned for Barry Goldwater, and accepted Richard Nixon's nomination to serve on the Court. Rehnquist used the case to offer the first systematic refutation of the "misleading" and "unnecessary" wall-of-separation metaphor, enunciated in the *Everson* case forty years earlier. Although Rehnquist accepted the incorporation doctrine, he declared that any decision drawing upon *Everson*'s "theory of rigid separation," including *Engel*, was simply wrong. A state was free, Rehnquist declared, to endorse school prayer as it saw fit. In short, Rehnquist believed, majorities should make political decisions involving religion, which invariably left out humanists and religious minorities, especially Jews, Muslims, and Buddhists.

Conservative Christians saw the ruling as a bitter defeat of their efforts to convince the Court to erase four decades of legal decisions, abandon the idea of a "wall of separation between church and state," and permit government to encourage religious activity. Beverly LaHaye of Concerned Women for America reacted with deep regret over this "act of war against this nation's religious heritage." Forest Montgomery, counsel to the 4.5 million-member National Association of Evangelicals, remarked that the Court's ruling would force state legislators to "play games" by pretending that no religious motivation underlies the enactment of moment-of-silence laws: "These laws usually come from a spiritual motivation. Everyone knows it, but you just can't say it." Pulitzer Prize–winning columnist George Will of *Newsweek* was disgusted with the Court's ruling because, he insisted, a moment of silence causes no injury, even if the state legislature hoped schoolchildren would pray during it. Will told the litigants to "buzz off."

As the U.S. Supreme Court and Congress proved uncooperative in permitting organized prayer, the Reagan administration searched for other ways to satisfy its restive conservative constituency. Noting that some schools forbade religious clubs out of a fear that they violated the establishment clause, the administration promoted the idea of allowing such clubs in school buildings after regular instruction ended. The administration justified the idea by changing the rate from freedom of religion to free speech, or, as one Senate aide put, from prayer as "good for kids" to "student rights," a cause that held wider appeal across the religious and political spectrums. Even civil libertarians, including Nat Hentoff of the *Village Voice* and Harvard law professor Laurence Tribe, supported the idea. But, most Jews and the American Jewish Congress opposed this "son of school prayer," afraid that the bill would be, as one Jewish lobbyist said, "the first step toward turning the public schools into beehives of religious proselytization."

Under the Equal Access Act, which passed in 1984, students in public schools could form religious groups, such as a Bible club, as long as their schools allowed nonreligious groups or clubs. A school did not have to allow any clubs, but if it allowed some, the school created a "limited open forum," which meant it had to allow all clubs that wanted to meet. Once a school allowed clubs, the law required that they be initiated by students and could not be sponsored by the school, interfere with educational activities, or regularly invite "nonschool persons." A delighted Jerry Falwell commented, "We knew we could not win on school prayer, but equal access gets us what we want."

The constitutionality of the Equal Access Act would be tested in a case arising in Omaha, Nebraska, that conservatives hailed as their best chance in years to defend their civil rights and put organized religious devotions back in the schoolhouse. In 1984, Bridget Mergens, a seventeen-year-old senior at Westside High School, sought approval for a Bible club modeled after other high school Christian clubs in the area. An enthusiastic member of the Assemblies of God denomination, Mergens discovered that her best friend was also Christian, and she "thought it would be neat if we could get some kids together at school and study the Bible." Mergens expected that a Bible club would help her faith mature and help troubled teenagers deal with violent drug gangs. Although Westside High already had sanctioned thirty clubs focusing on interests ranging from chess to scuba diving, school officials asserted, somewhat dubiously, that the Equal Access Act did not apply to the school because all clubs were directly rooted in the school curriculum. School board policy recognized the clubs as a "vital part of the total education program as a means of developing citizenship, wholesome attitudes, good human relations, knowledge, and

proposed clubs had been denied, including a soccer club,
and Dragons club, and another related to video games
sufficient interest or doubtful safety.

ames Findley, Bridget's homeroom teacher and "a close
iked the concept of a Bible club, but said it did not be-
ic school because the students were a "captive audience."
Findley also was concerned that a student Bible club would set a precedent requiring recognition of a Satanist club. Bridget was "shocked"
by Findley's ban, which she regarded as religious discrimination. "We
weren't asking for special treatment," Mergens insisted. "If we wanted
to do something destructive, like sacrifice dogs or cats or mess up the
school, I could understand it. But all we wanted to do was meet like
any other club."

Bridget sued her school with the help of Jay Sekulow, chief counsel for television evangelist Pat Robertson's new legal arm, the American Center for Law and Justice (ACLJ). Sekulow, a former Atlanta
real estate attorney who rejected his Jewish upbringing to become a
"Messianic Jew," emerged as the most visible and most successful liti-
gator for the religious right. After representing such groups as Jews
for Jesus and Christian Advocates Serving Evangelism, Sekulow now
headed what he called a "legal SWAT team" in defense of Christians'
right to exercise religious freedom in all areas of life, including public schools. With successes in prayer and abortion cases, the ACLJ
would grow to 700,000 members backed by a budget of $30 million,
a powerful counterweight to the ACLU, after which it was modeled.
Sekulow's brief in the *Mergens* case alleged that Findley's denial of the
Bible club violated the Equal Access Act and the students' rights of
free speech, freedom of association, and the free exercise of religion.

The U.S. Supreme Court was eager to take the case because lower
courts had created a hodgepodge of interpretations concerning the
legality of religious clubs. Writing for the majority in *Westside Community Schools v. Mergens* (1990), Sandra Day O'Connor, a nominal
Episcopalian, upheld the Equal Access Act because the law on its face
was "undeniably secular" and therefore satisfied the *Schempp* and
Lemon decisions. O'Connor's endorsement test helped her to explain
the essence of *Engel*: "There is a crucial difference between government speech endorsing religion, which the Establishment Clause forbids, and private speech endorsing religion which the Free Speech

and Free Exercise Clauses protect." For illustrative purposes, O'Connor mentioned that if students proposed clubs devoted to Judaism, Nietzsche's philosophy, and the Democratic and Republican Parties, the school would have to accept them. The *Mergens* case extended the Court's 1981 ruling, *Widmar v. Vincent*, which allowed religious groups to meet on state university campuses. O'Connor believed that high school students, like college students, are mature enough to understand that schools do not endorse religion by permitting a Bible club to meet on a nondiscriminatory basis.

The religious right was ecstatic about the decision. Pat Robertson called it "a tremendous victory . . . a fabulous decision!" High school students, he suggested, could now "meet together as Christians. It's opened the door wide for students to express their faith, to let students give out tracts, to carry their Bibles, to read the Bible, and to talk about Jesus and faith." Robert Simonds, president of the National Association of Christian Educators, believed the decision would finally enable the "500,000 born-again Christians working from 'inside' of the system to change it, and return the Christian ethic of morality and excellence to education." Armed with the *Mergens* ruling, evangelical Christian students formed 15,000 religious clubs at U.S. public high schools in a decade.

As the *Mergens* case was litigated, the Equal Access Act inspired young Baptists in a suburb of Fort Worth, Texas, to worship their God in a novel place. They met at the flagpole of their public school early each weekday morning. Proud of being Christians and eager to set an example for their classmates, the participants prayed, sang gospel music, read from the New Testament, and witnessed for their savior. The idea caught on like wildfire, and the religious ceremony became an annual event, involving 3 million students in all fifty states by 2000. As long as the ritual occurred outside school hours and without the direction or supervision of school authorities, "See You at the Pole" was authorized by the *Mergens* decision.

The *Mergens* decision seemed to portend a new direction in Supreme Court jurisprudence. Upon being elevated to chief justice by Reagan, William Rehnquist searched for a suitable case to dismantle the constitutional wall separating church and state. He pinned his hopes on the Rhode Island case of *Lee v. Weisman*. Much had changed since the *Jaffree* case, including his own promotion, the retirements of liberal justices William Brennan and Thurgood Marshall, and the appointment of several apparently conservative justices by Republican presidents, including Anthony Kennedy, David Souter, and Clarence Thomas. If those justices joined Rehnquist, Antonin Scalia, and Byron White, the Court's lone Democrat, *Engel* could be overturned.

The next major battle over school prayer stemmed from a 1986 graduation ceremony for eighth graders in Providence, Rhode Island, the most Catholic state in the Union. In line with long-standing practice, the principal of Nathan Bishop Middle School invited clergy to give an ecumenical invocation. But the Rev. Virgil Wood, a black Baptist minister, gave a sectarian prayer that asked students and their families to "thank Jesus Christ" for making "these kids what they are today."

The prayer was especially offensive to Daniel Weisman, a forty-three-year-old professor of social work at Rhode Island College. As the child of union activists and Communist Party members, Weisman was raised as a secular Jew whose obligation was to "repair the world through social action." An important part of his education took place each summer at the leftist Camp Hurley — the same camp that the Roth boys in the *Engel* case attended — and Weisman sent his own children there. In high school and college, Weisman "marched with Martin" Luther King Jr., boycotted the "duck and cover" atomic bomb drills, and demonstrated against the Vietnam War.

When confronted by the minister's prayer at his daughter Merith's graduation, Weisman found it "terribly uncomfortable and inappropriate . . . to have an activity sponsored by the state attack me on the basis of my religion." He noted that the audience included persons with a wide variety of personal beliefs, including animists, atheists, Buddhists, Hindus, and Satanists. Weisman fired off a protest letter to school officials, who never responded. With the immediate crisis over, the Weismans put the matter out of their minds.

Three years later, when the Weismans' younger daughter, Deborah, was to graduate with an award for "best school spirit," Daniel reminded the school about the establishment clause. Robert E. Lee, the new principal, tried to reassure the Weismans: "You don't have anything to worry about; we've gotten a rabbi this year." Lee had chosen Rabbi Leslie Gutterman of Temple Beth-El — the leader of Rhode Island's largest Reform temple — to deliver an invocation and benediction. To help the rabbi craft suitable prayers for the public event, Lee informed him that the prayers had to be nonsectarian and sent him a two-page leaflet entitled *Guidelines for Civic Occasions*, which had been prepared by the National Conference of Christians and Jews. The guidelines suggested that public prayer could acknowledge a divine presence and seek its blessing, but should not be occasions "to preach, argue, or testify." In essence, a government official was determining what kind of religious expression was permissible — the very control that the Supreme Court had forbidden. Daniel Weisman shook his head at Lee's plan, which was to foist Judaism, instead of Christianity, on the audience. Weisman remarked that the principal "didn't understand" the real issue. When the Weismans persisted, Lee dared the family to sue.

Daniel Weisman marched into court just days before graduation. He rejected the notion that graduation prayer was allowable because it was a long-standing tradition. "Not all tradition is worthy of preservation," he maintained. He noted that some time-honored practices had been abandoned, including lynchings, literacy tests, public floggings, and witch hunts. Besides, he knew that *Engel* had outlawed official prayer. As a social worker, he felt a commitment to help "vulnerable people," including religious minorities like him. Vivian Weisman, the assistant executive director of the Rhode Island chapter of the ACLU, recruited an attorney who had participated in the *Donnelly* crèche case to file a federal court injunction against the invocation. The court declined to issue one because of insufficient time to consider the matter.

Disregarding the threat of a lawsuit, the Nathan Bishop School District moved ahead with its plan for prayer at graduation. Principal Lee considered the Weismans' complaint "just a passing nuisance" that would go nowhere. As coached, the rabbi delivered what he termed "a typical Jewish family blessing" that was designed to be inoffensive. For the purposes of the suit, Deborah had to hear the invocation to the "God of the Free, Hope of the Brave," which turned out to be an amplified version of the New York regents' prayer. In what promised to be a replay of the *Engel* case, the Weismans sued in federal court to stop such government-sponsored prayers once and for all.

Gearing up for reelection, the first George Bush administration asked the U.S. Supreme Court to accept the Rhode Island case and broaden its scope considerably. U.S. Solicitor General Kenneth Starr hoped that *Weisman* would provoke a church-state showdown to smash through Jefferson's "wall" metaphor and flatten the *Lemon* test, which prohibited aid to sectarian schools. Justice Department attorneys, including John Roberts, Jr., who would later replace Rehnquist as chief justice, mounted a sweeping attack on the Court's interpretation of the establishment clause. They argued that the Court should abandon its "rigid doctrinal framework" and ban government actions only if they directly benefited one religion or compelled individuals to participate in religious worship. Starr denied that the administration wanted to overturn *Engel* and *Schempp*, conceding, "It is a violation of liberty to coerce a person to participate." Graduation prayer, he argued, was different from classroom prayer because graduations are celebratory, not instructional, events.

In *Lee v. Weisman* (1992), the U.S. Supreme Court rebuffed the Bush administration in a surprising five to four decision, upholding the ban on officially sponsored prayers at public school graduations. Anthony Kennedy, a devout Roman Catholic and former altar boy, ruled that the prayers were illegal, despite the brevity of the prayers, their allegedly nonsectarian character, and the supposedly voluntary nature of the exercise. All three issues had been decided by the Court decades earlier, and Kennedy deferred to this settled law. For Kennedy, the real issue was coercion, even though *Engel* had found coercion unnecessary in striking down religious practices in public schools. The government's involvement in the religious activity had been "pervasive" because school officials directed the performance of formal religious exercises at graduation ceremonies, making such prayers obligatory in that setting. The ceremony itself weighed heavily in Kennedy's thinking: "The Constitution forbids the state to exact religious conformity from a student as the price of attending her own high-school graduation," which, "everyone knows," is "one of life's most significant occasions."

What made Kennedy's decision all the more remarkable is that, in the crèche decision three years earlier, he had called for a reappraisal of the Court's establishment clause precedents. It was Kennedy, Reagan's appointee, who fouled up Rehnquist's calculations in overturning *Engel*. At the same time, Kennedy's coercion test, which prevailed over O'Connor's endorsement test, did not apply the more far-reaching *Lemon* test, amounting to a pyrrhic victory for liberals who cheered *Weisman.*

Whereas Vivian Weisman "screamed with joy" over Kennedy's decision, prayer supporters were dismayed. In an election year, a "very disappointed" President Bush, an Episcopalian, could not condemn the High Court ruling fast enough. He knew that his denunciation would earn him valuable points with the religious right, which he had been ardently courting. Bush implicitly promised that his next appointment to the U.S. Supreme Court would tip the balance in favor of school prayer. Solicitor General Starr called the decision "just stunning" because of the Court's "willingness to strike down a well-settled traditional and historical practice." At the same time, he believed that student-initiated prayers might be permissible. Gary Bauer, Reagan's former chief domestic adviser who championed the "profamily, pro-life, and pro–free enterprise" agenda of the Christian right, was especially embittered over "out-of-control judges." He commented acerbically: "Of the five new justices added to the court by Presidents Reagan and Bush, three joined in today's travesty. At that rate, one has to wonder why liberal interest groups bother fighting Republican nominees to the court. Why not just support them and watch them 'grow'?"

When President Bush lost his reelection bid to Bill Clinton (for reasons unrelated to school prayer), the Republican Party seized upon a bold plan to recover its political power. During the 1994 congressional election campaign, U.S. House Minority Whip Newt Gingrich of Georgia proposed a conservative manifesto — "Contract with America" — designed to unite the Republican Party's factions and to provide a contrast to the Democrats. Among other ideas, the contract proposed balancing the federal budget, reforming welfare, and strengthening a recent crime bill; it said nothing about the most polarizing issues — abortion or school prayer — because, Gingrich asserted, "the elite media would immediately turn the contract into a Christian Coalition document" and ignore the other issues. The contract proved popular, helping Republicans gain control of the House of Representatives for the first time in a half-century.

Once victorious, Gingrich, now elevated to Speaker of the House, promised to hold nationwide hearings on a school prayer amendment. He remarked that the *Engel* decision was "bad law, bad history, and bad culture. . . . And if the Court doesn't want to reverse itself, then we have an absolute obligation to pass a constitutional amendment to instruct the Court on its error." Initially, however, the Republicans focused on economic issues, as they had under Reagan.

Changing political circumstances left President Bill Clinton, a Southern Baptist and a "new Democrat," in a ticklish situation. To placate civil libertarians in his party, he tried to blunt Republican efforts for a school prayer amendment; but he also needed to appeal to religious conservatives who held the balance of power in many electoral districts. In April 1995, Secretary of Education Richard Riley released a document entitled "Religion in the Public Schools: A Joint Statement of Current Law," which was based on fifty years of court rulings and an understanding of U.S. religious diversity. The joint statement was drafted in consultation with leading separationist and accommodationist groups, including the ACLU, American Jewish Committee, American Muslim Council, Anti-Defamation League, Baptist Joint Committee on Public Affairs, Christian Legal Society, General Council of Seventh-Day Adventists, National Association of Evangelicals, National Council of Churches, People for the American Way, and Union of American Hebrew Congregations.

Within limits, the guidelines declared, public school students could wear religious symbols, pray or read the Bible as individuals or in groups around the flagpole, organize religious clubs, speak or write about religion, distribute religious material in the same way and time periods as other material unrelated to school activities, be excused from lessons that were religiously objectionable, and attend private baccalaureate services. At the same time, the guidelines prohibited school officials from organizing religious activities, prohibited religious education on campus during school time, and prohibited students from praying if they were disruptive or harassed other students. Schools could stop students' oral presentations that converted classrooms into churches. The guidelines acknowledged that some practices were in a gray area, especially student-led graduation prayer.

The Clinton guidelines did not mollify many in the religious right. With the support of House Speaker Newt Gingrich and conservative Christian groups, such as Concerned Women for America, the Rutherford Institute, and the Traditional Values Coalition, Republican congressmember Ernest Istook, a Mormon from Oklahoma, pressed

for a religious freedom amendment to overturn U.S. Suprem
decisions that had "attacked, twisted, and warped the Firs'
ment." After considerable redrafting, the Istook Amendm

> To secure the people's right to acknowledge God according to ᴧ
> dictates of conscience: Nothing in this Constitution shall prohibit
> acknowledgments of the religious heritage, beliefs, or traditions of
> the people, or prohibit student-sponsored prayer in public schools.
> Neither the United States nor any State shall compose any official
> prayer or compel joining in prayer, or discriminate against religious
> expression or belief.

Istook maintained that his amendment would "put God back into our
schools" and help stop mindless violence in the classroom.

In the congressional debate, Istook emphasized religious liberty in
arguing for school prayer: "You don't have the right to shut people up
and censor them just because you choose to be thin-skinned and intolerant when someone else is trying to express their faith." The amendment, he continued, would simply prevent federal courts from being
able to "tell you to sit down and shut up." Convinced that a clear
majority of the American people wanted the amendment, Istook
believed that its passage was assured now that Republicans controlled
both houses of Congress.

Critics believed that the Istook Amendment would allow student-
led prayers over public address systems, preaching from the Bible at
graduations, the teaching of creationism, and the use of tax monies to
support parochial schools. Melvin Watt, a black Democratic representative from North Carolina, accused Istook of insensitivity and angrily
shouted him down: "What you are saying is that you want to amend
the Federal Constitution to give that control to the majority, and I can
understand your desire to do that because you are a member of the
majority religion and the majority race in this country." Even the conservative *Chicago Tribune* opposed the measure because it "overrides the
wisdom" of the First Amendment. The Interfaith Alliance, a new separationist group, refuted the notion that anyone who questioned school
prayer was anti-God. Along with Christians and Jews, the alliance
attracted clergy from across the religious spectrum, including Buddhists,
Hindus, Muslims, Shintoists, Sikhs, Taoists, Wiccans, and Zoroastri-
ans. With such opposition, Istook's proposal fell short of passage in

1998, though a majority of representatives favored it. No "amen amendment," including those of 1964, 1966, 1971, and 1984, has ever received the required two-thirds vote in a single house of Congress.

As Congress debated the Istook school prayer amendment, a Texas case raised yet another question regarding *Engel*. Could students, as opposed to public school officials and designated clergy, lead prayers at school events? In the fall of 1995, hundreds of students and sports fans attended a public school football game in Santa Fe (which means "holy faith" in Spanish), a bedroom community of 4,000 mostly white inhabitants 20 miles northwest of Galveston, Texas. Before the opening kickoff, school officials handed a microphone to a student "chaplain" elected by his or her classmates and that person recited a Protestant prayer over the public address system. In the process, members of every other religious tradition were shunted to the side, including Jews who prayed in Hebrew (and English), Muslims in Arabic, Buddhists in Chinese, and Shintoists in Japanese, to say nothing of pagans who prayed to the goddess Sophia and atheists who found the idea of praying to a divine being a figment of an overactive imagination. Two students — one Roman Catholic, the other Mormon — found the broadcast prayer unacceptable. Their parents enlisted the ACLU to demand that school officials stop the game-day prayer. When school officials refused, the parents filed a lawsuit.

The lawsuit shocked Santa Fe, which was saturated with religion. With more churches (primarily Southern Baptist) than restaurants, the community never expected to become ground zero in the protracted national war over school prayer. According to School Board President John Couch II, an overwhelming majority of residents saw nothing wrong with starting a football game with a devotion because prayer established "the appropriate environment for the competition."

Since the lawsuit did not name the complainants, school officials tried to smoke out the objecting students by circulating two bogus petitions — one for students who supported the prayer and the other for those who opposed it. Anyone who did not sign was naturally suspect. Eventually, U.S. District Judge Samuel Kent stopped such petitions as not-so-subtle intimidation, warning school officials that they could face criminal liability: "Anybody who violates this order, no kidding, is going to wish that he or she had died as a child when this court gets through with it."

The Santa Fe School District had crossed the church-state line numerous times before this latest dust-up. Fourth graders who refused to recite a Protestant prayer were denied lunch. Teachers had pressured their students to attend evangelical revival meetings. District officials had granted permission to Christian missionaries to distribute Gideon Bibles at the schoolhouse door. When Jennifer Mason, an American Baptist, declined the offer, several students asked whether she was a "devil worshipper." Mason understood the core of the problem: "If the school got everything they wanted, we all know what religion Santa Fe High would be — Baptist. They basically want a private religious school that has public funding." When the Mormon student who objected to the game-day prayer was in seventh grade, David Wilson, her Texas history teacher, invited her to attend a Southern Baptist church meeting. The student asked if non-Baptists were welcome to attend. Upon learning that the student was Mormon, Wilson launched into a tirade against the "non-Christian, cult-like nature of Mormonism." Wilson was later forced to apologize.

When the Fifth U.S. Circuit Court of Appeals ruled that football games were "hardly the sober type of annual event that can be appropriately solemnized with prayer," some students in Texas were infuriated. A seventeen-year-old girl stormed into the press box during a high school football game in Justin, seized the microphone, and broadcast an evangelical prayer to the crowd. Fourteen-year-old Tiffany Bridwell recorded a similar invocation for a country music radio station that would be broadcast before kickoff at Andrews High School. In Stephenville, students circumvented a ban on saying prayers over the school's loudspeaker by smuggling a portable public address system into the stadium.

Faced with mounting pressure to act, the Santa Fe School Board adopted a new policy allowing students to open games with "an invocation and/or message." The students elected Marian Ward, the daughter of a Baptist minister, to say a few words to set an appropriate mood before the all-important football games, which were attended by 3,000 people. School officials warned Ward that she would be disciplined if she delivered an openly Christian prayer. Defiantly, she stepped to the microphone and asked for God's blessing for the players and spectators. She closed her invocation with the words, "In Jesus' name, I pray." The cheering audience gave her a standing ovation. "She was absolutely great," said one spectator, Norine Delanoix. "Just about everyone in these stands is 1,000 percent behind Marian. If you can't praise God, what *can* you do?"

Conservative Texas politicians sensed an opportunity to score valuable points with their constituencies. Texas Republicans in the state legislature approved a nonbinding resolution backing "student-initiated prayer" at public school sporting events. Several members of the Texas delegation to Congress, led by Republican Henry Bonilla, a Southern Baptist, and Democrat Charles Stenholm, a Lutheran, introduced a nonbinding resolution urging the U.S. Supreme Court to allow such prayers because they purportedly "contribute to the moral foundation of our nation." Bonilla wondered aloud, "If we can start each day in Congress with a prayer, why can't the students in our schools do the same before their football games?" The U.S. House of Representatives approved the resolution by a voice vote.

Texas governor George W. Bush, a Republican presidential candidate who regularly attended Methodist services with his wife, Laura, also backed the "student-led prayer." In an argument that would have turned *Engel* on its head, Bush instructed Texas Attorney General John Cornyn to file a brief insisting that the Court should "focus on the rights of the speakers, not of the listener. Constitutionally speaking, the majority view is just as valid as the minority view."

In the case of *Santa Fe Independent School District v. Doe* (2000), the U.S. Supreme Court soundly rejected student-led prayers in the public schools, insisting yet again that the Constitution requires a strict separation of church and state. Writing for the six to three majority, as he had in the *Jaffree* case, Justice John Paul Stevens refused to play the school district's game of "pretend." Relying heavily on the *Weisman* opinion, Stevens declared that the entire purpose of the school's student-led prayer policy was to promote religion, not some other kind of speech, such as "commentary on foreign policy." This system, he wrote, "encourages divisiveness along religious lines and threatens the imposition of coercion upon those students not desiring to participate in a religious exercise." The result was to brand nonparticipants as "outsiders." Ironically, it was the district's own machinations that sank the prayer. Stevens charged, "The majoritarian process implemented by the District guarantees, by definition, that minority candidates will never prevail and that their views will be effectively silenced." The ruling undercut a Christian legal strategy to convert the school prayer issue into another right guaranteed by the First Amendment — free speech. Even though most Americans continued to support school prayer, the Court again refused to budge from *Engel.*

Most religious right groups were infuriated by the *Santa Fe* decision. Jim Weidmann, vice chair of the National Day of Prayer Task Force, asserted, "It seems that people of faith are systematically being stripped of their abilities to express their beliefs. Supporters of the freedom of expression stand for protection of the rights of a third-grader to walk into his school's library and look at pornography on the Internet. Yet a student would be defying the law if he led a prayer before a sporting event. It is truly a sad commentary on how far our country has drifted from its spiritual heritage." The Rev. Richard Land, who earned a doctorate from Oxford University and served as president of the Southern Baptist Convention's Ethics and Religious Liberty Commission, remarked: "I don't care if a prayer is offensive to someone. There's no constitutional right against being offended. Nowhere does it say that you have a right not to be offended by your peers in high school."

As of this writing, *Santa Fe* is the last school prayer case to have been decided by the U.S. Supreme Court. The emotional reaction to *Engel,* which was handed down almost a half century ago, has largely spent its force. Congress is not tied up in knots over school prayer, and except for the odd school board race, no known election has ever been decided by it. Politicians need only mention their endorsement of school prayer to retain conservative support; they need not do anything about it. On one level, this political inaction seems surprising. According to the most recent Gallup public opinion survey (August 2005), 76 percent of Americans favor a constitutional amendment for "voluntary prayer in public schools" — a figure that has not changed appreciably since *Engel* was decided.

What has changed remarkably in the intervening years is the social, legal, and political landscape. The scourges of war, disease, and poverty have propelled millions of Muslim, Buddhist, and Hindu immigrants (among others) to the United States, making this nation even more religiously diverse. With four more decisions on school prayer, the Supreme Court itself has forbidden organized devotions under any circumstance in public schools. In addition, Congress has been unwilling to enact a school prayer amendment. As a compromise, it passed the Equal Access Act, which permits students to pray and study the Bible on their own before or after the school day. Even if Americans could obtain a prayer amendment, 69 percent favor a moment of silence, not spoken prayer. Other issues now dominate political discourse, particularly the hot-button issue of abortion, as well as war, energy, and the environment. Arguably, the most important reason that school prayer has receded from U.S. public life is that *Engel* has not impaired the ability of Americans to worship freely.

Despite the ongoing battle over school prayer and occasional cries for an "amen amendment," Lawrence Roth, Steven Engel, Monroe Lerner, Daniel Lichtenstein, and Lenore Lyons won their battle against "an establishment of religion." For more than forty years, neither the U.S. Supreme Court nor Congress has ever sanctioned government-sponsored prayer in the public schools. As William Butler, the plaintiffs' attorney, observed: "I think it's written in stone — *Engel v. Vitale*. Every year since then, there's been an attempt to introduce a constitutional amendment to overrule the case. That has never happened. It can't. For that to happen, they'd have to monkey around with the First Amendment. They can't do that." The Court has held consistently that the Founding Fathers, although steeped in Judeo-Christian values, designed the United States as a secular republic in which all citizens, regardless of religious convictions, are equal under the law. The lesson that Lawrence Roth drew from the case is that "you can fight city hall should the need arise."

Despite the torment he endured, Daniel Roth thought the whole episode was a necessary one because the Constitution is a "difficult instrument" that needs continuous "refinement." In his mind, *Engel* clarified the First Amendment, not to suppress one's faith but to implement the "blueprint" of religious liberty laid out by the Founding Fathers. In the process, Roth concluded, the case was widely misunderstood, producing "one of the great tectonic plates in this country to this day, one of the great divides in this country between one side and the other in the culture wars." Reflecting on his family's leading role and considerable sacrifice in pursuing the suit, Daniel Roth remarked: "What my father did was a really courageous thing. I have a lot of respect and admiration for my father. It wasn't fun and it wasn't easy."

The *Engel* case plainly affected the plaintiffs' children. Although several of them still carry emotional scars from the abuse they endured, all of them have led interesting and successful lives. One became an organic geochemist, another a psychiatrist, while others entered teaching, music, business, midwifery, and the film industry. A few of the children continued the social activism of their parents.

Naomi Lichtenstein became deeply involved in the civil rights, anti-war, and gay rights movements. No one was more active than Wendy Lyons, who as a Trotskyite, devoted her life to liberating oppressed peoples, including blue-collar workers, women, African Americans, and immigrants. To be close to the working class, she took industrial jobs such as meatpacker, joined the United Food and Commercial Workers Union, and held out for 144 days during a strike/lockout. "Industrial workers will change the world," she says. "If we build a big enough movement, we can unleash the power to create what we, the working people, need." To carry out her vision for a more just society, the sixty-year-old Lyons ran for mayor of Los Angeles in 2005 on the Socialist Workers Party line. She advocated a massive public works program, an end to police brutality, and the "immediate and unconditional withdrawal" of U.S. troops from Iraq. In a twelve-way race against politicians, attorneys, and businesspeople, Lyons received less than half of one percent of the vote.

Joe Roth suffered as much as, if not more than, any of the other petitioners' children, but he ultimately became enormously successful. Following high school graduation, Roth studied communications at Boston University, then moved to the West Coast, where he and an aspiring young actress established what became a large San Francisco commune that alienated his family and nearly ruined him. A lucky break came his way when he landed a job as a movie production assistant. Working his way up from the bottom, the street-smart Roth moved from gofer to chair of Walt Disney Studios. Among Joe Roth's dozens of films are hits such as *Home Alone, Maid in Manhattan, Mrs. Doubtfire,* and *White Men Can't Jump,* a semiautobiographical account of his days as a high school basketball player. A show business attorney concedes that "Joe is one tough dog, even if he doesn't bark much. He knows exactly what he wants." Having reached the pinnacle of Hollywood success, Roth resigned from Disney in 2000 and founded Revolution Studios, a $1 billion corporation named for the Beatles' counterculture anthem. Roth chose the name to transform the copycat film industry, but it evoked his antiestablishment past and recalled the leftwing fervor of his father. For his diverse civic and charitable activities, Joe Roth has received awards from the Variety Clubs, the National Multiple Sclerosis Society, and the National Conference for Community and Justice (formerly the National Conference of Christians and Jews).

Despite Joe Roth's amazing success — more probably because of it — his father, the one-time radical activist, long refused to see any of Joe's films. In contrast to his father, Joe has devoted his life to making money, achieving power, and supporting mainstream institutions. Joe's drive to succeed can be traced to his strained relationship with his father, the challenges of surviving in a highly competitive industry, and the loss of his first child, Alexis, from sudden infant death syndrome. Shocked by this tragedy, Joe Roth poured himself into his career and, at the same time, became what a colleague calls "a true-blue family man" who put his children's athletic contests ahead of his work schedule. As for his commercially successful films, Joe says simply, "Sometimes you make compromises." For Lawrence Roth, compromising one's ideals was unthinkable, especially concerning religion. When he objected to his granddaughter Julia's Bas Mitzvah, Joe pointedly asked his father to keep his comments to himself: "Dad, now isn't the time or place to protest." The bitterness over *Engel* and its aftermath lingered on in the Roth family.

Decades after the storm subsided, Steven Engel has mixed feelings about the epic case named after him: "I know my name is in history, but I really wish it could have been resolved with the board of education." When asked if he would file the lawsuit again, he responded, "Knowing what happened . . . somebody had to do it. If religious freedom was going to have any meaning in America, somebody had to do it." Still, Engel doubts whether he and his wife, Thelma, would stick their necks out again because the price was very high for their young children. "I don't think I would do it again if the price was their involvement and the price was what they would have to pay . . . because it's such a horrific experience. In a way, you're a dissident. No less a dissident than some of the Soviet dissidents, and it's not easy being a dissident. It's not easy at all." He pointed out that unpopular lawsuits affect everyone around the litigant: "The thing is, you do not get involved on your own. You get involved, your whole family's involved, and it's difficult. I can say for myself — the kids went through a tough time." Nevertheless, Engel was "proud of one thing — that I fought the good fight."

Although praising Justice Hugo Black for a brilliant decision in the school prayer case, Engel insists that the U.S. Supreme Court did not make public schools religion-free zones: "You can pray in school, read your Bible in school, even proselytize in school *as an individual* in school, but when the state or an agent of the state enters this arena to propose, promote or conduct prayer, then it's a violation of church and state." He says flatly, "We haven't stopped prayer in the school."

Indeed, religion remains an important focus in many schools. Students pray in several ways, including silently by themselves, openly at the flagpole before school, as part of a Bible-study group after school, and at graduation ceremonies. Children may recite the Pledge of Allegiance with the phrase "one nation under God," sing patriotic songs that mention a deity, join the Fellowship of Christian Athletes, and buy their school lunches with money imprinted with "In God We Trust." The Bible may be studied objectively for its history, literature, art, and philosophy. Today, there are more than 1,000 released-time programs involving 250,000 students.

As for the Herricks School District where the case arose, much has changed during the past half century. Not only was the regents' prayer outlawed in 1962, but the school board has long since abandoned the daily moment-of-silence it adopted after *Engel* was decided. The district still provides an excellent education, but the student body, which was once all white and primarily Catholic, Protestant, and Jewish, looks very different now. The Jewish population in Nassau County dropped by one-third in the 1980s alone, as baby boomers left home for college and careers and their parents moved to the sun-belt. In Herricks today, half the students are Asian (primarily Indian, Korean, Chinese, and Pakistani), 45 percent are white, 4 percent are Hispanic, and less than 1 percent African American, with twelve religions represented.

To reflect changing realities, the school has prepared an inclusive calendar that acknowledges significant events across the religious spectrum, including Birth of the Báb (a Baha'i holiday) and Dusserah (a Hindu and Jain festival), along with the more familiar Roman Catholic holidays such as All Saints' Day, and Jewish holidays such as Sukkot, Yom Kippur, and Rosh Hashanah. Herricks School Board President Paul Ehrbar remarked, "Everyone knows when Christmas is, but not everyone knows about Ramadan [an Islamic holiday]. But people do in Herricks." Clergy of several faiths, including St. Aidan's Roman Catholic Church in Williston Park, Temple Judea in Manhasset, and the Islamic Center of Long Island in Westbury, have formed a community coalition to encourage cultural forums and other exchanges among students as early as first grade. These yearlong events culminate in a well-attended community day at which many different customs and foods are freely shared. A *Newsday* headline in 1998 declared: "Vibrant Herricks Proud of Diversity." The *Engel* decision helped pave the way for that spirit of greater tolerance.

Without question, the battle over school prayer changed the United States. The *Engel* decision marked the end of Protestant domination of public education and the ultimate triumph of the doctrine known as separation of church and state. More profoundly, as University of Michigan law professor Paul Kauper observed, *Engel* signaled that Protestantism could "no longer claim a dominating position in shaping the American *ethos.*" This realization helps to explain why the public reaction to *Engel* was so heated. Conservatives feared that the school prayer decision would dry up religious sentiment and thereby produce an amoral society that would provoke divine wrath. God, it was thought, would repudiate a people who had repudiated him. Certainly, social mores have changed over the years, but such metamorphosis is inexorable and, arguably, has nothing to do with the perfunctory recital of a short prayer written by the state. In what has been a doomed effort, some presidents and many congressmembers have sought to return to the days of Protestant control of society by reviving government-sponsored prayer. These efforts have proved moribund, because most Americans have come to recognize that this landmark decision did not impair religious freedom, but safeguarded it.

Americans today are widely regarded as the most religious people in the industrialized world. This continuing pattern of religiosity prevails because Jefferson, Madison, and other Founding Fathers devised a recipe for freedom that protects religious minorities of all kinds, even nonbelievers, and that allows religion to flourish by removing its dependence on the state. Even after two generations have been reared without organized school prayer, 90 percent of Americans tell pollsters of their belief in God. David Barton, the sky-is-falling historian of the religious right, was wrong.

1647	The Massachusetts General Court approves the "Old Deluder" Act, which requires towns to establish schools where children could acquire "knowledge of the Scriptures."
1785	James Madison's "Memorial and Remonstrance against Religious Assessments" objects to government funding of religion.
1786	Virginia enacts Thomas Jefferson's Statute for Religious Freedom.
1791	The First Amendment to the U.S. Constitution is ratified; it declares in part that "Congress shall make no law respecting an establishment of religion, or prohibiting the free exercise thereof."
1802	President Jefferson describes the First Amendment as "building a wall of separation between church and state."
1826	Massachusetts law mandates Bible reading in public schools.
1838	Horace Mann issues his "First Report" to the Massachusetts Board of Education, in which he tries to establish a nonsectarian Protestant system of education.
1840	Bishop John Hughes of New York demands public funding of Roman Catholic schools.
1842–1844	Bishop Francis Kenrick petitions public schools in Philadelphia, Pennsylvania, to let Roman Catholic children read from the Catholic Bible, touching off deadly riots.
1854	The Maine Supreme Court upholds expulsion of Roman Catholic students for refusing to participate in Bible reading.
1859	The Eliot School Rebellion in Boston, Massachusetts, ends with pupil Tom Whall being beaten for not reading from the King James Bible.
1869	The Cincinnati School Board prohibits Bible reading, igniting the Cincinnati Bible War.

1875	The Blaine Amendment proposes to prohibit state funding of parochial schools; although it never passes in Congress, the measure inspires many states to pass their own such laws.
1903	New Jersey law requires public schoolteachers to read from the Bible.
1905	The Baltimore School Board requires Bible reading in public schools.
1913	Pennsylvania law requires Bible reading in public schools.
1914	Released time for religious instruction begins in Gary, Indiana.
Feb. 10, 1947	In *Everson v. Board of Education*, the U.S. Supreme Court interprets the establishment clause as erecting a "wall of separation" between church and state.
Mar. 8, 1948	In *McCollum v. Board of Education*, the U.S. Supreme Court prohibits religious instruction within public schools.
Nov. 30, 1951	The New York State Board of Regents writes an official prayer for public schools.
Apr. 28, 1952	In *Zorach v. Clauson*, the U.S. Supreme Court upholds released time for religious instruction away from public school grounds.
July 8, 1958	The Herricks School Board in Nassau County on Long Island directs district teachers to recite the New York regents' prayer.
Dec. 4, 1958	Lawrene Roth, Steven Engel, Monroe Lerner, Daniel Lichtenstein, and Lenore Lyons send a letter to Herricks School Board President William Vitale, Jr., demanding an end to the regents' prayer.
Aug. 24, 1959	In *Engel v. Vitale*, Justice Bernard Meyer of the New York Supreme Court (Nassau County) rules that the regents' prayer is constitutional, provided that parents give their express approval and that teachers neither comment on who participates nor request certain posture or dress on the students' part.
Oct. 17, 1960	The Appellate Division of New York's State Supreme Court unanimously upholds the regents' prayer.

July 7, 1961	The New York Court of Appeals upholds the regents' prayer because it is not "religious education" or an "establishment of religion."
June 25, 1962	In *Engel v. Vitale*, Justice Hugo Black and the U.S. Supreme Court ban official prayer from all public schools.
Summer 1962	Most politicians, clerics, and the public express great dismay over *Engel v. Vitale*.
June 18, 1963	In *Abington v. Schempp*, the U.S. Supreme Court bars mandatory Bible reading in Pennsylvania and the Lord's Prayer in Maryland.
Apr.–June, 1964	Republican Long Island congressmember Frank Becker pressures the U.S. House Judiciary Committee to hold the first hearings on school prayer amendments.
Sept. 21, 1966	The U.S. Senate rejects Illinois Republican Everett Dirksen's "Amen Amendment."
Nov. 8, 1971	The U.S. House of Representatives rejects Ohio Republican Chalmers Wylie's prayer amendment.
June 17, 1978	The Kentucky legislature requires public schools to post the Ten Commandments in every classroom.
Apr. 22, 1980	In *Florey v. Sioux Falls School District*, the U.S. Eighth Circuit Court of Appeals permits Christmas concerts when the music program is not primarily sectarian.
Nov. 17, 1980	In *Stone v. Graham*, the U.S. Supreme Court prohibits Kentucky public schools from posting the Ten Commandments in classrooms.
Mar. 20, 1984	The U.S. Senate rejects President Ronald Reagan's prayer amendment.
Aug. 11, 1984	The Equal Access Act allows students, not school officials, to form extracurricular religious clubs, such as Bible clubs.
June 4, 1985	In *Wallace v. Jaffree*, the U.S. Supreme Court strikes down an Alabama law that requires a moment of silence before the school day; the Court found that the law, although worded neutrally, had a clearly religious purpose.
June 4, 1990	In *Board of Education of Westside Community Schools v. Mergens*, the U.S. Supreme Court sanctions the Equal Access Act, which permits Bible clubs outside of regular school hours.

June 24, 1992	In *Lee v. Weisman*, the U.S. Supreme Court forbids clergy-led prayers at high school graduation ceremonies.
July 12, 1995	President Bill Clinton declares that schools are not "religion-free zones," and identifies religious rights that students possess.
June 4, 1998	The U.S. House of Representatives rejects Oklahoma Republican Ernest Istook's prayer amendment.
June 19, 2000	In *Santa Fe Independent School District v. Doe*, the U.S. Supreme Court bars school officials from allowing students to lead stadium crowds in prayer before football games.

RELEVANT CASES

Board of Education of the City of Cincinnati v. Minor, 23 Ohio 211 (1872)

Board of Education of Westside Community Schools v. Mergens, 496 U.S. 226 (1990)

Cantwell v. Connecticut, 310 U.S. 296 (1940)

Chamberlin v. Dade County Board of Public Instruction, 377 U.S. 402 (1964)

DeSpain v. DeKalb County Community School District, 384 F.2d 836 (7th Cir. 1967), cert. denied, 390 U.S. 906 (1968)

Donahoe v. Richards, 38 Maine 379 (1854)

Doremus v. Board of Education, 342 U.S. 429 (1952)

Engel v. Vitale, 370 U.S. 421 (1962)

Everson v. Board of Education, 330 U.S. 1 (1947)

Florey v. Sioux Falls School District, 619 F.2d 1311 (8th Cir.), cert. denied, 449 U.S. 987 (1980)

Ill. ex rel. McCollum v. Board of Education, 333 U.S. 203 (1948)

Lee v. Weisman, 112 S. Ct. 2649 (1992)

Lemon v. Kurtzman, 403 U.S. 602 (1971)

Lynch v. Donnelly, 465 U.S. 668 (1984)

Minersville School District v. Gobitis, 310 U.S. 586 (1940)

Murray v. Curlett, 374 U.S. 203 (1963)

People ex rel. Ring v. Board of Education, 245 Ill. 334 (1910)

Reynolds v. United States, 98 U.S. 145 (1879)

Santa Fe Independent School District v. Doe, 530 U.S. 290 (2000)

School District of Abington Township v. Schempp, 374 U.S. 203 (1963)

State ex rel. Weiss v. District Board, 76 Wis. 177, 44 N.W. 967 (1890)

Stein v. Oshinsky, 348 F. 2d 999, cert. denied, 382 U.S. 957 (1965)

Stone v. Graham, 449 U.S. 39 (1980)

Tudor v. Board of Education of the Borough of Rutherford, 14 N.J. 31, 100 A. 2d 857 (1953), cert. denied, 348 U.S. 816 (1954)

United States v. Carolene Products, 304 U.S. 142, 152 (1938)

Wallace v. Jaffree, 472 U.S. 38 (1985)

West Virginia State Board of Education v. Barnette, 319 U.S. 624 (1943)

Zorach v. Clauson, 343 U.S. 306 (1952)

Major U.S. Supreme Court Religion Cases

Case	Year	Petitioner(s)	Petitioner's Religion	Place	Issue	Petitioner's Counsel	Majority Opinion	Strict Separation?
Cantwell v. Connecticut	1940	Jesse Cantwell	Jehovah's Witness	New Haven, CT	Proselytism	Jehovah's Witnesses	Owen Roberts	Yes
Minersville SD v. Gobitis	1940	Walter Gobitas	Jehovah's Witness	Minersville, PA	Pledge of Allegiance	ACLU	Felix Frankfurter	No
WV Bd. of Ed. v. Barnette	1943	Walter Barnette	Jehovah's Witness	West Virginia	Pledge of Allegiance	Holt Wooddell	Robert Jackson	Yes
Everson v. Bd. of Ed.	1947	Arch Everson	Atheist	Ewing Township, NJ	Bus reimbursement	Edward Burke	Hugo Black	No
McCollum v. Bd. of Ed.	1948	Vashti McCollum	Humanist	Champaign, IL	Released time	Walter Dodd	Hugo Black	Yes
Zorach v. Clauson	1952	Esta Gluck Tessim Zorach	Jew Episcopalian	New York, NY	Released time	ACLU	William O. Douglas	No
Engel v. Vitale	1962	Steven Engel Monroe Lerner Daniel Lichtenstein Lenore Lyons Lawrence Roth	Jew Humanist Jew Unitarian Atheist	New Hyde Park, NY	Regents' prayer	ACLU	Hugo Black	Yes

Major U.S. Supreme Court Religion Cases *(Continued)*

Case	Year	Petitioner(s)	Petitioner's Religion	Place	Issue	Petitioner's Counsel	Majority Opinion	Strict Separation?
Abington v. Schempp	1963	Ellory Schempp	Unitarian	Abington, PA	Bible reading	ACLU	Tom Clark	Yes
Murray v. Curlett	1963	Madalyn Murray	Atheist	Baltimore, MD	Lord's Prayer	Leonard Kerpelman	Tom Clark	Yes
Lemon v. Kurtzman	1971	Alton Lemon	Humanist	Rhode Island	Parochial school aid	ACLU	Warren Burger	No
Stone v. Graham	1980	Anne Bowers Patricia Bricking Martin Perley Sydell Stone	Nonbeliever Roman Catholic Jew Unitarian	Kentucky	Ten Commandments	ACLU	Unsigned	Yes
Lynch v. Donnelly	1984	Daniel Donnelly	Roman Catholic	Pawtucket, RI	Crèche	ACLU	Warren Burger	No
Wallace v. Jaffree	1985	Ishmael Jaffree	Humanist	Mobile, AL	Moment of silence	Ronnie Williams	John Paul Stevens	Yes
Bd. of Ed. of Westside v. Mergens	1990	Bridget Mergens	Assemblies of God	Omaha, NE	Bible club	ACLJ	Sandra Day O'Connor	No
Lee v. Weisman	1992	Daniel Weisman	Jew	Providence, RI	Graduation prayer	ACLU	Anthony Kennedy	Yes
Santa Fe ISD v. Doe	2000	Anonymous Anonymous	Roman Catholic Mormon	Santa Fe, TX	Football game prayer	ACLU	John Paul Stevens	Yes

BIBLIOGRAPHIC ESSAY

Note from the series editors: The following bibliographic essay contains the primary and secondary sources the author consulted for this volume. We have asked all authors in the series to omit formal citations in order to make our volumes more readable, inexpensive, and appealing for students and general readers. In adopting this format, Landmark Law Cases and American Society *follows the precedent of a number of highly regarded and widely consulted series.*

The following books are excellent introductions to the historical controversy over religion in U.S. public education: Warren Nord, *Religion and American Education: Rethinking a National Dilemma* (Chapel Hill: University of North Carolina Press, 1995) and Joan DelFattore, *The Fourth R: Conflicts over Religion in America's Public Schools* (New Haven: Yale University Press, 2004). Classic works on this topic include R. Freeman Butts, *The American Tradition in Religion and Education* (Boston: Beacon Press, 1950); Anson Stokes, *Church and State in the United States* (New York: Harper, 1950); Frank Sorauf, *The Wall of Separation: The Constitutional Politics of Church and State* (Princeton: Princeton University Press, 1976); and Rodney Smith, *Public Prayer and the Constitution: A Case Study in Constitutional Interpretation* (Wilmington, DE: Scholarly Resources, 1987).

I learned a great deal about the subject of school prayer from older works, including William Muir, *Prayer in the Public Schools* (Chicago: University of Chicago Press, 1967); Donald Boles, *The Bible, Religion, and the Public Schools* (Ames: Iowa State University Press, 1965) and *The Two Swords: Commentaries and Cases in Religion and Education* (Ames: Iowa State University Press, 1967); Alvin Johnson, *The Legal Status of Church-State Relationships in the United States with Special Reference to the Public Schools* (Minneapolis: University of Minnesota Press, 1934); Alvin Johnson and Frank Yost, *Separation of Church and State in the United States* (Minneapolis: University of Minnesota Press, 1948); Paul Kauper, *Religion and the Constitution* (Baton Rouge: Louisiana State University Press, 1964); Richard McMillan, *Religion in the Public Schools* (Macon, GA: Mercer University Press, 1984); Robert Michaelsen, *Piety in the Public School: Trends and Issues in the Relationship between Religion and the Public Schools in the United States* (New York: Macmillan, 1970); V. T. Thayer, *The Attack upon the American Secular School* (Boston: Beacon Press, 1951); and William Fleming, *God in Our Public Schools* (Pittsburgh: National Reform Association, 1944).

Regarding the Founding Fathers devising the First Amendment and safeguarding religious liberty, one might profitably consult William Lee Miller, *The First Liberty: Religion and the American Republic* (New York: Knopf, 1986); Thomas Curry, *The First Freedoms: Church and State in America to the Passage* of the First Amendment (New York: Oxford University Press, 1986); Edwin Gaustad, *Proclaim Liberty throughout the Land: A History of Church and State in America* (New York: Oxford University Press, 2003); and Frank Lambert, *The Founding Fathers and the Place of Religion in America* (Princeton, NJ: Princeton University Press, 2003). For a more general discussion of the First Amendment, see Robert Alley, *James Madison on Religious Liberty* (Buffalo, NY: Prometheus Books, 1985) and Akhil Amar, *The Bill of Rights: Creation and Reconstruction* (New Haven, CT: Yale University Press, 1998).

The meaning of the First Amendment is of crucial importance because the U.S. constitutional system relies heavily on the doctrine of originalism. This doctrine asserts that the U.S. Supreme Court must ascertain the meaning of the federal Constitution by looking at the intentions of the Founding Fathers. Among the more authoritative works in this regard are Edwin Scott Gaustad, "A Disestablishment Society: Origins of the First Amendment," *Journal of Church and State* 11 (1969): 409–425; Donald Drakeman, "Religion and the Republic: James Madison and the First Amendment," *Journal of Church and State* 25 (Autumn 1983): 427–445; Douglas Laycock, "The Origins of the Religion Clauses of the Constitution: 'Nonpreferential' Aid to Religion: A False Claim about Original Intent," *William and Mary Law Review* 27 (1986): 875–923; Leonard Levy, *The Establishment Clause: Religion and the First Amendment* (Chapel Hill: University of North Carolina Press, 1994); Derek Davis, *Religion and the Continental Congress, 1774–1789: Contributions to Original Intent* (New York: Oxford University Press, 2000); Philip Hamburger, *Separation of Church and State* (Cambridge: Harvard University Press, 2002); and Daniel Dreisbach, *Thomas Jefferson and the Wall of Separation between Church and State* (New York: New York University Press, 2002). Other scholars maintain that a rigid separation between church and state is a misreading of U.S. history and jurisprudence. See Robert Cord, *Separation of Church and State: Historical Fact and Current Fiction* (New York: Lambeth Press, 1982) and Michael McConnell, "The Origins and Historical Understanding of Free Exercise of Religion," *Harvard Law Review* 103 (May 1990): 1409–1517.

The "warfare" thesis posits that the history of church and state in the United States can be summed up by the conflicts that occurred, chiefly between Protestants and Catholics and between Protestants and Jews. Certainly, much evidence exists to support this long-standing argument. See the old standard — Ray Allen Billington, *The Protestant Crusade, 1800–1860: A Study of the Origins of American Nativism* (New York: Macmillan, 1938) — as well as Diane Ravitch, *The Great School Wars: New York City, 1805–1973, A History of the Public Schools as Battlefield of Social Change* (New York: Basic Books, 1974); Michael Feldberg, *The Philadelphia Riots of 1844: A Study of Ethnic Conflict* (Westport, CT: Greenwood, 1975); Stephan Brumberg, "The Cincinnati Bible War (1869–1873) and its Impact on the Education of the

City's Protestants, Catholics, and Jews," *Hebrew Union College Journal* 54 (April 29, 2004): 11–46; and John McGeevy, *Catholicism and American Freedom: A History* (New York: Norton, 2003).

People have long assumed that formal religion always existed and was pervasive in public schools. This view has been sharply challenged by R. Laurence Moore, "Bible Reading and Nonsectarian Schooling: The Failure of Religious Instruction in Nineteenth-Century Public Education," *Journal of American History* 86 (March 2000): 1581–1599. Benjamin Justice provides a particularly valuable discussion of New York public schools in the late nineteenth century in *The War That Wasn't: Religious Conflict and Compromise in the Common Schools of New York State, 1865–1900* (Albany: State University of New York Press, 2005). For older works on this subject, consult Samuel Brown, *The Secularization of American Education, as Shown by the State Legislation, State Constitutional Provisions, and State Supreme Court Decisions* (New York: Russell and Russell, 1912) and William Dunn, *What Happened to Religious Education? The Decline of Religious Teaching in the Public Elementary School, 1776–1861* (Baltimore: Johns Hopkins University Press, 1958).

Several excellent scholarly studies in the period since World War II have examined the critical role that Jews and Jewish defense organizations played in trying to keep a strict separation between church and state. See especially Naomi Cohen, *Jews in Christian America: The Pursuit of Religious Equality* (New York: Oxford University Press, 1992) and Gregg Ivers, *To Build a Wall: American Jews and the Separation of Church and State* (Charlottesville: University Press of Virginia, 1995).

As the Roman Catholic Church increasingly demanded parochial school funding after World War II, voices arose to challenge the church. No one was more significant than Paul Blanshard, whose works have been viewed as anti-Catholic polemics. See Blanshard's *American Freedom and Catholic Power* (Boston: Beacon Press, 1949); *God and Man in Washington* (Boston: Beacon Press, 1960); and *Religion and the Schools* (Boston: Beacon Press, 1963). Blanshard's views were carried into court by Protestants and Other Americans for Separation of Church and State (POAU), an organization for which he worked. In this connection, see Lawrence Creedon and William Falcon, *United for Separation: An Analysis of POAU Assaults on Catholicism* (Milwaukee: Bruce, 1959).

The organization most responsible for bringing First Amendment lawsuits to the U.S. Supreme Court has been the American Civil Liberties Union (ACLU). The ACLU's archives at the Seeley G. Mudd Library, Princeton University, Princeton, New Jersey, contain a wide variety of materials of interest to the student of school prayer. Another valuable source is the *New York Civil Liberties Union Weekly Bulletin*, which was published by the ACLU affiliate that brought the case. Histories of the national organization do not delve deeply into religious establishment cases, especially *Engel,* but see Samuel Walker, *In Defense of American Liberties: A History of the ACLU* (New York: Oxford University Press, 1990). An ACLU founder has written his memoir: Arthur Garfield Hays, *City Lawyer: The Autobiography of a Law Practice* (New York: Simon and Schuster, 1942).

Leo Pfeffer, a prime architect of religious establishment cases (especially religious instruction, school prayer, and Bible reading in public schools) in the formative period after World War II, was a prolific writer and influential interpreter of the First Amendment. See his many works, including *The New York Regents' Prayer Case* (Engel v. Vitale*): Its Background, Meaning, and Implications* (New York: Commission on Law and Social Action of the American Jewish Congress, 1962); *Church, State, and Freedom* (Boston: Beacon, 1967); *God, Caesar, and the Constitution* (Boston: Beacon, 1975); and *Religion, State, and the Burger Court* (Buffalo, NY: Prometheus Books, 1984). Pfeffer's papers are at the George Arendts Research Library, Syracuse University, Syracuse, New York. A festschrift by Pfeffer's admirers was compiled by James Wood, Jr., *Religion and the State: Essays in Honor of Leo Pfeffer* (Waco, TX: Baylor University Press, 1985).

There is no full-length academic study of the *Engel* case in all its dimensions, particularly an examination of the petitioners and their community. Lynda Fenwick's book, *Should the Children Pray? A Historical, Judicial, and Political Examination of Public School Prayer* (Waco, TX: Baylor University Press, 1989), concentrates on the colonial and constitutional periods before skipping to the period after World War II. Books for juveniles include Carol Haas, Engel v. Vitale: *Separation of Church and State* (Hillside, NJ: Enslow, 1994); Mark Dudley, Engel v. Vitale *(1962): Religion and the Schools* (New York: Twenty-First Century, 1995); Tricia Andryszewski, *School Prayer: A History of the Debate* (Hillside, NJ: Enslow, 1997); and Julia Loren, Engel v. Vitale: *Prayer in the Public Schools* (San Diego: Lucent Books, 2001).

None of the principals in the *Engel* case has written his or her story. No petitioner, no petitioner's spouse or child, no classmate, no teacher, no administrator, no attorney, no judge or justice connected in some way to the case has written an essay, much less published a book about the case. To my knowledge, only Steven Engel and Lawrence, Daniel, and Joseph Roth have been interviewed at any length about the case prior to the research for this book. My study of Lawrence Roth — the key figure in the *Engel* lawsuit — and his family leans on a variety of sources, including the U.S. Census; *Fort Wayne City and Allen County Directory* (Fort Wayne, IN: R. L. Polk, 1897–1916); John Ankenbruck, *Twentieth Century History of Fort Wayne* (Fort Wayne, IN: Twentieth Century Historical Fort Wayne, 1975); *Fort Wayne Daily*; *Pittsburgh Post-Gazette*; *Braddock Herald*; *Wilmerding News-Tribune*; *Borough of Turtle Creek Centennial: 1892–1992* (Turtle Creek, PA: Centennial Committee, 1992); and

Memories of U (the Union High School yearbook). Personal information about the litigants can be found in Nathaniel Lehrman, "The Psychological Warfare Campaign against Long Island's Public Schools," *Journal of Church and State* 2 (November 1960): 137–155; William Kunstler, "Five Against God," in *And Justice for All* (Dobbs Ferry, NY: Oceana Publications, 1963), pp. 210–229; Fred Friendly and Martha Elliott, *The Constitution: That Delicate Balance* (New York: Random House, 1984); Fred Schruers, "Crossing Over," *Premiere* 3 (April 1990): 124–131; and Maximillian Porter, "The Insider," *Gentlemen's Quarterly* 72 (March 2002): 304–309, 356.

This book relies substantially on oral history interviews with participants and contemporary observers. Of course, such narratives must be handled with care and, when possible, supported by written records. Most valuable of all, I spoke to at least one member of all five petitioner families, something that no other scholar has done. With the recent deaths of Monroe Lerner and Lawrence Roth, the sole surviving petitioner is Steven Engel of Great Neck, New York. Engel's wife Thelma is also living, as are Julia Lerner and Ruth Lichtenstein and, as far as can be determined, all of the petitioners' children. For a full list of interviewees, see the "Acknowledgments" section of this book.

The most significant archival materials on the case are in the Herricks School District administration building. There, one finds school memoranda, school board minutes, letters to school officials, petitions, yearbooks (*Tartan*), and so forth. William Butler, the petitioners' lead attorney, has an archive at the Robert S. Marx Law Library, University of Cincinnati College of Law, Cincinnati, Ohio, but this collection is useful primarily for its scrapbooks of newspaper clippings. Barbara Kantowitz, an alumna of Herricks High School, wrote a useful study of her school and community, which was ground zero in the school prayer fight: "*Engel v. Vitale*: Local Reaction to Religion in the Schools," Senior Seminar Essay (New York: Barnard College, 1964).

Newspapers have been indispensable to my work. Most scholarship on the *Engel* case relies on the *New York Times*, but much more of the story can be found in local newspapers, especially *Newsday*, and, to a lesser extent, the *New Hyde Park Courier*, *Long Island Advocate*, *Long Island Catholic*, *Long Island News*, *Long Island Post*, *Long Island Press*, *Long Island Star-Journal*, *Mineola American*, *Roslyn News*, and *Williston Times*. The *Herricks Highlander*, the student newspaper, did not contain information about the case per se; it did provide insights into the school district and the extent of religious practices in the schools. Besides the *New York Times*, the papers in the Big Apple carried many detailed and analytical accounts of the case, including the *New York Daily News*, *New York Herald Tribune*, *New York Journal-American*, *New York Mirror*, *New York Post*, and *New York World-Telegram*. For other school prayer cases, read articles in the *Baltimore Sun*, *Birmingham News*, *Christian Science Monitor*, *Louisville Courier*, *Los Angeles Times*, *Mobile Register*, *Philadelphia Bulletin*,

Philadelphia Inquirer, Philadelphia Sunday Bulletin, Providence Journal-Bulletin, Wall Street Journal, Washington Post, and *Washington Star.*

In addition, I examined a wide variety of periodicals, including *The Nation, National Review, New Republic, Newsweek, Time,* and *U.S. News World & Report.* The journals that follow issues relating to church and state most closely are the respected *Journal of Church and State,* which is published by the J. M. Dawson Institute for Church and State at Baylor University, and *Church and State,* the journal of Americans United for Separation of Church and State. Because this book necessarily focuses on religious communities for their involvement in and reaction to school prayer cases, I consulted many Protestant, Catholic, and Jewish periodicals.

Many primary source materials on *Engel* and associated cases can be found in published form. For an overview of the issues and justices involved in *Engel* and other establishment cases in New York State, see Bernard Meyer, Burton Agata, and Seth Agata, *The History of the New York Court of Appeals, 1932–2003* (New York: Columbia University Press, 2006). Robert Sikorski has edited legal documents relating to school prayer in *Prayer in Public Schools and the Constitution, 1961–1992,* vols. 1–3 in the Controversies in Constitutional Law Series, Paul Finkelman, ed. (New York: Garland, 1993). For a transcript of the Supreme Court's conference discussion of *Engel,* see Del Dickson, ed., *The Supreme Court in Conference (1940–1985): The Private Discussions behind Nearly 300 Supreme Court Decisions* (New York: Oxford University Press, 2001). Supreme Court briefs and oral arguments in *Engel* are reprinted in Philip Kurland and Gerhard Casper, eds., *Landmark Briefs and Arguments of the Supreme Court of the United States* (Washington, DC: University Publications of America, 1975).

The papers of justices of the U.S. Supreme Court are useful too. They contain multiple drafts of opinions and memoranda helpful for understanding the internal workings of the Court as it struggled with these matters. Indispensable in this regard are the papers of Hugo Black, the prime architect of church-state jurisprudence, along with William Brennan, William O. Douglas, and Earl Warren, all of which are stored at the Library of Congress in Washington, DC. Potter Stewart's papers at Yale University have not yet been made accessible to the public.

Many fine commentaries and sourcebooks exist on the U.S. Supreme Court and religion. Among the better works are Henry Abraham, *Freedom and the Court: Civil Rights and Liberties in the United States* (New York: Oxford University Press, 1988); Robert Alley, *The Supreme Court on Church and State* (New York: Oxford University Press, 1988); Robert Miller and Ronald Flowers, *Toward Benevolent Neutrality: Church, State, and the Supreme Court* (Waco, TX: Baylor University Press, 1992); Terry Eastland, ed., *Religious Liberty in the Supreme Court: The Cases That Define the Debate over Church and State* (Washington: Ethics and Public Policy Center, 1993); Ronald Flowers, *That Godless Court? Supreme Court Decisions on Church-State Relationships* (Louisville: Westminster John Knox Press, 1994); Peter Irons, *A People's History of the Supreme Court* (New York: Penguin, 1999); John Johnson, ed., *Historic U.S. Court Cases: An Encyclopedia*, 2nd ed., vol. 2 (New York: Routledge, 2001); Melvin Urofsky, *Religious Freedom: Rights and Liberties under the Law* (Santa Barbara, CA: ABC-CLIO, 2002); Paul Finkelman and Melvin Urofsky, *Landmark Decisions of the United States Supreme Court* (Washington: Congressional Quarterly Press, 2003); and David Schultz and John Vile, eds., *The Encyclopedia of Civil Liberties in America* (M.E. Sharpe, 2005).

A number of judicial biographies, autobiographies, and studies have been helpful in examining religious establishment. For an introduction, see Melvin Urofsky, ed., *The Supreme Court Justices: A Biographical Dictionary* (New York: Garland, 1994). The following books delve into the lives and decisions of members of the U.S. Supreme Court from the Great Depression to the attack on the World Trade Towers in 2001: Alpheus Mason, *Harlan Fiske Stone: Pillar of the Law* (New York: Viking, 1956); Melvin Urofsky, *Felix Frankfurter: Judicial Restraint and Individual Liberties* (Boston: Twayne, 1991); F. William O'Brien, *Justice Reed and the First Amendment: The Religion Clauses* (Washington, DC: Georgetown University Press, 1958); John Ferren, *Salt of the Earth, Conscience of the Court: The Story of Justice Wiley Rutledge* (Chapel Hill: University of North Carolina Press, 2004); Eugene Gerhart, *America's Advocate: Robert H. Jackson* (Indianapolis: Bobbs-Merrill, 1958); Sidney Fine, *Frank Murphy: The Washington Years* (Ann Arbor: University of Michigan Press, 1984); Earl Warren, *The Memoirs of Earl Warren* (Garden City, NJ: Doubleday, 1977); Tinsley Yarbrough, *John Marshall Harlan: Great Dissenter of the Warren Court* (New York: Oxford University Press, 1992); Kim Eiser, *A Justice for All: William J. Brennan, Jr., and the Decisions That Transformed America* (New York: Simon and Schuster, 1993); Bruce Allen Murphy, *Wild Bill: The Legend and Life of William O. Douglas* (New York: Random House, 2003); Stephen Monsma, "Justice Potter Stewart on Church and State," *Journal of Church and State* 36 (Summer 1994): 575–577; Donald Beschle, "The Conservative as Liberal: The Religion Clauses, Liberal Neutrality, and the Approach of Justice O'Connor," *Notre Dame Law Review* 62 (1987): 151–192; Robert Sickels, *John Paul Stevens and the Constitution: The Search for Balance* (University Park: Pennsylvania State University Press, 1988); and Richard Brisbin, Jr., *Justice Antonin Scalia and the Conservative Revival* (Baltimore: Johns Hopkins University Press, 1997).

The central figure in church-state jurisprudence was U.S. Supreme Court justice Hugo Black, and the literature about him is voluminous: for example see Hugo Black and Elizabeth Black, *Mr. Justice and Mrs. Black: The Memoirs of Hugo L. Black and Elizabeth Black* (New York: Random House, 1986); Barbara Perry, "Justice Hugo Black and the 'Wall of Separation between Church and

State,'" *Journal of Church and State* 31 (1989), pp. 55–72; James Simon, *The Antagonists: Hugo Black, Felix Frankfurter, and Civil Liberties in Modern America* (New York: Simon and Schuster, 1989); and especially Roger Newman, *Hugo Black: A Biography* (New York: Fordham University Press, 1997).

For information on the Warren Court at the time of *Engel*, see H. C. Hudgins, *The Warren Court and the Public Schools* (Danville, IL: Interstate Printers and Publishers, 1970); Thomas Mengler, "Public Relations in the Supreme Court: Justice Tom Clark's Opinion in the School Prayer Case," *Constitutional Commentary* 6 (1989): 331–349; Morton Horwitz, *The Warren Court and the Pursuit of Justice* (New York: Hill and Wang, 1998); and Michal Belknap, *The Supreme Court under Earl Warren, 1953–1969* (Columbia: University of South Carolina Press, 2005).

The adverse reaction to the *Engel* decision was enormous, shaped in large measure by the negative press coverage: see Chester Newland, "Press Coverage of the United States Supreme Court," *Western Political Quarterly* 17 (March 1964): 15–26. For congressional reaction following *Engel*, see John Laubach, *School Prayers: Congress, the Courts, and the Public* (Washington, DC: Public Affairs Press, 1969); Edward Schapsmeier and Frederick Schapsmeier, *Dirksen of Illinois: Senatorial Statesman* (Urbana: University of Illinois Press, 1985); Edward Keynes and Randall Miller, *The Court versus Congress: Prayer, Busing, and Abortion* (Durham, NC: Duke University Press, 1989); Garry Wills, *Under God: Religion and American Politics* (New York: Simon and Schuster, 1990); David O'Brien, *Storm Center: The Supreme Court in American Politics* (New York: Norton, 1993); and Lucas Powe, Jr., *The Warren Court and American Politics* (Cambridge: Harvard University Press, 2000).

The first great moment for political reform came with the 1964 Becker Amendment, which would have allowed formal school prayer. In this regard, see William Beaney and Edward Beiser, "Prayer and Politics: The Impact of *Engel* and *Schempp* on the Political Process," *Journal of Public Law* 13 (1964): 475–503; Richard McBrien, *Caesar's Coin: Religion and Politics in America* (New York: Macmillan, 1987); Steven Green, "Evangelicals and the Becker Amendment: A Lesson in Church-State Moderation," *Journal of Church and State* 33 (Summer 1991): 541–567; and Robert Alley, *School Prayer: The Court, the Congress, and the First Amendment* (Buffalo, NY: Prometheus, 1994).

Perhaps the most studied aspect of the *Engel* case is educational compliance: see Raymond Celada, *The Supreme Court Opinion in the School Prayer Case (*Engel v. Vitale*): The Decision, the Reaction, the Pros and Cons* (Washington, DC: Library of Congress Legislative Reference Service, 1963); Richard Johnson, *The Dynamics of Compliance* (Evanston: Northwestern University Press, 1967); H. Frank Way, Jr., "Survey Research on Judicial Decisions: The Prayer and Bible Reading Cases," *Western Political Quarterly* 21 (June 1968): 189–205; and Kenneth Dolbeare and Phillip Hammond, *The School Prayer*

Decisions: From Court Policy to Local Practice (Chicago: University of Chicago Press, 1971).

Fortunately, there are audio recordings of court proceedings and videotaped interviews with key figures in the school prayer cases. Oyez.org contains the recordings of these cases, and I have listed the specific site for the *Engel* case: http://www.oyez.org/media/item?type=audio&id=argument&parent= cases/1960-1969/1961/1961_468. See also Peter Irons and Stephanie Guitton, eds., *May It Please the Court: 23 Live Recordings of Landmark U.S. Supreme Court Decisions* (Princeton, NJ: Films for the Humanities and Sciences, 2000); CBS News, *Landmark U.S. Supreme Court Decisions, Part 1: The School Prayer Case* — *Engel v. Vitale* (Princeton, NJ: Films for the Humanities and Sciences, 1963); Bill Moyers, *In Search of the Constitution, Part 9: For the People* (New York: Public Affairs Television, 1987); CBS News, *Landmark U.S. Supreme Court Decisions, Part 2: Bible Reading in the Public Schools* — *The* Schempp *and* Murray *Cases* (Princeton, NJ: Films for the Humanities and Sciences, 1963); *One Nation Under God? School Prayer and the First Amendment* (Alexandria, VA: Close Up Foundation, 1995); and *School Prayer: A Community at War* (Public Broadcasting Service, 1999).

Excellent books on the plaintiffs in religious liberty cases, including school prayer, are Peter Irons, *The Courage of Their Convictions* (New York: Free Press, 1988) and Robert Alley, *Without a Prayer: Religious Expression in Public Schools* (Amherst, NY: Prometheus, 1996). Joseph Lewis, a pioneer in challenging religion in public education, discusses his perspective in *An Atheist Manifesto* (New York: Freethought Press, 1954). Vashti McCollum's *One Woman's Fight* (Garden City, NY: Doubleday, 1951) chronicles her victory over released-time programs in public schools. Ellory Schempp discusses "My Supreme Court Case," in remarks found at http://www.secularstudents.org/node/403. Without question, Madalyn Murray O'Hair was the most flamboyant plaintiff to take a school prayer case to the U.S. Supreme Court and win. She gives her side of the story in *An Atheist Epic: The Complete Unexpurgated Story of How Bible and Prayers Were Removed from the Public Schools of the United States* (Austin, TX: American Atheist Press, 1989). *American Atheist* magazine, which was published by O'Hair, pulls no punches in criticizing religion in general and school prayer in particular. O'Hair's controversial life and death are chronicled in Bryan Le Beau, *The Atheist: Madalyn Murray O'Hair* (New York: New York University Press, 2003) and Ted Dracos, *Ungodly: The Passions, Torments, and Murder of Atheist Madalyn Murray O'Hair* (New York: Free Press, 2003). O'Hair's oldest son, William Murray, presents her in a critical light in *My Life without God* (New York: Thomas Nelson, 1983) and *Let Us Pray: A Plea for Prayer in Our Schools* (New York: Morrow, 1995). Ishmael Jaffree outlines his views in "The Quest for Humanist Values," *African-American Humanism: An Anthology*, Norm Allen, Jr., ed. (Buffalo, NY: Prometheus

Books, 1991). For Daniel Weisman's recollections of the graduation prayer case that bears his name, see "My Journal: The Education of an Un-Reformed Red Diaper Baby," http://www2.ric.edu/itl/volume_04_weisman_v4.php.

Conservative Christians — loosely divided into fundamentalists and evangelicals — despised the *Engel, Schempp*, and *Murray* rulings, and organized as the religious right to reverse them: see Erling Jorstad, *The New Christian Right, 1981–1988* (Lewiston, NY: Edwin Mellon Press, 1987); Walter Capps, *The New Religious Right: Piety, Patriotism, and Politics* (Columbia: University of South Carolina Press, 1990); Eugene Provenzo, Jr., *Religious Fundamentalism and American Education: The Battle for the Public Schools* (Albany: State University of New York Press, 1990); Michael Lienesch, *Redeeming America: Piety and Politics in the New Christian Right* (Chapel Hill: University of North Carolina Press, 1993); Clyde Wilcox, *God's Warriors: The Christian Right in Twentieth-Century America* (Baltimore, MD: Johns Hopkins University Press, 1993); Fritz Detwiler, *Standing on the Premises of God: The Christian Right's Fight to Redefine America's Public Schools* (New York: New York University Press, 1999); and Steven Brown, *Trumping Religion: The New Christian Right, the Free Speech Clause, and the Courts* (Tuscaloosa: University of Alabama Press, 2002). In *School Prayer and Discrimination: The Civil Rights of Religious Minorities and Dissenters* (Boston: Northeastern University Press, 1999), Frank Ravitch argues that Christians are the aggrieved minority in the culture wars.

Accounts by religious right activists include Tim LaHaye, *The Battle for the Public Schools* (Old Tappan, NJ: Revell, 1983); Jay Sekulow, *From Intimidation to Victory: Regaining the Christian Right to Speak* (Lake Mary, FL: Creation House, 1990); and Jesse Helms, *Here's Where I Stand: A Memoir* (New York: Random House, 2005). John Whitehead's *The Rights of Religious Persons in Public Education* (Wheaton, IL: Crossway Books, 1991), provides a manual of the civil liberties of evangelical Christians in public schools. No one has been more prominent in the rise of the religious right than Jerry Falwell: see his manifesto *Listen, America!* (Garden City, NY: Doubleday, 1980); see also Dinesh D'Souza, *Falwell before the Millennium: A Critical Biography* (Chicago: Regnery, 1984). Other members of the religious right have set forth their own convictions about U.S. history: see David Barton's *America: To Pray or Not To Pray?* (Aledo, TX: WallBuilder Press, 1988), *A Guide to the School Prayer and Religious Liberty Debate* (Aledo, TX: Rebuilder Press, 1995), and *The Myth of Separation* (Aledo, TX: WallBuilder Press, 1989).

Critics of the religious right are legion: see especially Rob Boston, *Why the Religious Right Is Wrong about Separation of Church and State* (Buffalo, NY: Prometheus Books, 1993). Boston also wrote a review of the legal battle over devotions since *Engel*: "Forever and Ever Amen: The 30 Years' War over Prayer and Bible Reading in the Public Schools," *Church and State* 46 (June 1993): 7-10. For additional critical assessments of the religious right, consult

David Bollier, *Liberty and Justice for Some: Defending a Free Society from the Radical Right's Holy War on Democracy* (Washington, DC: People for the American Way, 1982); Flo Conway and Jim Siegelman, *Holy Terror: The Fundamentalist War on America's Freedoms in Religion, Politics, and Our Private Lives* (Garden City, NY: Doubleday, 1982); Mel White, *Religion Gone Bad: The Hidden Dangers of the Christian Right* (New York: Tarcher/Penguin Books, 2006); and Barry Lynn, *Piety & Politics: The Right-Wing Assault on Religious Freedom* (New York: Harmony Books, 2006). Regardless of how one feels about the religious right, this group's anger over the school prayer decisions fueled powerful resentment that spawned cultural conflict. Jonathan Zimmerman, *Whose America? Culture Wars and the Public Schools* (Cambridge, MA: Harvard University Press, 2002), has written an authoritative account.

Chief Justice William Rehnquist hoped to level Jefferson's metaphoric wall and reverse *Engel*, but his grand plan never succeeded: see Derek Davis, *Original Intent: Chief Justice Rehnquist and the Course of American Church/State Relations* (Buffalo, NY: Prometheus Books, 1991) and Gregg Ivers, *Lowering the Wall: Religion and the Supreme Court in the 1980s* (New York: Anti-Defamation League, 1991).

One of the greatest pleasures of this book has been following in the academic footsteps of my father, Richard Dierenfield, a noted authority on school prayer. The statistics compiled in his book, *Religion in American Public Schools* (St. Paul, MN: Public Affairs Press, 1962) and articles, including "Religious Influence in American Public Schools," *Clearing House* 59 (May 1986): 390–392, have been cited repeatedly in the literature I have examined and are, to a limited extent, reprinted here. Like my father, I have long found school prayer to be an interesting subject: see Bruce Dierenfield, "Secular Schools? Religious Practices in New York and Virginia Public Schools since World War II," *Journal of Policy History* 4, no. 4 (1992): 361–388; "Rooting out Religion: Devotions in Minnesota Public Schools since 1950," *Minnesota History* 58, no. 3 (Winter 1993): 294–311; "The Amen Amendment: Doomed to Failure?" *Religion and Education* 22 (Fall 1995): 40–48; "'A Nation under God': Ronald Reagan and the Crusade for School Prayer," in *Ronald Reagan's America*, Eric Schmertz, Natalie Datlof, and Alexej Ugrinsky, eds. (Westport, CT: Greenwood Press, 1997), pp. 215–247; "'Somebody is Tampering with America's Soul': Congress and the School Prayer Debate," *Congress and the Presidency* 24, no. 2 (Autumn 1997): 167–204; "Steven Engel and Lawrence Roth: 'The Supreme Court Has Held That God Is Unconstitutional,'" in *100 Americans Making Constitutional History*, Melvin Urofsky, ed. (Washington, DC: Congressional Quarterly Press, 2004): 48–51; "*Engel v. Vitale*," in *The Public Debate over Controversial Supreme Court Decisions*, Melvin Urofsky, ed. (Washington, DC: Congressional Quarterly Press, 2006): 215–225.

After the Supreme Court outlawed organized school prayer, proponents of religion in the schools searched for another means to permit devotions. One such means is a moment of silence, which allows students an opportunity to pray or meditate. See Walter Dellinger, "The Sound of Silence: An Epistle on Prayer and the Constitution," *Yale Review* 95 (July 1986): 1631–1646; Douglas Laycock, "Equal Access and Moments of Silence: The Equal Status of Religious Speech by Private Speakers," *Northwestern University Law Review* 81 (1986): 1–67; and Nadine Strossen, "A Constitutional Analysis of the Equal Access Act's Standards Governing Public School Student Religious Meetings," *Harvard Journal of Legislation* 24 (1987): 117–190.

A compromise of sorts between separationists and accommodationists has been the Equal Access Act of 1984, which permits students to form religious clubs as long as they are student-run and meet outside of regular school hours: see Bill Hewitt, "Bridget Mayhew's Desire for a Bible Club in School Redrew the Boundary between Church and State," *People Weekly* (June 25, 1990): 67–68; Rosemary Salomone, "From *Widmar* to *Mergens*: The Winding Road of First Amendment Analysis," *Hastings Constitutional Law Quarterly* 18 (Winter 1991): 295–323; and Frank Jimenez, "Beyond *Mergens*: Ensuring Equality of Student Religious Speech under the Equal Access Act," *Yale Law Journal* 100 (May 1991): 2149–2168.

Another long-standing practice in U.S. public schools was to have clergy recite a brief prayer at commencement exercises. For a discussion of this practice and the Supreme Court case that ended it, see James Conn, "Graduation Prayers and the Establishment Clause," *America* 167 (November 14, 1992): 380–382; Suzanna Sherry, "*Lee v. Weisman*: Paradox Redux," *Supreme Court Review* (1992): 123–153; and Paula Cohen, "Psycho-Coercion, A New Establishment Clause Test: *Lee v. Weisman* and Its Initial Effect," *Boston University Law Review* 73 (May 1993): 501–521.

Doubtless, we have not heard the last of these proposals to introduce devotions in the public schools. The question then will be whether the U.S. Supreme Court upholds its epic decision on school prayer — *Engel v. Vitale* — one more time.

Abington High School, 163
  Bible reading at, 168
Abington School District, 164, 167
  appeal by, 169
  establishment clause and, 166
Abortion, 4, 134, 188, 189, 212
  dispute over, 51
Adams, John, 11
African Americans, 74, 177
Agostini v. Felton (1997), 105
Aguilar v. Felton (1985), 105
Alexander, Dan, 195
Allen, James, 159
  criticism of, 79
  Engel and, 160
  racial desegregation and, 160
  regents' prayer and, 133
  school prayer and, 160
  Ten Commandments and, 78
Alliance Defense Fund, 189
All Souls Unitarian Church, 49, 128
America (magazine), 156–57
  Schempp and, 180
"America" (song), 70, 134, 160, 182
American Bar Association, 44, 136,
  153
American Center for Law and
  Justice (ACLJ), 189, 200
American Civil Liberties Union
  (ACLU), 43, 70, 133, 156–57,
  176, 188
  ACLJ and, 200
  Engel and, 112
  formation of, 41
  game-day prayer and, 208
  Hawthorne and, 62
  Jews and, 74
  joint statement and, 206
  Kent and, 93

Lemon and, 185
Lerner and, 98
McCollum and, 53
Murray and, 171, 172
regents' prayer and, 69, 94
Roth and, 91, 137
Schempp and, 164–65, 166
Ten Commandments plaques
  and, 191–92
Weisman and, 203
Zorach and, 58, 59
American Coalition for Traditional
  Values, 188
American Ethical Union, 122
American Freedom and Catholic Power
  (Blanshard), 128
American Friends Service
  Committee, 91
Americanism: atheism and, 59
  Protestantism and, 27
  religion and, 18–19, 65
American Jewish Committee, 38,
  62, 74, 94
  Engel and, 155
  Pfeffer and, 54
  regents' prayer and, 122
American Jewish Congress, 38, 41,
  52, 62, 74, 94, 105, 182
  America editorial and, 157
  Engel and, 155, 156
  Gluck and, 58
  Pfeffer and, 53
  regents' prayer and, 69
  school prayer and, 199
American Jewish World, 155
American Legion, 77, 145, 147
  Project America and, 181
American Muslim Council, 206
American Nazi Party, 141

American Protestant Association, 22

American Republican Party, 18

Anderson, Arthur, 143

Andrews, George, 147

Andrews High School, 209

Anglican Church, 6, 8, 10
disestablishment of, 9

Anti-Catholicism, 22, 32, 51, 52, 128, 153
Blaine Amendments and, 33
Kennedy and, 150
public schools and, 17, 29, 157

Anti-Defamation League of B'nai B'rith, 74, 79, 94, 206
Engel and, 155
Pfeffer and, 54
regents' prayer and, 122
Ten Commandments and, 77

Anti-Semitism, 53, 54, 73, 75, 87, 139, 141, 142, 170, 176
Catholics and, 157
return of, 156–157

Archer, Glenn, 51

Armey, Dick, 189

Assimilation, 18
Catholics and, 34
cultural, 43
Jews and, 19, 37

Atheism, 57, 113, 120, 153, 162, 175
Americanism and, 59
Catholicism and, 29
religious education and, 40
religious freedom and, 45

Atlanta Constitution, 135

Bach, Johann Sebastian, 90

Back to God Committee, 77

Backus, Isaac, 8, 9

Baker, Howard, 184, 185, 192

Baldwin, Roger, 44, 93

Balin, Herbert, 80, 81

Baltimore Department of Public Welfare, 174–75

Baltimore School Board, 174, 220

Baltimore Sun, 135
Murray and, 170

Bapst, John, 23–24

Baptist Joint Committee on Public Affairs, 179, 206
Engel and, 155

Baptists, 3, 6–7, 8, 17, 51, 201
church-state separation and, 179
Engel and, 152, 154–55

Barton, David, 1, 217

Battle for the Public Schools, The (LaHaye), 189

Bauer, Gary, 205

Baum, Douglas, 82, 83

Baum, Leone, 82

Baum, Robert, 82

Bayh, Birch, 184

Becker, Frank, 147
school prayer amendment and, 181, 221

Becker Amendment, 181, 182, 192

Bedock, George, 117, 118

Bermingham, Charles, 83

Bernreider, William, 151

Bible club: access for, 199–200, 201
permitting, 221

Bible reading, 15, 16, 21–22, 24, 27, 29, 33
banning, 30–31, 36, 166, 167, 168, 182, 221
Catholics and, 19
continuing, 161, 181
Jews and, 167
laws on, 183, 184, 219
opposition to, 17, 35–36, 165, 174, 175
poll on, 65
public schools and, 163

spending on, 34–35, 63
support for, 66, 67, 180, 189, 201
Bibles: banning, 16, 31
　distribution of, 191 (*see also*
　　Catholic Bible)
　Douay-Rheims Bible, 21, 35, 36
　Gideon Bibles, 63–64
　King James Bible, 20, 30, 176
　New Testament Bibles, 3
　Protestant Bible, 23, 31
Bible study, 40, 161, 216
Biggs, John, Jr., 168
Bigotry, 10, 26, 29, 142, 150
Bill of Rights, 12, 48, 92, 152
　absolutes of, 49l
　church-state questions and, 13
　Founding Fathers and, 94
　McCollum and, 60
　minorities and, 11
　political controversy and, 44
　religion and, 112
　school prayer and, 120
Birch, Anne, 81, 102
Birnbaum, Art, ix
Black, Hugo, 1
　on Bill of Rights, 49
　church-state relations and, 54, 130
　Constitution and, 49
　criticism of, 56, 135, 149, 152–53
　deliberations by, 127–28
　Douglas and, 60
　Engel and, 47, 49, 120, 128, 131,
　　153, 215
　establishment clause and, 130
　Everson and, 48, 50, 52, 55
　First Amendment and, 44, 48, 50,
　　130–31
　Gobitis and, 42–43
　Jackson and, 51
　judicial restraint and, 42
　Kerpelman and, 175
　McCollum and, 54, 55, 56

regents' prayer and, 129, 130
reimbursement plan and, 50
religion and, 48, 49, 130
Schempp and, 176
school prayer and, 119, 221
Vitale and, 133
Blaine, James, 32
Blaine Amendment (1875), 32–33,
　220
Blanshard, Paul, 128
*Board of Education of the City of
　Cincinnati v. Minor* (1872),
　30–31, 223
*Board of Education of Westside
　Community Schools v. Mergens*
　(1990), 200–201, 221, 223
Bobek, Emil, 77, 159
Boehm, Charles, 182
Bonilla, Henry, 210
Book of Mormon, 35, 124
Boss, Harold, 105
Boston Globe, 135
Boyd, Charlene, 193, 194
Brain, George, 180
Brennan, William, 64, 202
　Engel and, 146
　Schempp concurrence and, 193
　on teaching religion, 124
Bridwell, Tiffany, 209
Brind, Charles, 159
Brooklyn Catholic Diocese, 68
Brooklyn Protective Association,
　139
Brosnan, John, 68, 72
Brown, Carl, 171
Brown v. Board of Education (1954),
　46, 133, 150
　criticism of, 147, 152
　Engel and, 155
Buddhists, 4, 176, 211
Bunyan, John, 128
Burch, Francis, 180

Burg, Victor, 2
Burger, Warren, 198
  Lemon test and, 185, 197
Burton, Harold, 55
Bush, George H. W., 203–204
  Weisman and, 205
Bush, George W., 210
Bush, Laura, 210
Bushnell, Horace, 22
Butler, William, 116
  Daiker and, 122
  Engel and, 92, 93, 125, 133, 213
  establishment clause and, 115
  human rights and, 93
  oral arguments by, 120, 127
  Pfeffer and, 105
  regents' prayer and, 92, 94,
    113–14, 117, 123, 124
  released time and, 125
  Roth and, 92, 94, 142
  suit and, 102–103, 104
  Zorach and, 124–25
Butler, Jablow, and Geller (law
  firm), 92
Byrnes, James, 44
Byron, Lord, 50–51
Byse, Charles, 166

Camp Hurley, 90, 202
Camp Siegfried, 73
Campus Crusade for Christ, 188
Cantor, Eddie, 72
Cantwell, Newton, 41
Cantwell v. Connecticut (1940), 41,
  42, 223
Carbone, Michael, 83
Carlson, C. Emmanuel, 179
Carter, Jimmy, 189
Case, Clarence, 62
Castro, Fidel, 129
Catholic Bible, 17, 37, 219
  Protestant Bible and, 35

Catholic Chronicle, 56
Catholic Herald, 21
Catholics: anti-Semitism and, 157
  assimilation and, 34
  Bible reading and, 19
  devotions and, 28
  Engel and, 156
  Everson and, 51
  immigration of, 16, 27
  marginalization of, 23
  parochial schools and, 66
  Protestants and, 17, 18
  public education and, 19
  religious education and, 40
  school prayer and, 187
Catholic Standard and Times, 156
Catholic War Veterans, 181
Catholic World, 28
Celler, Emanuel, 181
Center for Emotional Re-
  Education (CER), 140
Center Street Elementary School,
  74, 83
Central Conference of American
  Rabbis, 38
  America editorial and, 157
*Chamberlin v. Dade County Board of
  Public Instruction* (1964), 172,
  223
Chandler, Porter, 113, 115
  Engel and, 134
  First Amendment and, 126
  Ford and, 109–10
  free exercise and, 126–27
  Spellman and, 109
Channing, William Ellery, 6
Chicago Sun-Times, 135
Chicago Tribune, 135
  on Grant speech, 32
  on Istook Amendment, 207
Christian Advocates Serving
  Evangelism (CASE), 200

Christian Century, 154
    regents' prayer and, 68
Christian Coalition, 188, 189
Christian Crusade, 180
Christianity Today, 154
Christian Legal Society, 189, 206
Christian Voice, 188
Christmas programs, ix, 3, 79, 90,
    133, 159, 216, 221
    Jews and, 37–38
Churchill, Winston, 48
Church of Christ, Scientist
    (Christian Science), 16
Church of England. *See* Anglican
    Church
Church of Jesus Christ of Latter-
    Day Saints (Mormons), 16
Church of Scientology, 3
Church, State, and Freedom (Pfeffer),
    105
Church-state relations, 37, 105, 127
    balance in, 162
    common sense approach to, 61
Church-state separation, 5, 12,
    33, 48, 51, 54, 60, 71, 77, 82,
    104, 108, 119, 121, 133, 160,
    220
    defining, 56
    regents' prayer and, 69
    upholding, 47, 138, 210
    violation of, 78
Cincinnati Bible War, 31, 219
Cincinnati Enquirer, 135
Cincinnati Gazette, 30
Cincinnati School Board, Bible
    reading and, 29, 30, 219
Citizens Congressional Committee,
    180
Citizenship, 5, 12, 27, 163
    education and, 199–200
    immigrants and, 18
    regents' prayer and, 69

Citizens Union, 69
Civil liberties, 44, 58, 86, 179
Civil religion, 65, 125
Civil rights, 37, 89, 199, 214
Clark, Tom, 59
    Engel and, 153
    Schempp opinion by, 176–78
    on school prayer/Founding
        Fathers, 177
Cleveland Plain Dealer, 135
Clinton, Bill, 1, 206, 222
Cold War, 64, 66, 69, 129, 175
    fighting, 73
    patriotism/religion and, 59
Commager, Henry Steele, 96
Committee for a Sane Nuclear
    Policy (SANE), 89
Committee for Better Schools, 90
Committee for the Survival of a
    Free Congress, 188
Committee to Restore God and
    Prayer in Our Schools, 151
Commonweal, *America* editorial and,
    157
Communism, 78, 144, 151
    Jews and, 89
    juvenile delinquency and, 77
    religion and, 145
    threat of, 179
Communist Party, 177
    Murray and, 174, 175
    Roth and, 89
    Weisman and, 202
Conant, James, 77
Concerned Women for America,
    188, 198, 206
Conference of State Governors,
    146
Congregational Church, 5–6
Congressional Record, on *Engel*, 148
Congress of Racial Equality
    (CORE), 89

Conservative Christians, 206
    Jaffree and, 198
    public school and, 189
    school prayer and, 187–88
Constitutional amendments. *See*
    First Amendment and
    Fourteenth Amendment
Constitutional Prayer Foundation,
    180
Cooke, McLaurin, 24
Coolidge, Calvin, 40
Cornyn, John, 210
Corwin, Erwin, 56
Couch, John, II, 208
Coudert-McLaughlin Religious
    Instruction Bill (1940), 57
Council for National Policy, 188
Council on Religious Education, 53
Cox, James, 87
Coxe, Spencer, 185
Crawford, Kenneth, 149
Creation, teaching, 191, 207
Cromwell, Arthur, 52
Cub Pack 521, 106
Culture wars, 213
Curlett, John, 174

Daiker, Bertram, 115, 116
    argument by, 114
    Butler and, 122
    civil religion and, 125
    Engel and, 104, 133
    pressure on, 122–23
    regents' prayer and, 104–105,
        114, 125, 126
    on school prayer, 131
    Warren and, 125–26
Daily Worker, 174
Dallas Morning News, 135
Darwin, Charles, 27, 189, 190
Davies, Samuel, 8
Davis, Hazel, 153

Declaration of Independence, 10,
    67
    supreme deity and, 125, 127, 131,
        146
DeKalb County Public Schools, 2
Delaney, Thomas, 109
Delanoix, Norine, 209–10
Dellinger, Walter, 1–2
Denton, Jeremiah, 189
Denton Avenue Elementary School,
    74
Derounian, Steven, 145
Desegregation, 147, 148, 150, 151,
    160
Des Moines Register, 135
Desmond, Charles, 118
Desmond, Henry, 35
*DeSpain v. DeKalb County
    Community School District*
    (1967), 223
Detroit Free Press, 135
Devotions, 3, 27, 148, 163
    opposition to, 28, 29, 36, 39, 171
    reciting, 176
    support for, 26, 145, 156
Dewey, John, 39, 68, 189
Dierenfield, Richard B., ix
DiGiovanna, Anthony, 59
DiLoretto, Richard, 144
Dirksen, Everett: prayer
    amendment and, 184, 221
    church-state separation and, 151
    Oshinsky and, 184
Disciples of Christ, 16
Dobson, James, 187
Dodd, Walter, 54
Donahoe, Bridget, 23
Donahoe v. Richards (1854), 223
Dorchester, Daniel, 22–23
Doremus, Donald, 62
Doremus v. Board of Education
    (1952), 62, 63, 94, 118, 223

Douay-Rheims Bible, 17, 163, 164
    using, 21, 33, 35, 36
"Double standard" doctrine, 40–41
Douglas, William O., 124
    Black and, 60
    church-state relations and, 129
    Engel and, 128, 131
    Everson and, 131
    on Frankfurter, 43
    Gobitis and, 42
    judicial restraint and, 42
    majority opinion and, 47
    McCollum and, 60
    regents' prayer and, 132
    released time and, 60
    religious establishment and, 131
    wall of separation and, 61
    Zorach opinion by, 60
Dual enrollment, 161
Duffett, Mrs., 82, 83
Dulles, Allen, 152
Dulles, John Foster, 152
Durant, H. F., 24–25
Dutch Reformed Church, 7, 73
Duval, Dorothy, 173
Dye, Marvin, 118, 119

East, John, 189
Eastland, James, 148
Eaton, Robert, 159
Edgerton School Board: King
    James Bible and, 35
    suit against, 34–35
Education: citizenship and, 199–200
    nonsectarian, 29
    religion and, 77
Edwards, Jonathan, 7
Ehrbahr, Paul, 216
Eichman, Adolf, 129
Eisenhower, Dwight D., 65, 119, 152
    Constitutional Prayer
        Foundation and, 180

desegregation and, 148
    Engel and, 145
    regents' prayer and, 132
Eisenhower, Milton, 152
Eliot School Rebellion, 24, 219
Emerson, Ralph Waldo, 144
Emmons, Nathaniel, 14
Endorsement test, 204
Engel, Michael, x, 108, 141
    regents' prayer and, 96, 100–101
Engel, Steven, x, 72, 97, 103, 106,
        119, 186
    criticism of, 141, 142
    Engel and, 104, 213
    harassment of, 138, 143
    Meyer ruling and, 117
    mixed feelings of, 215–16
    NYCLU and, 141
    regents' prayer and, 95–96,
        100–101, 220
    on religious freedom, 215
    state-sponsored religion and, 96
Engel, Thelma, x, 215
Engel v. Vitale (1962)
    analysis of, 135–36, 159
    challenging, 120, 150, 158, 190,
        193, 196, 202, 204, 207, 210
    commonsense interpretation of,
        149–50
    compliance with, 148, 158,
        159–60, 182, 183–84
    criticism of, 1, 131, 135, 138,
        144–48, 150, 152–53, 155,
        157–58, 187
    defense of, 153, 158, 159,
        160–61, 183–84, 195
    legacy of, ix, x, 148, 163, 173,
        192–93, 196, 200, 211–14, 217
    New York ruling in, 220
    opposition to, 106, 144–47, 152,
        155, 180, 184, 211, 221
    plaintiffs of, 72

Engel v. Vitale, continued
    ruling in, 221
    Schempp and, 178–79
    support for, 145, 154, 155, 156,
      160
Episcopal Church, 73
    disestablishment of, 13
    Engel and, 154
Equal Access Act (1984), 199, 212,
    221
    upholding, 200–201
E. R. Dickson Elementary School,
    prayer at, 193–94
Ervin, Sam, Jr., 148, 184
Establishment clause, 12, 13, 46, 47,
    48, 54, 61, 67, 93–94
    absolutist interpretation of,
      119
    cases involving, 109
    extending, 51
    Founding Fathers and, 118, 130
    oversimplification of, 178
    regents' prayer and, 129
    religious clubs and, 198–99
    understanding, 31
    violation of, 185
Ethical Culture Society, 80, 156
Ethic and Religious Liberty
    Commission (SBC), 211
European Enlightenment, 6, 7
Everson, Arch, 46
Everson v. Board of Education of
    Ewing Township (1947), 46, 47,
    62, 70, 109, 129, 131, 223
    criticism of, 152
    establishment clause and, 220
    First Amendment and, 52
    legacy of, 51
    released time and, x
    religious establishment and, 52
    separation and, 49, 50, 198
Ewing Township, 46, 50

Falwell, Jerry, 190
    equal access and, 199
    school prayer and, 187
    Stone and, 192
Family Life Seminars, 188
Farber, Andrew, 82
Farber, R. J., 82
Federal Bureau of Investigation
    (FBI), 174
Federalism, 11, 48
Fellowship of Christian Athletes,
    191, 216
Feuerstein, Moses, 155
Findley, James, 200
Finegan, Scott, 143
    on moment of silence, 158
    regents' prayer and, 83, 97
First Amendment, 12, 44, 50, 64,
    66, 91, 99, 116, 119
    attacking, 56, 207
    church-state questions and, 13,
      60
    defending, 86, 136, 152, 155,
      157, 182
    Engel and, 213
    establishment clause and, 47, 48,
      51, 93–94, 125, 130–31, 148,
      196
    Everson and, 52
    Founding Fathers and, 51, 114,
      213
    Fourteenth Amendment and, 196
    freedom of speech and, 211
    free exercise and, 120
    genius of, 130–31
    interpreting, 47–48, 49
    prayer amendment and, 184
    ratification of, 219
    regents' prayer and, 40, 41,
      113–14, 120, 185
    religious establishment and, 3,
      11, 187

school prayer and, 4, 136
violation of, 164, 165, 169
wall of separation and, 219
First Plenary Council, 23
Fittipaldi, Helen, 78
Flag Day, 44
Flag salute, 42, 43, 44, 73, 92–93,
104, 114, 127, 164
Florey v. Sioux Falls School District
(1980), 221, 223
Focus on the Family, 188
Ford, Gerald, 181, 197
Ford, Thomas, 117, 133–34
brief by, 121
Chandler and, 109–10
regents' prayer and, 109
Founding Fathers, 121, 134, 140
Bill of Rights and, 94
constitutional amendments and,
151
establishment clause of, 118, 130
First Amendment and, 51, 114,
213
religion and, 7, 10, 11, 48, 213
school prayer and, 177
Fourteenth Amendment, 56, 116
due process clause of, 12
Engel and, 147–48
establishment clause of, 51
First Amendment and, 196
religion clauses of, 41
Frankfurter, Felix, 121, 127, 129
on Black, 49
Butler and, 124
on civil liberties, 44
cultural assimilation and, 43
dissent by, 47
Everson and, 55
Gobitis opinion and, 43, 44
judicial restraint and, 42
McCollum and, 54, 55, 60–61
Murphy and, 47

on public schools/democracy, 56
Reed and, 55
symbols and, 43
Free exercise clause, 12, 41, 120–21,
132, 136, 178, 201
Free School Society (Public School
Society), 20
Free Speech Clause, 201
Freethinkers of America, 58, 93,
166
Freud, Sigmund, 189
Freund, Paul, 120–21
Fried, Philip, 81
Friendly Sons of St. Patrick, 68
Friends of New Germany, 73
Fry, Franklin Clark, 154
Fuld, Stanley, 118
Fuller, Edgar, 158
Fusey, Rhoda, 82
Fusey, Stephanie, 82

Gallup poll, 211
on Becker Amendment, 182
on belief in God, 65
on *Engel* ruling, 138
Gary Plan, 39
Gaustad, Edwin, 8
Gay rights movement, 151, 214
Geller, Stanley, 104
briefs by, 120
on courtroom atmosphere, 113
establishment clause and, 115
First Amendment and, 93–94
free exercise clause and, 121
Pfeffer and, 105
regents' prayer and, 94
General Council of Seventh-Day
Adventists, 206
General Federation of Women's
Clubs, 145
George III, 8
German-American Bund, 73

G.I. Bill of Rights, 72
Gibbons, Milton, 144
Gideon Bibles, 36, 64, 191, 209
Gideons International, Rutherford
    School Board and, 63
Gingrich, Newt, 205–206
Glatthorn, Allan, 164–65
Glenn, John, 129
Gluck, Esta, 58
Gobitas, Billy, 42
Gobitas, Lillian, 42
Gobitas, Walter, 42
God, 121, 126
Goddard, Percy, 154
Goldwater, Barry, 181, 192, 198
Gordon, Thomas, 7
Government, religion and, 130,
    178
Graham, Billy, 65
    on *Engel*, 155
    on *Schempp*, 179–80
    Tudor and, 64
Grant, Ulysses S., 32
Grayzel, Solomon, 166–67
Great Awakening, 6–7
Great Depression, 40
Greater New York Coordinating
    Committee on Released Time
    of Jews, Protestants, and
    Roman Catholics, 57, 70
Greatest Faith Ever Known, The
    (Sheen), 65
Greenberg, Hyman, 142
Griffin, Turene, 191
Griswold, Erwin, 136
Groh, Albert, 145
Gross, Calvin, 182
Guidelines for Civic Occasions, 203
Guild of Catholic Lawyers for New
    York, 109
Gunn, Neier, and Daiker (law firm),
    104

Gutchess, Celia, 28
Gutterman, Leslie, 202–203

Hand, W. Brevard, 196
"Hang Ten" movement, 191
Hanukkah, 79, 91, 133
Harding, Frank, 37–38
Harding, Warren G., 87
Hargis, Billy James, 180
Harlan, John Marshall, II, 123,
    124
Harriman, W. Averill, 111
Harris, William, 28
Harte, Mary, 81, 98, 134
    regents' prayer and, 80, 119,
    133
Hartford Courant, 135
Hawthorne Board of Education, 62
Hays, Arthur Garfield, 92, 93
Hays, Jane, 92
Hearst, William Randolph, Jr.,
    180
Helms, Jesse, 187
Henry, Patrick, 9
Henry Sibley High School, ix
Hentoff, Nat, 199
Herberg, Will, 65
Herbert, Augusta, 38
Herricks High School, 76, 143
    regents' prayer and, 84, 97
Herricks Junior High, 74
    Christmas program at, 90
    regents' prayer and, 97
Herricks Parent-Teacher
    Association, 107
Herricks School Board: church-
    state separation and, 121
    complaints against, 101
    Engel and, 125, 133
    letter to, 220
    Meyer and, 116
    Peck and, 80

regents' prayer and, 72, 80, 91,
105–106, 125, 220
suit and, 92, 103–104
Herricks School District, x, 71–72,
114, 145
bond issue and, 75–76
changes for, 216
conservatism of, 73
Engel and, 134
population of, 74
regents' prayer and, 74, 77, 97,
111, 129
religion and, 90
suit against, 95, 103, 108
Herring, David, 3
Herring, Paul, 3
Herring, Rachel, 3
Herring, Sarah, 3
Hicksville School Board, 159
Hilleboe, Guy, 63
Hillside Methodist Church, 82
Hilton, Conrad, 180
Hitler, Adolf, 73
Hobbs, Herschel, 155
Hobbs, Samuel, 56
Hollenberg, Henry, 109
Holmes, Donald, 197
Holmes, Oliver Wendell, 56
Holy Name Society of Notre Dame
Church, 80
Homeowners Association, 106
Hoover, Herbert, 145
Horace Mann Elementary School, ix
Hoshino, Robert, 159
Hughes, Charles Evans, 42, 43, 44
Hughes, John, 21
Catholic schools and, 219
public funding and, 20
public schools and, 29
Human rights, 41, 93
Hurley, Dennis, 61
Hyde, Henry, 192

*Illinois ex rel. McCollum v. Board of
Education* (1948), 59, 63, 69,
70, 129, 220, 223
church-state separation and, 56
criticism of, 152
establishment clause and, 54, 61
legacy of, 56, 57
precedent of, 120
released time and, x, 58, 114
Zorach and, 60
Illuminati, The, 188
Immigrants, 16, 22, 27
citizenship and, 18
transformation of, 19
Incorporation doctrine, 12–13, 51,
198
Indianapolis Star, 135
Institute for Creation Research, 188
Inter-Church Conference on
Federation, 39–40
Interfaith Alliance, 207
International Christian Youth, 181
International Commission of
Jurists, 93
International Council of Christian
Churches, 180
Irons, Peter, 190
Islamic Center of Long Island, 216
Istook, Ernest, 206–207, 222
Istook Amendment, 206–207
opposition to, 207–208

Jackson, Robert, 47, 55, 198
Bill of Rights and, 94
Black and, 51
bus reimbursement and, 50
on Douglas, 61
Frankfurter and, 44
McCollum and, 54
on religious freedom, 44
Jaffree, Chioke, 193–94, 195–96
Jaffree, Ishmael, 193–95

Jaffree, Jamael Aakki, 194, 196
Jaffree, Makeba, 194, 196
Jaffree, Mozelle, 194
James, Forrest "Fob," Jr., 195
James, Forrest, III, 195
Jansen, William, 58
Japanese Americans, Clark and, 177
Jefferson, Thomas, 8, 107
  Declaration of Independence
    and, 127
  establishment clause and, 48
  First Amendment and, 12, 13, 114
  government/religion and, 130
  influence of, 115
  religious freedom and, 9, 219
  religious minorities and, 217
  separationist views of, 49
  Virginia Statute for Religious
    Freedom and, 10, 47
  wall of separation and, 47, 132,
    180, 196, 204, 219
Jehovah's Witnesses, 4, 114
  attacks on, 44
  case of, 41–42
  rights of, 127
Jesus of Nazareth 2–3, 5, 7, 9–10,
    17, 30, 35, 37–38, 53, 62–63,
    90, 107, 164, 167, 169, 171,
    189, 197, 201–202, 209
Jews, 4, 7, 65, 113, 176
  ACLU and, 74
  America editorial and, 157
  "Anti-God" campaign and, 156
  assimilation and, 19, 37
  Bible reading and, 167
  Christians and, 59, 79
  Christmas programs and, 37–38
  communism and, 89
  devotions and, 28
  discrimination against, 73, 74
  education and, 19, 94
  Engel and, 141, 152, 155, 156

immigration of, 27
  loyalty of, 59
  public schools and, 66
  regents' prayer and, 81, 83, 85,
    96–97, 106
  released time and, 57
  religious education and, 40, 52
  religious freedom and, 45
  school prayer and, 77, 199
  sectarianism and, 29, 73–74
  Sunday-closing laws and, 37
Jews for Jesus, 200
Jim Crow, 133, 148, 177
John XXIII, 180
John Birch Society, 96, 151, 152,
    188
Johnson, Courtland, 111
Johnson, Lyndon B., 136
Jones, John Paul, 70
Judaism, denationalization of,
    29–30
Judeo-Christian heritage, 66, 146
Junior Order of United American
    Mechanics, 46
Juvenile delinquency, 67, 71, 116,
    143
  communism and, 77
  regents' prayer and, 125

Kansas City Star, 135
Kantowitz, Barbara, 84
Keirns, Billie Jean, 191
Kelley, Dean, 182
Kennedy, Anthony, 190, 202
  Engel and, 204
  establishment clause and, 204
  Weisman and, 204, 205
Kennedy, D. James, 187
Kennedy, Howard, 179
Kennedy, John F.: desegregation
    and, 148
  Engel and, 149–50, 155, 156

Kenrick, Francis, 21, 23, 219
Kent, Rockwell, 93
Kent, Samuel, 208
Kentucky Heritage Foundation, 191
Kent v. Dulles (1958), 93
Kerpelman, Leonard, 172, 175
Khrushchev, Nikita, 144
Kiernan, Owen, 160–61
King, Martin Luther, Jr., 89, 129, 202
King James Bible, 36, 163, 164
  reading from, ix, 6, 14, 16, 17, 18, 23, 24, 27, 29, 30, 34, 35, 38, 53, 95, 105, 111, 124, 176, 219
  rejection of, 63
  removing, 20
  passing out, 63
Klein, Anna, 62
Knights of Columbus, 66
Know Nothings, 18, 23–24
Koons, Edgar, 190
Koppen, Bernard, 143
Koster, Evelyn, 109
Ku Klux Klan, 46, 73
  Black and, 47, 135
  Roth and, 87
Kurland, Philip, 136

Ladies Auxiliary of the Veterans of Foreign Wars, 106
LaHaye, Beverly, 188, 198
LaHaye, Tim, 188, 189
Land, Richard, 211
Langley, Thomas, 76, 83, 97
Lawrence Berkeley National Laboratory, 168
Lecroy, W. A., 160
Lee, Charles, 82
Lee, Robert E., 202, 203
Lee v. Weisman (1992), x, 201–202, 204, 210, 222–223
  criticism of, 205–206

Lefkowitz, Louis, 159
Legal Services Corporation, 193
Lehman, Herbert, 57
Leland, John, 8
Lemon, Alton, 185
Lemon v. Kurtzman (1971), 185, 191, 197, 205
  criticism of, 185, 204
Lerner, Cynthia, x, 98, 100, 138
Lerner, Julia, x, 75, 98, 102, 142
  regents' prayer and, 99
Lerner, Monroe, x, 72, 97, 103, 106
  criticism of, 142
  Engel and, 213
  harassment of, 138
  NYCLU and, 141
  radicalism of, 98
  regents' prayer and, 99, 102, 220
Levittown School Board, 159
Lewis, Anthony, 149
Lewis, Joseph, 58, 61, 166
Liberty Lobby, 151
Lichtenstein, Daniel, x, 72, 76, 97–98, 103, 106
  criticism of, 142
  Engel and, 138, 213
  NYCLU and, 141
  regents' prayer and, 220
Lichtenstein, David, x, 98, 144
Lichtenstein, Judith, x, 84, 98, 144
Lichtenstein, Naomi, x, 98, 100, 214
Lichtenstein, Ruth, x, 76, 98, 138
Life Is Worth Living (Sheen), 65
Lilienthal, Max, 29
Lincoln, Abraham, 93
Locke, John, 8
Lockrem, Gar, ix
Loewe, Alfred, 80
Long Island Advocate, 76–77
Long Island Post, 111–12

Lord's Prayer, 29, 66, 158, 170, 176
    reciting, ix, 6, 23, 36, 38, 62, 111,
        133, 160, 163, 164, 165, 169,
        190
    spending on, 63
    stopping, 67, 168
Los Angeles Times, 135
Losgar, James, 143
Losgar, Joseph, 143
Louisville Courier-Journal, 135, 192
Luciano, Charles "Lucky," 119, 129
Luther, Martin, 17
Lutheran Church of America, 154
Lutherans, 7, 8, 73
    religious education and, 40
Lynch v. Donnelly (1984), 197, 203,
    223
Lyons, David, x, 99, 100, 106, 138
Lyons, Douglas, 99, 139, 144
Lyons, Jeanne, x, 99
Lyons, Lenore, x, 72, 103, 106
    criticism of, 142
    Engel and, 100, 213
    harassment of, 138
    regents' prayer and, 99, 220
Lyons, Wendy, x, 99, 100, 108, 214

Madison, James, 8, 11, 178
    First Amendment and, 13, 114
    freedom of religion and, 10
    government/religion and, 130,
        219
    influence of, 115
    religious minorities and, 217
    separationist views of, 49
Maine Supreme Court, 219
Malin, Patrick Murphy, 69–70, 112
Manhasset Republican Club, 145
Mann, Harriet, 107
Mann, Horace, 14, 15, 219
Mann, Stephen, 14
Marshall, Thurgood, 202

Martin, Clinton, 145
Maryland Court of Appeals, 174
Mason, Jennifer, 209
Masonic Lodges, 66
Massachusetts Bay Colony, 5
Massachusetts Board of Education,
    219
Massachusetts Citizens for Public
    Prayer, 181
Massachusetts General Court, 6,
    219
McCarthy, Joe, 159
McCarthy era, 89, 93, 96
McCollum, James Terry, 52, 53, 54
McCollum, Vashti, 62, 143
    criticism of, 54, 56
    religious instruction and, 52
    suit by, 53
McGinniss, James, 142
McGrath, J. Howard, 56
McGucken, Joseph, 180
McGuffey, William, 14
McGuffey's Eclectic Reader, 14
McIntire, Carl, 180
McIntyre, Francis, 180
McMurrin, Sterling, 158
Mead, Sidney, 19
"Memorial and Remonstrance
    against Religious Assessments"
    (Madison), 10, 219
Meredino, Joe, 144
Mergens, Bridget, 199–200
Methodists, 7, 16, 17, 51, 73
Meyer, Bernard, 113, 114
    establishment clause and, 115
    First Amendment and, 116
    Herricks School Board and, 116
    minorities and, 117
    opinion by, 111, 115–18, 220
    regents' prayer and, 116
    religious accommodation and,
        116

Middleton, John, 59, 68
Milwaukee Journal, 135
Minersville School District v. Gobitis
    (1940), 42, 92–93, 223
    criticism of, 43–44
Minneapolis Star, 135
Minorities: litigation by, 41
    protection of, 117
    religious, x, 33, 45, 136, 203
    rights of, 11, 41
Minton, Sherman, 59
Missionaries, 13, 209
Moment of silence, 85, 124, 196,
    212, 216
    authorization of, 193
    regents' prayer and, 158
    religious accommodation and,
    197
    religious motivation for, 198
Montgomery, Forest, 198
Moon, Sun Myung, 188
Morality, 6, 67, 70, 71, 163, 176,
    189, 201
Moral Majority, 188, 192
Mormons, 4
    school prayer and, 187. *See also*
    Church of Jesus Christ of
    Latter-Day Saints
Morse, Frederick, 159
Moss, Maximilian, 68, 69, 70
Murphy, Frank, 43, 55, 59
    belief system of, 46
    Gobitis and, 42–43
    religious freedom and, 47
    separation principle and, 47
Murray, Jon Garth, 186
Murray, Madalyn (O'Hair), 143
    ACLU and, 171, 172
    alienation of, 169–70
    anti-Semitism of, 170, 172
    atheism and, 177, 185
    death of, 186

harassment of, 173–74, 175
    Schempp meeting and, 175
    school prayer and, 169, 170,
    172
    suit by, 169, 172, 185
Murray, Robin, 186
Murray, William, III, 169, 175
    ACLU and, 171
    harassment of, 173
    on mother's murder, 186
    Murray and, 170, 172
Murray v. Curlett (1963), x, 163,
    170, 177, 223
Muslims, 136, 211

Nast, Thomas, 29, 33
Nathan Bishop Middle School, 202
Nathan Bishop School District, 203
National Association for the
    Advancement of Colored
    People (NAACP), 41
National Association of Christian
    Educators, 201
National Association of
    Evangelicals, 180, 198, 206
National Catholic Educational
    Association, 56
National Citizens' Council for
    Better Schools, 76
National Conference for
    Community and Justice, 214
National Conference of Christians
    and Jews, 203, 214
National Conservative Political
    Action Committee, 188
National Council of Churches in
    Christ, 154, 179, 182, 206
National Day of Prayer, 65
National Day of Prayer Task Force,
    211
National Education Association
    (NEA), 26, 31, 51

National Jewish Community Relations Advisory Council, 94, 122
America editorial and, 157
National Legal Foundation, 189
National Multiple Sclerosis Society, 214
National Organization for Women (NOW), 188
National Party, 141
National Radio Pulpit, 68
National Reform Association (NRA), 36
National Teacher's Association, 26
Nation's Schools, survey by, 157–58
Native American, 22
Native American Party, 18
Nazis, 40, 63, 141
New Hyde Park Courier, 75, 77, 144
on regents' prayer, 80–81
New Hyde Park Herald, 106
New Hyde Park School Board, 77, 78, 79, 159
New Hyde Park School District, 77, 79
New Orleans Times-Picayune, 135
New Republic, 43
Newsday, 91, 198, 217
Engel and, 135, 162
on juvenile delinquency, 71
Newsweek, 149
New Testament Bibles, distribution of, ix, 3, 63, 191
New York Association of Judges of Children's Courts, 68
New York Association of Secondary School Principals, 68
New York Board of Education, 159
New York Board of Rabbis, 69, 70
New York Board of Regents, 68, 79, 123
moral/spiritual training and, 71
prayer by, 67, 220

scholarships from, 76
school prayer and, 71, 125
New York City Board of Education, 68, 69, 182
New York City Board of Higher Education, 109
New York City Public Library, 115
New York Civil Liberties Union (NYCLU), 93, 133
Engel and, 102–103, 105, 112, 141
Roth and, 91, 92, 120, 141
New York Constitution, 111, 118
New York Court of Appeals, 59, 118, 221
New York Daily News, 135
New York Department of Education, 184
New York Herald Tribune, 135
New York Independent, 35
New York Journal-American, 135
New York Mirror, 135
regents' prayer and, 135
on school prayer, 110
New York Post, 135
New York Progressive Party, 92
New York School Boards Association, 68
New York Society of Ethical Culture, 69
New York Supreme Court, 145, 220
Meyer ruling and, 117–18
New York Teachers Guild, 69
New York Times, 129
Engel and, 135
regents' prayer and, 69
on southern Democrats, 149
New Yorker, 152
Newton, Louie, 155
Nietzsche, Friedrich, 189
Nixon, Richard, 136, 198
Northcott, Clifford, 53

North Dakota Council of Religious Education, 40
North Dakota State Department of Public Instruction, 40
Notre Dame Rosary Society, 106

O'Connor, Sandra Day, 190
    endorsement test and, 204
    Mergens opinion by, 200–201
"Old Deluder" Act (1647), 219
Olmstead, Wilbur, 84
O'Neil, John, 28
O'Neil, Julia, 28
Order of the Star-Spangled Banner, 24
Order of United Americans, 18
Orwell, George, 127
Oshinsky, Elihu, 184
Ostreicher, David, 82
Ostreicher, Herbert, 82
Ostreicher, Jane, 82
Ozone Park Catholic War Veterans, 145

Parents-Taxpayers League (PTL), 77
Parochial schools, 33, 34, 50, 51, 66, 80, 128, 161
    establishment of, 19
    opposition to, 154
    public funding of, 157, 219, 220
    public schools and, 75
    transportation to, 129
Paul of Tarsus, 32
Peale, Norman Vincent, 65, 68
Peck, George, 80
Peck, Lester, 75, 79–80
    regents' prayer and, 81, 82, 85
Pedersen, Frederick, 84
Penn, William, 5
People ex rel. Ring v. Board of Education (1910), 223

People for the American Way, 206
Pfeffer, Leo, 52, 62, 176
    brief by, 54, 55, 63
    Doremus and, 63
    Engel and, 105, 118, 155–56, 183, 184
    Gideon Bibles and, 63, 64
    McCollum and, 53
    regents' prayer and, 94, 122
    released time and, 58
    religious equality and, 179
    Schempp and, 183, 184
    sectarianism and, 22
    Zorach and, 59, 94
Philadelphia Bible riots, 132
Philadelphia Bulletin, 135
Philadelphia School Board, 21–22
Phillips, H. I., 110
Picciano, Frank, 78–79, 109
Pike, James, 154
Pike County Public Schools, 2
Pilgrim's Progress, The (Bunyan), 128
Pittsburgh Post-Gazette, 135
    on Roth death, 87
Pius IX, 34
Planned Parenthood, 188
Pledge of Allegiance, 65, 81, 118, 120, 124, 133, 165, 216
    reciting, 36, 42
Politics, religion and, 150
Polygamy, 13, 47, 48
Ponderosa Bible Camp, 2
Popular culture, religion and, 65
Pornography, 151, 188, 211
Port Huron Statement, 129
Power of Positive Thinking, The (Peale), 65
Prayer: game-day, 208–209, 210
    government-sponsored, 67, 130, 204, 213, 217
    graduation, 202–3, 204, 222
    nondenominational, 67

Prayer: game-day, *continued*
  nonsectarian, 159
  Protestant, 209
  reciting, 183, 184, 190–91, 208
  student-sponsored, 207, 210
  voluntary, 145, 150, 159, 187,
    193, 196, 197. *See also* School
    prayer
Prayer Rights for American Youth
  (PRAY), 184
Presbyterians, 6, 7, 8
Press, freedom of, 12–13, 44
Prinz, Joachim, 157, 182
Project America, 181
Property rights, human rights and,
  41
Protestant Bible, 29, 37
  Catholic Bible and, 35
  reading from, 1, 23
Protestantism, 7
  Americanism and, 27
  public education and, 19, 217
Protestants, 4, 7, 65
  Catholics and, 17, 18
  Engel and, 154, 156, 179
  shared time and, 161
Protestants and Other Americans
    United for Separation of
    Church and State (POAU), 51,
    52, 128
Public School Society, 20
Public schools: alternative to, 34
  attendance at, 33
  democracy and, 56
  parochial schools and, 75
  Protestant domination of, 19,
    217
  religion and, ix–x, 2–3, 2 (table),
    13, 21, 26, 52, 70, 71, 118, 133,
    169, 170, 179, 183 (table), 184,
    191, 194, 216
Purcell, John Baptist, 29

Purgar, Stanley, 77
Puritans, 5, 49

Quakers, 7
  Engel and, 152
  sectarianism and, 29

Reagan, Ronald, 205, 206
  autobiography of, 192–93
  campaign of, 189–90
  Engel and, 196, 204
  First Amendment and, 190
  school prayer and, 190, 192, 193,
    211
Reed, Ralph, 189
Reed, Stanley, 50, 55
Reehill, Dan, 134
Regents' prayer: adoption of, 71–72
  amendment for, 145, 150
  compliance with, 83
  criticism of, 68–69, 82, 100
  end to, 92, 129, 137–38, 216,
    220
  introduction of, 67–68, 80
  opposition to, 82, 95–96, 99,
    102–103, 107, 119, 122
  reciting, 84, 97, 117
  as religious practice, 126, 127
  substitute for, 134
  support for, 68, 94, 101, 106–107,
    113, 118, 119
Regner, Sidney, 157
Rehnquist, William, 190, 202
  church-state separation and,
    201–202
  Engel and, 204
  school prayer and, 198
  wall of separation and, 198
Released time, 61, 77, 93, 114, 125,
  216
  decision on, x, 220
  Jews and, 57

support for, 39, 52, 57–58, 59, 60–61

Religion: academic study of, 137
Americanism and, 18–19, 65
Bill of Rights and, 112
civil rights and, 37
communism and, 145
conflict over, 33–34
Founding Fathers and, 7, 10, 11, 48, 213
freedom of, 5, 8, 9, 12, 33–34, 40, 44, 48, 50, 59, 85, 92, 93, 101, 113, 115, 154, 155, 187, 189, 199, 200, 207, 217, 219
free exercise of, 10, 49, 126–27government and, 52, 130, 151, 178, 219
patriotism and, 73
politics and, 150
poll on, 65
public education and, ix–x, 2–3, 2 (table), 13, 21, 26, 52, 63, 70, 71, 77, 118, 133, 169, 170, 179, 183, 183 (table), 184, 191, 194, 216
removal of, 37
state-sponsored, 96, 169
teaching/teaching about, 124
Religion cases, 225–26 (table)
"Religion in the Public Schools: A Joint Statement of Current Law" (Riley), 206
Religious clubs, 200, 201, 206
establishment clause and, 198–99
Religious disestablishment, 8–9, 13
Religious diversity, 3, 6, 30, 91, 206
Religious education, 39, 77, 221
public funds for, 20, 133
Religious Education Committee, 100
Religious establishment, 7, 9, 11, 49, 131, 132, 168, 176, 187, 213, 219

disputes over, 51
regents' prayer and, 221
Religious exercises: graduation, 204
opposition to, 28
outlawing, 33, 129, 161
percent schools having, 15
Religious minorities, x, 136, 203
religious freedom and, 45
toleration by, 33
Religious right, 189, 206
school prayer and, 187–88
Stone and, 192
Weisman and, 205
Religious Roundtable, 188
Republican Club, 106
Republican Party, 33, 205
Revised Standard Version, 65, 164
Revolution Studios, 214
Reynolds, George, 47
Reynolds v. United States (1879), 47, 223
Riley, Richard, 206
Riner, Claudia, 191
Riner, Tom, 191
Ring v. Board of Education of District 24 (1910), 36
Rippon, Ruth, 97
Rivers, Mendel, 149
Robbins, Andrew, 84
Roberts, John, Jr., 204
Roberts, Owen, 41, 55
Robertson, A. Willis, 148
Robertson, Marion "Pat," 148
ACLJ and, 200
Mergens and, 201
school prayer and, 187
Robison, James, 187
Rockefeller, Nelson, 146, 159
Rockwell, George Lincoln, 141
Rocky Mountain News, 135

Roman Catholic Church:
  Cincinnati Bible War and, 31
  criticism of, 17–18, 41, 128
  doctrine of infallibility and, 32
  Engel and, 153–54
  non-denominationalism and, 28
  POAU and, 52
  public education and, 15
  regents' prayer and, 68
  religious instruction and, 70
  school system by, 4
  sectarianism and, 30
  shared time/dual enrollment and,
    161
  tradition and, 17
Roosevelt, Franklin D., 42, 43, 50
Roosevelt, Theodore, 37
Roslyn Civic Association, 107
Rotary Club, 106
Roth, Alexis, 215
Roth, Daniel, x, 88, 98
  described, 90
  Engel and, 213
  harassment of, 107–108, 143
  on neighborhood, 89
  Reagan and, 192–93
  regents' prayer and, 100
  school activities of, 144
  on Sokolsky, 112
Roth, Ethel Kline, 86
Roth, Frances Harris, x
  criticism of, 142
  harassment of, 143
  marriage of, 88
  radicalism of, 89
  regents' prayer and, 137
Roth, Joseph, x, 88, 90
  harassment of, 107–108, 139
  regents' prayer and, 100
  sports and, 140
  success for, 214, 215
  trials of, 141, 214

Roth, Julia, 215
Roth, Lawrence, x, 72, 97, 98, 106,
    186
  ACLU and, 91, 137
  brother's death and, 87–88
  Communist Party and, 89
  criticism of, 142
  determination of, 86, 101, 112
  Engel and, 86, 102, 104, 117, 137,
    213, 215
  on establishment clause, 119
  First Amendment and, 91
  harassment of, 88, 107, 139,
    140–41, 142–43
  ideals of, 215
  litigation and, 99
  marriage of, 88
  NYCLU and, 91, 92, 120, 141
  radicalism of, 89
  recruiting by, 95
  regents' prayer and, 88, 91, 102,
    107, 117, 220
  religion and, 87, 90, 92, 103
Roth, Sidney: death of, 87–88
Rubin, David, 84
Rundquist, George, 91–92, 112
Rutherford, Joseph, 42
Rutherford Institute, 189, 206
Rutherford School Board, 63
Rutledge, Wiley, 44, 47, 55, 197
  church-state separation and, 54
  death of, 59
  on religious freedom, 50
Ryan, Stephen, 28

Sander, Harold, 107
San Francisco Chronicle, 135
San Francisco News-Call Bulletin, 135
Santa Fe High School, 209
*Santa Fe Independent School District
    v. Doe* (2000), x, 210, 223
  criticism of, 211

Santa Fe School Board, 209
Santa Fe School District, 208–209
Satterfield, John, 136
Saunders, George, 128
Saunders, Richard, 81
Sawyer, Henry, III, 175–76
Scalia, Antonin, 190, 202
Schechter Poultry Corp. v. United States (1935), 151
Schempp, Donna, 164, 166
Schempp, Edward, 164
  Bible reading and, 168
  harassment of, 167–68
  Murray meeting and, 175
  suit and, 167–68
Schempp, Ellory, 163
  ACLU and, 164–65, 166
  Bible reading and, 168
  First Amendment and, 164, 165, 166
  suit and, 167–68
Schempp, Roger, 164, 167
School District of Abington v. Schempp (1963), x, 105, 163, 172, 192, 223
  Bible reading and, 221
  compliance with, 182, 183–84
  criticism of, 179–80
  defiance of, 181, 183–84
  dissent in, 178
  Engel and, 178–79
  legacy of, 196, 200
  Lemon test and, 185
  opinion in, 176–78
  support for, 179
School Law (1827), 14
School prayer, 22, 40, 79–80
  Bill of Rights and, 120
  controversy about, 3–4, 35–36, 77, 202, 213, 217
  deliberations over, 129
  end of, 1, 134, 159, 212
  First Amendment and, 136

Founding Fathers and, 177
government-sponsored, 87, 190
Jews and, 77, 199
laws on, 87, 131, 159, 183, 184, 221
opposition to, 153, 154, 165, 189, 199
poll on, 65
support for, 66, 67, 93, 134, 149, 180, 187, 189, 190, 211
voluntary, 211
School prayer amendment, 147, 150, 151, 184, 211–13, 221, 222
  failure of, 193, 206
  First Amendment and, 184
  hearings on, 181
  opposition to, 192, 207–208
  support for, 180, 190
Schug, Philip, 53
Scully, William, 68
Searingtown School, 74, 96
Seattle Times, 135
Second Great Awakening, 16
Second Plenary Council of Baltimore (1866), 28
Sectarianism, 15, 20, 21, 22, 26, 32, 37, 39, 66, 69, 78
  complaints about, 29
  fighting, 19
  Jews and, 29, 73–74
Secular humanism, 189, 196
Secularism, 51, 53, 61, 155, 156
  momentum of, 57
  religion of, 178
Seeger, Pete, 90
"See You at the Flagpole," 201
Sekulow, Jay, 200
Seton, Elizabeth, 22
Seventh-Day Adventists, 16, 206
Seward, William, 21
Shared time, 62, 161

Sheen, Fulton, 65
Sheldon, Louis, 187
Shepard, Sophia, 24
Shipman, Jeannette, 81
Shipman, Magill, 81, 85
Siler, Eugene, 148
Simonds, Robert, 201
Skura, John, 143
Smith, Adam, 7
Smith, Gerald L. K., 180
Smith, Rodney, 145–46
Snyder, John, 134
Socialist Workers Party, 214
Society for Ethical Culture, 98, 103,
    185
Sockman, Ralph, 68
Sokolsky, George, 111–12
Souter, David, 202
Southern Baptist Convention
    (SBC), 155, 211
Southern Democrats: criticism of,
    149
  Engel and, 147–148
Southern Methodist Church, 16
Sparkman, John, 181
Speech, freedom of, 12, 44, 152,
    199, 200, 211
Spellman, Francis, 109, 153–54, 180
Spencer, John, 116
Spiritual training, 67, 70, 71
St. Aidan's Holy Name Society, 106
St. Aidan's Roman Catholic
    Church, 80, 83, 216
Stam, Jacob, 63, 64
St. Andrew's Episcopal Church, 106
Starr, Kenneth, 204, 205
"Star-Spangled Banner," 106, 132,
    159
*State ex rel. Weiss et al. v. District
    Board* (1890), 35, 223
Stearns, Harry, 161
Stein v. Oshinsky (1965), 184, 223

Stenholm, Charles, 210
Stephens, Rual, 160
Stevens, John Paul: *Jaffree* opinion
    by, 197
  Santa Fe opinion by, 210
Stewart, Potter, 123, 127
  free exercise and, 132
  Kerpelman and, 175
  on official religion, 132
  regents' prayer and, 119, 124
  Schempp and, 178
St. John's Lutheran Church Men's
    Club, 106
St. Louis Post-Dispatch, 43
  Engel and, 135
Stone, H. V., 77
Stone, Harlan Fiske, 40, 44
Stone v. Graham (1980), 191–192,
    221, 223
Strong, Josiah, 27
Students for a Democratic Society,
    129
Stull, W. Eugene, 165, 168
Sunday-closing laws, 37
Sunday schools, 38, 39, 49, 52, 98,
    109, 161, 189
Superior Court of Cincinnati, 30
Supreme Court of Ohio, 30
Sweet, Ossian, 92
Sybert, C. Ferdinand, 174
Syllabus of Errors (Pius IX), 34
Synagogue Council of America:
    America editorial and, 157
  Engel and, 155
  regents' prayer and, 69, 122

Tablet, The, 68
Taft, Alphonso, 30
Taft, William Howard, 30
Talmadge, Herman, 148
Taxpayers Party, 106
Temple Brotherhood, 66

Ten Commandments, 42, 66
  posting, 77, 78, 191–92, 221
  prohibition on, 192, 221
  reading, 24, 36
  secular application of, 191
  studying, 192
  suit about, 24–25
Ten Commandments, The (movie), 65
Textbooks: banning, 35
  bigoted, 19, 29
This Week (magazine), Clark in, 153
Thomas, Clarence, 202
Thurmond, Strom, 148
Time magazine, 65
"To Our Jewish Friends" (*America*), 156–57
Toy, Henry, Jr., 76–77
Traditional Values Coalition, 206
Trenchard, John, 7
Tribe, Laurence, 199
Trilateral Commission, 188
Truman, Harry, 59, 149, 177
Tudor v. Board of Education of the Borough of Rutherford (1954), 63, 223
  criticism of, 64

Unification Church, 188
Union High School, 88
Union of American Hebrew Congregations, 206
  America editorial and, 157
  Engel and, 155
Union of Orthodox Jewish Congregations in America, 38, 155
Union Street Benevolent Society, 139
Unitarian Church, 6, 99, 103, 175
Unitarians, 113, 164
  Engel and, 156
  religious education and, 40

religious freedom and, 45
sectarianism and, 29
United Food and Commercial Workers Union, 214
United Nations, 93, 188
United Parents Association, 69
United Presbyterian Church, 179
United States v. Carolene Products (1938), 40, 223
Universalists, 29
Urane, Andrew, 87
U.S. Circuit Court of Appeals
  Eighth, 221
  Fifth, 209
U.S. Department of Justice, 204
U.S. House Judiciary Committee:
  Becker Amendment and, 182
  school prayer amendment and, 180, 221
U.S. House of Representatives, 221
U.S. Senate Judiciary Committee, 148
U.S. Steel Corporation, 39, 87
U.S. Supreme Court
  criticism of, 51, 56–57, 61, 64, 134–36, 138–58, 179–82, 187–190, 198, 205–207, 211
  defiance of, 2–3, 158–161, 183, 190–191, 195
  support for, 61, 64, 133–38, 149–50, 154–58, 160, 162, 179, 201, 205, 207
  See also specific cases and justices

Van Allen, Howard, 159
Variety Clubs, 214
"Vibrant Herricks Proud of Diversity" (*Newsday*), 217
Vietnam War, 129, 187, 202
Village Voice, 199
Vinson, Fred, 59, 120
Virginia Assembly, 9, 10

Virginia Statute for Religious
    Freedom (1786), 10, 47, 219
Vitale, William, Jr., 81
    Black and, 133
    Engel and, 104
    Meyer ruling and, 116–17
    Picciano and, 109
    regents' prayer and, 101–102, 220
Vorspan, Albert, 157

Waite, Morrison, 47
Waite Court, 48
WallBuilders, 1
Wall of separation, 5, 12, 47, 48, 49,
    50, 51, 54, 59, 61, 117, 121,
    132, 175, 180, 219, 220
    refutation of, 196, 198, 204
Wallace v. Jaffree (1985), x, 196–97,
    202, 210, 221, 223
Wallace, George, 146–47, 181,
    195
Walt Disney Studios, 214
Walters, Harold, 90
Walworth, Graham, 144
Ward, Marian, 209–10
Ward, Philip, 176
Warren, Earl, 150
    criticism of, 151–52
    Daiker and, 125–26
    deliberations by, 127–28
    Engel and, 120, 128, 131–32, 146
    regents' prayer and, 120
    Schempp and, 176
Warren Court: criticism of, 134–35,
    147, 190
    desegregation and, 147
    Engel and, 133
    judicial revolution by, 151
    school prayer and, 4
    support for, 134–35
Washington, George, 13
Washington Post, 135, 174

Washington Star, 135
Watt, Melvin, 207
Webster's Speller, 14
Weicker, Lowell, 192
Weidmann, Jim, 211
Weiland, Mrs. Irving, 107
Weisgal, Fred, 171, 172
Weisman, Daniel, 202, 203
Weisman, Deborah, 202, 203
Weisman, Merith, 202
Weisman, Vivian, 203, 205
Welch, Robert, Jr., 151
Westside High School, 199
*West Virginia State Board of
    Education v. Barnette* (1943),
    44–45, 114, 223
Whall, Thomas, 24–25, 219
Whistler, James, 152
White, Byron, 120, 198, 202
    devotions and, 176
    Engel and, 129
White, E. E., 31
Whitefield, George, 7
Whitehead, John, 187
Whitestone Elementary School,
    184
Whittaker, Charles, 119, 120, 129
"Why the Bible Should Not Be
    Read in the Public Schools"
    (pamphlet), 38
Wickshire Elementary School, 74
Widmar v. Vincent (1981), 201
Wiget, Bernardine, 24
Wildmon, Donald, 187
Will, George, 198
Williams, John Bell, 148–49
Williams, Roger, 5, 79, 123
Williston Park Reformed Church,
    109
Williston Times, 106
Wilson, David, 209
Wirt, William, 39

Wise, Isaac Mayer, 29
Wolfman, Bernard, 166
Wood, Virgil, 202
Woodbourne Junior High School,
170, 172
World Council of Churches, 154
Wundt, William, 189
Wylie, Chalmers, 184–85, 221

Young, Brigham, 47

Zorach, Tessim, 58
Zorach v. Clauson (1952), 60, 62, 64,
94, 109, 178, 180, 223
criticism of, 124–25
establishment clause and, 116
First Amendment and, 118
McCollum and, 60
reception of, 59, 61
released time and, x, 61, 220
Zuckerman, Judah, 100